IMAGES OF WOMEN IN PEACE AND WAR

C

(

1

Images of Women in Peace and War

Cross-Cultural and Historical Perspectives

Edited by

Sharon Macdonald,
Pat Holden
and
Shirley Ardener

The University of Wisconsin Press

Published in the United States of America in 1988 by
The University of Wisconsin Press
114 North Murray Street
Madison, Wisconsin 53715

Published in Great Britain in 1987 by
THE MACMILLAN PRESS LTD
Houndmills, Basingstoke, Hampshire RG21 2XS
and London

Printed in Great Britain

Library of Congress Cataloging-in-Publication Data
Images of women in peace and war.
   1. Women and the military.2. Women and war.
I. Macdonald, Sharon.II. Holden, Pat. III. Ardener,
Shirley.
U21.75.I48   1987   355'.0088042   87—40518
ISBN 0–299–11760–X
ISBN 0–299–11764–2 (pbk.)

BOOKS SPONSORED BY THE OXFORD UNIVERSITY WOMEN'S STUDIES COMMITTEE

Images of Women in Peace and War: cross-cultural and historical perspectives
edited by Sharon Macdonald, Pat Holden
and Shirley Ardener, 1987.

Contents

vii

List of Plates

Acknowledgements

The editors and publishers acknowledge with thanks permission from the following to reproduce the cover photograph and illustrations in the text:

Mary Evans Picture Library for the cover photograph; Mary Evans/Fawcett Library for the illustration of Boadicea in Plate 1; The Trustees of the National Museum of Scotland for the illustration of an Inka vase in Plate 2; IDAF for the illustration of women SADF members in Plate 3; Paula Allen for the illustration of women at Greenham Common in Plate 4; Catriona Howse for the illustration from the Dragon Action leaflet in Plate 5.

The editor and publishers also acknowledge with thanks permission from the following to reproduce extracts in the text: Department of Sound Records, Imperial War Museum; and CND for quotes from an unpublished independent report of research which it commissioned.

Notes on the contributors

Shirley Ardener, of the Centre for Cross-Cultural Research on Women, Queen Elizabeth House, University of Oxford, is the author of numerous publications and editor of *Perceiving Women*, 1975, *Defining Females*, 1978, *Women and Space*, 1981, *The Incorporated Wife* (with Hilary Callan), 1984 and *Visibility and Power, Essay on Women in Society and Development* (with Leela Dube and Eleanor Leacock) 1987. She is a social anthropologist who has carried out extensive fieldwork in Cameroon.

Margaret Brooks is Keeper of Sound Records at the Imperial War Museum, London.

Penny Dransart is undertaking research at the Ethnology Department, University of Oxford. She has done fieldwork in Peru, Chile and Bolivia.

Pat Holden is a Research Associate at the Centre for Cross-Cultural Research on Women, Queen Elizabeth House, Oxford. She is the editor of *Women's Religious Experience*, 1983 and of *Anthropological Approaches to Nursing* (forthcoming). She has lived and worked in Uganda, Malawi, Nigeria and Egypt.

Lynne Jones read human sciences at Oxford. A medical doctor who has lived at Greenham Common Peace Camp for extended periods of time, she is a regular contributor to the *New Statesman* and editor of *Keeping the Peace*, 1983.

Tabitha Kanogo lectures in the department of History at Kenyatta University College, Nairobi. She was recently Rhodes Fellow,

Somerville College, University of Oxford. She is author of *Squatters and the Roots of Mau Mau, 1905–1963* (1987).

Ilse Kirk was formerly Research Fellow at the Institute of Ethnology and Anthropology, University of Copenhagen, with a project called 'Women in the Stone and Bronze Ages', and at the Centre for Cross-Cultural Research on Women at Oxford.

Sharon Macdonald, who read human sciences at St Catherine's College, Oxford, is carrying out research in social anthropology at the Institute of Social Anthropology, Oxford. She was awarded a Sir John Rhŷs Studentship for Celtic Studies in 1986. She has recently carried out fieldwork in the Isle of Skye.

Jessica Mayer is doing research at the University of Sussex and teaching part-time at Goldsmith's College, London. She has done fieldwork in New Guinea.

Rosemary McKechnie is undertaking research in social anthropology at the Institute of Social Anthropology, Oxford. She has recently returned from fieldwork in Corsica.

Ruth Roach Pierson is Associate Professor at the Ontario Institute for Studies in Education. She is the author of *They're Still Women After All: The Second World War and Canadian Womanhood*, 1986, and the editor of *Women and Peace*, 1987.

Elaine Unterhalter is Senior Research officer in the Department of Sociology, University of Essex. She is a member of the Women in South African History Study Group.

Preface

This volume is the latest in the series sponsored by the Oxford University Women's Studies Committee; previous titles are listed in the front of this book. The editors have selected studies which consider women's direct involvement as *active participants* in both peace movements and in wars, and also studies which discuss the more diffuse, pervasive, *realm of ideas* which conjures up images identifying women sometimes as warriors, sometimes as peace-makers. We were aware, of course, that the distinction is not absolute since the reification of women – whereby they do duty as manipulable symbols – bears crucially upon the world of practice.

The definition of 'war' has always been problematic – as declared war shades through guerrilla-type resistance movements into urban violence, for example. Different interpretations of a conflict and its context may co-exist, though not necessarily in harmony. For example, there may be differing views even as to whether a state of peace or war exists. A particularly acute awareness of definitional problems has arisen in recent years with the existence of nuclear weapons; these are claimed by one side as evidence for the keeping of the peace in Europe and by the other as evidence of a permanent state of war. The terminology 'cold' applied to war is itself suggestive. The problem of apparent identities masking difference is illustrated by women's peace-movements which have been in existence for a long time but today are a response to a new set of ideas, circumstances and techniques, firmly located in feminism. The term 'Amazon', as Isle Kirk shows (Chapter 2), has been applied in widely different contexts; these range from the original ancient European texts to the female militia of nineteenth-century Dahomey (see the cover). Further, peace and war are indefinable one without the other and the varied nature of women's involvements in both is explored in this book.

Just as ideas of war and peace are mutually defined, so concepts of men and women are mutually contrasted and reflected. The wide variety of historical and cross-cultural situations addressed here show that women's roles in both war and peace-movements are very much determined by broader perceptions of gender and notions of appropriate female roles held by the societies to which they belong.

Stereotypes of maleness – particularly those evoked in time of war – throw into exaggerated contrast imagery and symbolism associated with women. Compatabilities and inconsistencies become especially critical when women are incorporated into active military service. Further, women in war situations often form organisations that structurally replicate those of men, but which express very different sets of values and self-perceptions. On the other hand some contemporary peace-movements in Britain have attempted to dissolve certain common institutional structures, and in doing so pose a challenge to the much wider arena of perceptions of gender-difference, thus evoking both praise and criticism.

As social anthropologists, the editors ensured that the book would not be restricted to contemporary British material, but would range widely over time and space: that it would be cross-cultural. Of course, the limitations of book length posed problems for such ambition. A selection of available material has had to be made; a certain arbitrariness has been inevitable. But we make no apologies for adopting this course even though darting across contours of space and time may open us to charges of lack of comprehensiveness and consistency. The avoidance of complete ethnocentricity makes this worthwhile.

The studies selected were drawn from different sources. Three derive from a seminar series convened by the editors for the Oxford University Women's Studies Committee in 1983: those by Jessica Mayer, Lynne Jones and Margaret Brooks. The papers by Sharon Macdonald, Rosemary McKecknie, Tabitha Kanogo and Penny Dransart were first given at the Oxford Women's Social Anthropology Seminar.[1] The papers by Ilse Kirk, Ruth Roach Pierson[2] and Elaine Unterhalter were written especially for this volume.

Discussions during the seminars referred to, and informally afterwards, have played an important part in forming some of the ideas expressed in this book, and we are grateful to those who participated. Timothy Ashplant helped plan the Committee's seminar, and Alison Smith, Helen King and Jill Cook all offered useful editorial advice: we thank them. While editing this book has been a co-operative excercise, we wish to acknowledge the special role of Sharon Macdonald who not only wrote the Introduction, but shouldered a disproportionate part of the editorial function.

SHIRLEY ARDENER, PAT HOLDEN

Queen Elizabeth House, Oxford

Notes

1. Attention is drawn to a number of papers given in the women's Studies Committee's programme and at the Oxford Women's Social Anthropology Seminar which could not be included in this book, so that readers may consult those in print elsewhere and may contact the authors of others. Thus at the Committee's seminar, Anne Armstrong (Anne Mayo) formerly of the British Army, currently editor of *Neighbours* (the journal of the British Army wives' club), gave a paper on 'Women in the British and US Armed Forces' which included some comparative material from other armies. Lindiwe Guma and Elaine Unterhalter spoke on 'Women in the National Liberation Struggle of the ANC'. Anne Summers gave a paper which now forms part of her book *Angels and Citizens: British Women as Military Nurses 1854–1914* (Routledge & Kegan Paul). Marina Warner's talk on 'The Language of War in the Allegories of Virtue: from Nike to Margaret Thatcher' is embodied in her *Monuments and Maidens. The Allegory of the Female Form* (Weidenfeld & Nicholson, 1985), Mandy Merck's contribution on Amazons was based on her paper in *Tearing the Veil* (ed. Susan Lipshitz, Tavistock, 1978).

   Papers given at the social anthropology seminar of special relevance to the themes of this book include 'Women Warriors in Traditional Ethiopia' by Tsehai Berhane Selassie, a version of which has appeared in the *Journal of the Anthropological Society of Oxford* (JASO XII, 1, 1981) as '"Centre" and "Periphery" in History; The Case of Warriors and Women in traditional Ethiopia'. Sabine Willis spoke on 'Anzac Day and Women' (see 'Rape – Our Window of Vulnerability' in *Social Alternatives* I, 3, 1984). Ilse Kirk gave a paper on 'The Ibo Women's War' which is soon to be published in Denmark, as well as a paper on the so-called 'Amazons of Dahomey' in West Africa. A short version of Audrey Wipper's paper on 'Riot and Rebellion among African Women: three examples of women's political clout', can be found in *Perspectives on Power* (ed. Jean O'Barr, Durham USA, 1982). Jean O'Barr, of Duke University, in her seminar paper on Kenyan writers, prefigured her Introductory Essay to *Passbook Number F.47927: Women and Mau*

Mau in Kenya by Muthoni Likimani, published by Macmillan Education in this series (1985). See also Mona Macmillan's Study 'Camp Followers: A Note on Wives of The Armed Services' in *The Incorporated Wife*, eds. H. Callan and S. Ardener (Croom Helm, 1984).

2. An earlier version of the paper by Ruth Roach Pierson was delivered at the Conference on 'Gender and War: Historical, Political and Cross-Cultural Perspectives', sponsored by the Program in Women's Studies and the Shelby Cullom Davis Center for Historical Studies, Princeton University, 17 March 1984.

1

Drawing the lines – gender, peace and war: an introduction

SHARON MACDONALD

In recent years there have been two notably different strands in the ways in which Western women have viewed and attempted to transform the prevailing imagery of gender, peace and war in their societies. Some women have set up women's peace-movements and peace-camps, drawing on what they see as the special connection between women and peace. Part of their aim is to alter the evaluation and perceptions of women, as well as those of peace. Other women, however, consider that the symbolic links between women and peace must be denied if women's status is to be truly transformed, and some argue that this can only be fully and effectively done if women are accepted into the military on equal terms with men. In this book, we explore the nature of the intricate symbolic network of gender, peace and war, and examine some of the concepts and associations that lie at its heart.

Women's experience of warfare, and their participation in peace-movements, are still relatively uncharted areas. Much of written history is the record of warfare – of conquest and revolution, of battles fought and treaties signed, of military and political tactics, of great leaders, and of heroes and enemies. In this history, women rarely figure. All we have are a few exceptional historical figures – mythological women leaders or warriors like Joan of Arc and Elizabeth I or like the Amazons and Boadicea discussed in this volume (Chapters 2 and 3). In more recent times, women may find brief mention in accounts of the revolts of unruly masses, as have the Inka and Kikuyu women described more fully here (Chapters 4 and 5); and occasionally their presence in state militaries is made an issue (see the South African example in Chapter 6). We have even less record of women as victims of war (like the internees in the Far East in Chapter 9), or of women otherwise caught up in violent struggle;[1] or of women whose lives are defined by ideas of warfare even in 'peacetime' (such as the women associated with the Foreign Legion and New Guinea warriors, discussed here in Chapters 7 and 8). Of peace-movements, and of women's participation in particular, the historical record virtually draws a blank. For many people, the women's peace-camp on Greenham Common probably seems unprecedented and exceptional, and yet as we see in this book, there is a long history of women opposing war – a history which is only now being unearthed. As is shown in the case-studies here of women warriors, of women who have fought in struggles for the freedom of their people, and of women 'fighting' for peace, creating or maintaining a voice in history is itself a constant struggle with imagery (Chapters 10 and 11).

In this book we are concerned with looking behind the face of the superficial images of women in peace and war, and analysing the ways in which these images are constructed, and their place within the wider social order. We consider the ways that women perceive themselves and are perceived by others, and the ways that women may themselves become symbols of the human qualities epitomised by peace and war. The selection of essays is wide in scope, the intention being to illustrate the range and persistence of the symbolic links between gender, peace and war. Each essay explores a particular dimension of women's participation in activities connected with war – from women as warriors, soldiers and freedom-fighters, to women as wives, mothers, war-victims and peace-activists. These categories of women form part of a network of concepts, a semantic grid, and the nature of any one category is better understood in relation to the others. Although the case-studies cover a broad historical and cultural range, all may be said to throw light on contemporary Western culture.[2] The 'other cultures' dealt with here either form part of the Western tradition, or else are analysed at the point of contact with the West.

The power of imagery

In all of the case-studies in this book we find the use of sexual imagery to delineate women's proximity to what seems so often to be an exclusively male arena, warfare. Even where women are supposed to be participating on equal terms with men, gender is an issue, although this is often demonstrated at the level of symbol and ritual rather than spoken statements. We are concerned here particularly with these more subtle forms of ideology, and our contention is that these are in many instances more potent and powerful than the more readily recognised and acknowledged public sets of rules governing behaviour.

Because imagery works on a less easily articulated level it is difficult to challenge, for the dominant 'language' of challenge is more blatant and less intricate than that of the underlying imagery. This is why women have had to develop their challenge to the status quo not just through 'objective' 'rational' argument, but also through symbolism, and subversion of the imagery itself. Recourse to such means of challenge is typical of 'muted groups' (S. Ardener, 1975a, 1975b; E. Ardener, 1975); it is the 'power of the powerless' (Ridd, 1986); and as a 'tradition among women – typically – isn't even dignified by a name' (Spender, 1985, p. 52). The essays in this book frequently demonstrate women's resilience and innovative-ness, and their ability to subvert the symbolism which muffles their voice.

Imagery, like myth, 'transforms history into nature' (Barthes, 1973, p. 129). To be effective, therefore, any challenge must confront not only the status quo, but the whole understanding of 'the way things are'. We should not be surprised then that challenge is usually localised and of short duration. The challenge is, after all, to what is already defined as unchallengeable.

In the realm of gender, peace and war the 'unchallengeable' seems particularly entrenched, and this is manifest in the complex network of imagery that is dealt with here. To consider the imagery of women in peace and war is to face arguments about the very nature of the sexes and of human needs and instincts. Within modern Western culture, explanations both of warfare itself, and of gender differences in participation, are nearly always based on suppositions of biological, evolutionary drives. These explanations do not attempt to deal with the complexities of imagery and symbolism and the cross-cultural variability encountered in this book, though they do provide rationalisations of why warfare seems so often to be an exclusively male preserve. These rationalisations in their turn are used to support the status quo.

It is not possible to deal in any detail here with the various sociobiological rationalisations of warfare and sex-difference, though put very briefly they can mostly be said to rest on the idea that evolution has favoured males being aggressive, and females maternal (usually conceived as caring and passive). The evidence for sex difference in instinct is far from conclusive, however, and the investigations themselves often employ the sorts of associations and images which are the topic of this book (see Sayers, 1982, pp. 65–83). Investigation of human nature is, of course, necessarily through the filter of socialisation, and even in those social behaviours which exhibit a high degree of cross-cultural concurrence, the exceptions should warn us against any simple determinist inference. As can be seen in some of the case-studies here, what counts as 'male-warfare' behaviour may be transmuted into other activities (see especially Mayer in Chapter 8 below); and where women use what might be called 'aggressive' tactics, these may be redefined. A sensitivity to the terms employed, and to the process of definition, should be, it seems, the starting point to a proper analysis of women in peace and war.

Nevertheless, there are as we shall see common features in the imagery of women, peace and war in very different circumstances, and the exigencies of female biology, especially motherhood, are frequently invoked in explanations of why women are not or should not be warriors. Biology has its own suggestiveness, and it is not particularly surprising if many cultures take the hints in similar ways; this is a phenomenon well documented in social anthropology (see for example, Douglas, 1966, 1970; Needham (ed.), 1973; S. Ardener, 1975a, 1978, 1987). Sociobiological speculations might themselves be seen as examples of the creation of conceptual systems on just such suggestiveness. In the creation of a well-ordered ideology, dualities such as all women as potential mothers and all men as potential warriors have their own rationale, even – or perhaps especially – if they mask a much more complex reality. Many of our most potent oppositions may use the perceived duality of gender as metaphor, or even be based upon it: for example, active and passive, nature and culture, public and private.[3] In the case-studies in this book we are interested both in the extent to which woman may become a 'natural symbol' for peace, home and protected society, and in the ways in which gender is incorporated into wider and more complex symbolic systems.

The first five studies in this book (Chapters 2–6) look at examples of women participating in armies or on the battlefield, and the last five (Chapters 7–11) give attention to the consequences for women, and women's actions, of men's warfare. All of the essays consider not only women's actions, but the ways in which these actions are perceived and represented; and this has bearing on the wider problems for feminists of presenting aims and ideals through imagery, and through language which is unavoidably rich in imagery (see below). On one level, the first half of the book may be read as an exploration of the potential of the female fighter as an image for strong liberated women. The inherent problems and potentials of such an image are well brought out by juxtaposition of these various case-studies. The representation – or *mis*representation – of women in history is a central theme here; and it is well illustrated that the uses and interpretations of imagery are deeply embedded in the social life.

In the second half of the book these and further themes are illustrated in relation to other images of women in peace and war. There is greater concentration on peace here; though, sadly, it seems that 'peace' has its most prominent sense in our culture not as a state in its own right, but as a concomitant to 'war': 'Freedom from or cessation of war' is the first interpretation given in the *Concise Oxford English Dictionary* (1976). As Marina Warner has put it: 'The idea of peace seems difficult to seize without referring to the absence of war, and thus making war present as a standard' (Warner, 1986, p. 26). In these essays we see war's presence in the definition of peace, and the definition of lives during 'peacetime'. Rosemary McKechnie and Jessica Mayer, in two very different cases (Chapters 7 and 8), both consider the impact on women of living with soldiers/warriors, and in particular the impact of this when the men are no longer engaged in active warfare as they used to be. The women internees discussed by Margaret Brooks in Chapter 9 are not themselves at war, though their lives are circumscribed by it. However, even these women who are in 'about as passive a position as possible' (p. 166) create their own definitions and social order, and even use imagery to manipulate events, albeit in limited ways. Women's peace-movements, analysed in the final two studies (Chapters 10 and 11), seem to generate a whole complex of images, created by both themselves and outsiders (mainstream society). Their attempt is to alter the social order and redefine prevailing constructions of gender and of peace and war, and this necessarily entails a 'battle' of sorts through symbolism and imagery.

Female fighters and male myths

Where war is defined as a male activity, and where highly-valued masculine characteristics are often associated with war, a female warrior must be seen as inherently unsettling to the social order. The circumstances under which this potentially disruptive figure finds her way into society and mythology, and the ways in which her actions are limited, defined or forgotten, are examined here in mythological instances of female fighters, and in modern case-studies of women's participation in an army and a liberation struggle. In this introduction to the papers, I am particularly concerned to illuminate the interrelationship between imagery and society; and to show how the images of women that we find on the sidelines of the domain of warfare are not simply accidentally or irrelevantly there, but rather that they play an important part in defining the domain, and in 'symbolically articulating' the social order and its values.

Ideal or unnatural? Images of ancient warrior women

Amazons are probably the archetypical female warriors. They have been used both by feminists to represent the power of women and an idealised alternative society; and by others as caricatures of 'over-masculine', 'unnatural' women. In her analysis of these uses of Amazon imagery, Ilse Kirk (Chapter 2) gives an account of the nature of Amazons in classical mythology, and the role of Amazon tales in Ancient Greece. She describes how, although Amazons were not portrayed as ridiculous or warmongering figures in the mythology, they were nevertheless presented as antithetical to the interests of Greek (Athenian) society. The production of the next generation of male warriors was of critical importance to the Athenian patriarchy, and the Amazons reject marriage and sons. Their independence is not idealised in the mythology: they either fight against the Greeks and are defeated, or else they are transformed into 'proper' women through marriage. It is only as wives that the Amazons may *enter* society, otherwise they are located *outside* or on its *borders*. In this, they act as metaphor for unmarried Athenian women: it is only marriage which successfully classifies and controls the unspoken threat that women pose to male-dominated society. The Amazons are also outside, or marginal to, the accepted classificatory scheme: they confound the normally distinct categories of warriors (men) and women. In representing women who remain outside patriarchal classification, they throw the patriarchal ideals into relief. We find this use of warriors or armies to mark the boundaries of society or the social order at large in many of the essays in this book. As those boundaries alter, however, the prevailing imagery will also be reset. Thus as Ancient Greek society breaks down, the Amazons may enter the city (p. 32).

The ancient British warrior queen, Boadicea (Chapter 3), has at times been accepted into society to the extent of making her a national heroine. However, her intrinsic disruptiveness, as woman warrior, is effectively negated in the recastings of her story in ways which are, perhaps, symptomatic of the means by which female warrior figures, or strong women in general, are 'disarmed'. Put somewhat simplistically, we might say that this is done in one of two ways. Either her womanliness is stressed and she is made to uphold honourable female virtues (chastity, shame, maternal concern),[4] her role as warrior being downplayed or shown to be due to exceptional circumstances. Or else, where the emphasis is on her warrior qualities, she is shown to be not thoroughly womanly, in some sense 'unnatural', and therefore not identifiable with 'normal' women in the society recipient of the myth. It is only as idealised woman, and not as warrior, that she can be admitted into the dominant world-view as a model for the society's women. In some women's iconography, however, Boadicea *as warrior* is used as a symbol for women's strength and determination to fight for their objectives. This seditious interpretation of a national icon is, I should note, relatively hidden from view in the very literal sense that the material is much less accessible in major libraries, galleries and public places; a phenomenon which, it seems, is typical of women's voice in history.

The cases of Boadicea and the Amazons in some ways raise rather pessimistic questions for the enterprise of finding historical or mythological embodiments for feminist ideals, for even these ostensibly strong independent women are shown to be predominantly part of a mythology whose message is at odds with strength and independence in women. Uncovering this bias is an accepted part of feminist analysis, for the processes in play are seen as a continuing part of women's experience today. The problem for women's own reading of iconography is how to make this 'public' and preserve it intact over time.

Social struggle and the imposition of imagery

The problem of protecting one's self-identity is not exclusive to women. Whole cultures may have their traditions and histories forgotten or recast by the newly dominant social and political order; a process which results in many cases in women's actions and interpretations being 'doubly muted', doubly difficult to exhume from history. The difficulty here is not simply one of finding reliable reports, for as we see in the careful analyses of the Inka and Kikuyu peoples, by Penny Dransart and Tabitha Kanogo respectively (Chapters 4 and 5), misunderstandings by the foreign reporters may well have occurred at a deeper, semantic level.

In the case of the non-literate Inka civilisation, conquered over 400 years ago, uncovering the indigenous concepts and understandings is a particularly delicate task. The Inka women who fought on the battlefield during the Spanish invasion are assumed by the Spanish – who ignore the impact of the invasion itself – to have been fulfilling a role normally open to women in Inka society. There is the possibility here, as raised in the historiography of Boadicea, that presenting female warriors as a *normal* part of an alien social order was a means of highlighting its perceived peculiarity of primitiveness. It is only through chinks in the historical record that we can glimpse a world-view in which women's place and warfare itself were rather differently conceived from our own.

Tabitha Kanogo, investigating a much more recent and successful struggle,[5] is able to present a detailed picture of women's changing roles (and the perception of those roles) over the period of the Mau Mau rebellion and its aftermath. Because she includes material from interviews (most of which she conducted herself) with women who participated in Mau Mau, she is able to reveal women's own perception of the roles and stereotypes ascribed them. Women's experience of national liberation struggles and revolutions has achieved some attention from theorists interested in whether the greater equality of roles often achieved during disruption will be continued into peace-time.[6] As Jean O'Barr has pointed out, however, we still have insufficient material on *women's own* responses to struggle: 'The story of women freedom-fighters has yet to be written' (O'Barr, 1985, p. 2).

When war intrudes *into* society – as in the case of invasion or colonialism – it may become very difficult to maintain the traditional social order, and boundaries, such as those of gender, may well break down. We see this very clearly in the desperate fight of the Inkas against the *conquistadores*. In the case of Mau Mau, women's participation is initially clearly circumscribed in terms of role, though as the struggle goes on and women prove themselves, they increasingly take on traditionally male roles. In the midst of this apparent blurring of boundaries, however, there is a fervent production of symbolism going on, much of it sexual. The boundaries of the newly formed Mau Mau organisation, which might split neighbour from neighbour, or even husband from wife, were marked by ritual which often included sexual acts deemed quite unacceptable under normal circumstances. Such inversion of social mores in ritual is not uncommon cross-culturally, and would seem to act as a means of making the boundaries more distinct and less easily impeachable (see, for example, Douglas, 1966). The *sexual* content of the ritual highlights gender distinction, though it may also be used to symbolise more general social concerns.[7] The Kikuyu women's own tradition of manipulation of sexual symbolism is discussed below.

Social roles during and after conflict will to an extent be mapped onto previous social models. Inka women had previous experience of the battlefield and use of some weapons; and Kikuyu women were traditionally keepers of the home, yet also had a tradition of political protest. Classificatory systems demonstrate an inertia which is not easily broken without serious disruption from outside; and the tendency to revert to the old hierarchies is prevented only by public articulation of previous inequalities and grievances.

For many Western feminists, the consequences for women's roles and status of the majority of revolutions and independence-movements has been disappointing. As Berkin and Lovett point out, however, from the (albeit rather inadequate) evidence available, it does not seem that the women involved have in most cases perceived themselves as victims of a callous 'preservation of male values' (Berkin and Lovett (eds), 1980, p. 82). Kimble and Unterhalter (1982) have argued, in a discussion of women's participation in the African National Congress, that Western feminists' disappointment in women freedom-fighters' return to the apparently traditional spheres of home and childcare, is based upon an ethnocentric perspective. The family in the new social-order, they maintain, is not an instrument of women's oppression in the same way as it is seen to be under capitalism. African Nationalist ideology specifically articulates that the oppression of women would be abhorrent, for it would parody the structure of oppression that has been endured by the people as a whole. Compare this also, for example, with the case of the Zimbabwe liberation struggle: 'men realise that if Zimbabwe must be free, that women must be free' (Nhiwatiwa, 1982, p. 249). What happens in the new society, it is argued, is not that women are forced *out* of political roles, but that traditional female roles *become* political and are given increased importance. As Naomi Nhiwatiwa puts it of the Zimbabwean example, childbearing is made 'accountable to the Zimbabwean people' just as any 'public' role would be (Nhiwatiwa, 1982, p. 249).

Perhaps what is crucial in this apparent reordering of social values is whether women *also* retain a presence and voice in public politics. Otherwise we might be tempted to suspect, along with Berkin and Lovett, that 'patriotic motherhood . . . [has] its origins . . . in the determination of political leadership to preserve patriarchy' (Berkin and Lovett (eds), 1980, p. 212). Motherhood and family life do, of course, have very real practical and symbolic importance after a conflict, in that they re-establish stability and promise a future for the people. It will only be through thorough analysis of women's post-conflict experience , and their perception of that experience, however, that we will be able fully to solve the question of whether 'patriotic motherhood' is an image imposed upon the women, or one which they truly choose for themselves.

Social order and the female soldier

After some liberation struggles, in which women's equality was specifically enshrined as one of the canons of the new society, women have remained in the military. Even in these situations, however, the presence of women is not wholly unproblematic. Even in one of the most famous examples of women's military participation today – the Sandanista military in Nicaragua – most women are trained apart from the men. This is explained by the male director of the military school as follows:

> The need to train women separately is not because of any limitations the women have. In fact you might say it's because of failing on the part of some men. Our army has many new soldiers, comrades who haven't had the experience of fighting alongside women, and they aren't always able to relate to a woman as just another soldier. They still tend to see them as women. (Quoted in Enloe, 1983, p. 171; from Randall, 1981)

Part of the problem, it is sometimes said, is that the men will desire to 'protect' the women, and so be distracted from the job at hand.

Where women are enlisted into armies they are almost always segregated from the men in terms of the jobs they do, by the creation of separate regiments for women, and – particularly relevant to our theme – by the use of significata which at one level seem inconsequential. The paradox facing armies is how to preserve sex-difference, while controlling sexuality. The agitation during the First World War over whether the uniforms of British service-women should have a breast pocket is one illustration of this. The final decision was that the pocket should be removed as it emphasised the bust (Goldman and Stites, 1982, p. 27). Within the British military at this time, two contradictory policies on sex-difference were being battled out. While on the one side the attempt was to minimise any signs of difference, on the other,

> commanders successfully resisted identical uniforms and insignia and discouraged the female use of the salute. Women enrolled instead of enlisting, had no ranks and titles equivalent to those of males, and had officials instead of officers. These officials were called controllers and administrators or, for NCO levels, fore-women. (Goldman and Stites, 1982, pp. 27–8)

In this way women were marked as 'other', while the specifically *sexual* – or sexually attractive – aspect of that 'otherness' was denied. We also see here that recourse to classification through what are often regarded as rather trivial means – such as dress, gesture and title – is not exclusive to women. The 'otherness' which is marked by these details is not, of course, gender-neutral: it is through such means that the image of the woman soldier is subtly portrayed. That *Killing Me Softly*, along with other 'suitably feminine songs', is 'a favourite tune in the WRAC [Women's Royal Army Corps]' (Polly Toynbee, *Guardian*, August 1983) is not fortuitous.

Even in the celebrated case of the Israeli army, which has provided many a glossy magazine with pictures of uniformed women touting rifles and driving tanks, women today are unlikely to be assigned to combat positions, and a gender boundary is in many respects marked out. During the military struggle before and during the early period of the formation of the State of Israel, social disruption meant that it was difficult to maintain such boundaries, for as the war entered the settlements, women found themselves on the battle 'front' (though they were redefined to the 'rear' once this had been established). Today, however, despite the persistence of the image of the tough Israeli woman soldier, women in the military mostly occupy traditional female 'support' roles. In 1980, women were engaged in only 270 of the 850 military positions available, and 65 per cent of women occupied secretarial, administrative and clerical positions (Yuval-Davis, 1981; Bloom, 1982). The myth nevertheless persists even for Israeli servicewomen themselves, as was graphically illustrated in a film made by Shuli Eshel, which showed women cadets as they finished their training and were assigned their future jobs in the army. First, each woman stands proudly with her rifle for the official photograph, and then as the assignments are announced 'secretary, clerk, secretary . . . one woman soldier after another spontaneously breaks into tears' (Enloe, 1983, pp. 155–6). Israeli servicewomen belong to a special Women's Corps whose name, 'Chen', means 'charm' (Yuval-Davis, 1981, p. 76). The women are expected to add charm to the Israeli Defence Army by preserving their femininity (they are given advice on cosmetics), and by giving the army a humanitarian and social face (Yuval-Davis, 1981, p. 76). Imagery can capture the paradoxes and contradictions which if more clearly articulated would be easily ridiculed. In the image of the Israeli woman soldier we see both the tough egalitarian optimism of Israeli youth, and also the traditional qualities of gentle supportive femininity.

We see similar paradoxes in the imagery of women in the South

African military, though these are to be understood, of course, within the particularities of the South African context. It might initially seem surprising that in South Africa, where there is little women's rights activism, that (white) women have been recruited into the military for some time. However, Elaine Unterhalter shows how this can be comprehended against the backdrop of the government's wider concerns with its own image, and with upholding apartheid. The South African army, like many other militaries, 'projects itself as an exemplar for the rest of society' (p. 114); and, for South Africa, women's presence is used to symbolise a white unity that overrides gender and class differences. However, at times, for the outside world, the South African military attempts to use women's presence to project a wholly different message by making an analogy betwen sexual and racial equality. The suggestion is that the presence of women in the military illustrates the State's willingness to lessen all forms of discrimination. The ironies are rife here, of course, for neither women nor non-whites have equality in either the military or society at large. The fact that the message is disingenuous is demonstrated at one level by the conservative 'controls' on women soldiers. Their occupations are traditional female ones for the most part, and their otherness – femininity – is not forgotten.

Maternity and militaries

Significantly, however, the South African women soldiers' 'femininity' is not constructed to incorporate caring, 'maternal' images. We don't have any information on whether women are expected to leave the army when they become pregnant (as is the case in the Israeli army, for example), but it is clear that, ideologically, mothers are excluded. The exclusion of maternity from military contexts is very common. Taking a brief overview of the case-studies in this book, we find a persistent concern with motherhood. In the Ancient Greek and British examples, the concurrence of motherhood and war is presented in the imagery as unnatural or exceptional; and the Amazons themselves are, of course, devoid of socially *significant* maternity in that they abandon their sons. In Andean ritual battles only unmarried women fight (see Dransart,

Chapter 4, p. 71); and in the examples of the Foreign Legion and the Ommura of New Guinea, the exclusion or control of mothers is an aspect of the men's martial self-identity. In Mau Mau it was usually single women who went to the forest, and the sexual ritual of Mau Mau oath ceremonies may have been in part a dramatic encoding of the taboos against sex and pregnancy in the forest. If a woman were to find herself with child she would 'lose the rifle' (p. 88).

Somewhat paradoxically, however, within many countries newly emergent from liberation struggle, including some in which women did not engage in combat duties, the image of the woman with a rifle over one shoulder and a baby in her arms, is very popular. The symbolism here is potent, for the image of the mother protecting her child is a highly emotive one – it is after all our original 'protector'/'protected' relationship. On one level it may be read as the Mother Country protecting her people, the female form being particularly suited to the expression of such general abstract ideas (see Warner, 1985, p. 12). It is difficult to imagine a poster designed showing a male soldier which would project the ideas of 'the protected' and 'the future' (as represented by the child) without misunderstanding, and with such force and sentiment. Imagery, being polysemic, also speaks at a specific level, in this case at that of gender. The woman soldier, the poster implies, is also a (potential or actual) mother. The image is one of 'patriotic motherhood', and can be interpreted either as a significant re-evaluation of motherhood, or – more cynically – as a way of leaving women 'holding the baby' and excluding them from the political domain when the struggle is over.

Another female figure who might initially seem to contradict the idea of motherhood being excluded from the arena of warfare is the nurse, who in some ways epitomises caring maternal qualities. Yet institutionalised war nursing by women is a relatively recent phenomenon in Western Europe,[8] and the nurse is quite frequently defined as not part of the military itself, as in the South African example. Furthermore, nursing units are rarely positioned on what is defined as the battle-front, though they may well in fact be directly in the line of fire (see Enloe, 1983, Chapter 4); and nurses, of course, are necessarily dealing with 'fallen' incapacitated soldiers, and not with men whose active military roles are, on the actual and symbolic levels, polarised with the activities of nurses. The power of this symbolism is well illustrated in a description by a woman internee of an occasion when the women donned nurses uniforms to 'protect' themselves (successfully) from rape by their captors (pp. 173–4).

Mothers – and maternal characteristics – in their very difference from the qualities necessitated by war, and in their power to remind the individual soldier of an intimate relationship, pose 'special' classificatory problems within the male-militarised social order. In so doing, they often act as stencils against which the outlines of other categories of women may be sketched. It is small wonder, as we see in the final two studies in this book (Chapters 10 and 11), that motherhood has also been a concern for women who actively oppose war.

Women where men wage war

It is not only the female fighter who is given a carefully defined place within military imagery; indeed, her presence is an exception rather than the rule. Ordinary, less glamourised women may also find their lives brought under the sway of a military ideology in which images of women play a crucial role in the military's definition of itself. In a world in which gender is a principal articulator of the social order, and in which it is men who wage war, women may take on a particular objectified importance as 'the protected', or even as the custodians of the social values that the men are fighting for.

In armies, men's lives are submitted to the most rigorous sets of rules, as well as the powerful controls of imagery. It has been argued that it is only by such pervasive and unremitting regulation that the individual can be made to subdue personal feelings and emotions, and obey commands without hesitation; and to accept an existence that is very much harsher and less exciting than the romantic fantasies promised. For the new recruit, the imagery is still important, but now in addition to the vaunted masculine figures (the hero, comrade, 'real' man, and so on), he is also goaded with negative images. Very frequently these are female or homosexual images, and they are used to represent the weak and ineffective qualities in the recruit. Wayne Eisenhart, an American marine, recalled,

While in basic training, one is continually addressed as a faggot or a girl. These labels are usually screamed into the face from a distance of two or three inches by the drill instructor, a most awesome, intimidating figure. During such verbal assaults one is required, under threat of physical violence, to remain utterly passive. (Quoted in Michalowski, 1982, p. 330)

In this 'transaction' non-masculinity is equated with ineffectiveness and passivity; and masculinity with power and aggression (see Michalowski, 1982). The young soldier, however, does not easily transform himself into the masculine side of the equation, for in the submission to authority required of him, he is taking on a typically 'feminine' role. This tension at the heart of the imagery serves the army well, however, for the insecurity it generates can be countered only by the man *proving* his masculinity along the lines laid down by the military ideology. Were he already assured of his manly status, he wouldn't have the same incentive to demonstrate it: his sexual status is always 'on the line'. The rape of women in warfare is another means by which a man may attempt to prove his masculinity and symbolically surmount the 'feminine' characteristics that he has been made to denigrate. Although rape may be officially discouraged by military regulations, it nevertheless fulfils the military association of masculinity, aggression and depersonalisation, and it is for this reason that some feminists see warfare as inextricably bound up with violence against women (see Brownmiller, 1976, Chapter 3; Stiehm, 1982; Erika, 1984).

While in one respect femininity is associated in military ideology with (desirable yet despicable) submission, in another – and quite paradoxically – it is associated with a wholly undesirable and 'dangerous' individualism. Women offer the potential of an individual relationship, and perhaps, in particular, the 'protector'/'protected' relationship on an individual scale. It might be argued that motherhood, in being a primary individual 'protector'/'protected' relationship, and one in which it is the woman who takes on the active role, is particularly problematic for military imagery. Wives and consorts of soldiers are living examples of the threatening individualism women pose, and for this reason their lives, like those of the men they have relations with, must also be governed by the military.

Everyday lives and sexual identities

Rosemary McKechnie, in a sensitive analysis of the lives of women connected with the French Foreign Legion in Corsica, unpacks the semantic layers of the rich sexual symbolism that defines and restrains both the women and the legionnaires. She shows how, now that the men are no longer so frequently away at war, women's presence – and the loyalties that a woman may demand – constitute a threat to a man's commitment to his military life. This threat is contained, however, by a complex of ideals, rules and trivial social norms (for example, what time the floor is washed). Women's studies and social anthropology often pay attention to detail typically overlooked by more traditional disciplines; and it is well illustrated in Rosemary McKechnie's study (Chapter 7) just how significant such 'minutiae' may be. It is a characteristic experience of women (and, indeed, 'muted groups' in general) that their own perception and reformulation of the socially dominant imagery, should be classified as socially irrelevant – as 'prattle', 'gossip', 'rubbish', 'beside the point', 'caprice', 'women's stuff' and so forth (cf., for example, S. Ardener, 1978, p. 21; Spender, 1980). Yet within such 'unimportant' areas we may well find – as we do in this case – that many women discard or even deride socially acceptable classifications.

The Foreign Legion, as Rosemary McKechnie notes, is in some ways an archaic form of military within Europe; and it seems as though it may be in a transitional period between excluding women associated with the lower ranks, by classifying them as troublesome camp-followers, and incorporating them, to an extent, as part of a new 'cleaner' image (note the vetting of wives' credentials). Such a transition has been charted in Britain between 1850 and 1880 by Myna Trustram, who has shown how problems of enlistment, and the unacceptable immoral image of the armed forces within the wider context of Victorian society, created the need to transform camp-followers into respectable wives (Trustram, 1984).[9] Whether the Legion will fully make this transition is, of course, questionable, especially given its more tenuous attachment to a country, and the abundance of men keen to be recruited.

Incorporated by the military as morale-boosters and supporters, wives' lives are no less subject to the minutiae of social regulation than are those of the excluded wives and consorts – witness the identical furnishings of army accommodation, and the housing inspection in the British services. As one woman interviewed by Cynthia Enloe put it so aptly: '"Six spoons, six knives, six forks". It makes you feel like a child!' (Enloe, 1983, p. 51). Within such a context the stashing away of the cutlery at the back of the drawer and the use of one's own cheerfully nonstandard tableware constitutes a type of rebellion. However, such rebellion draws its impetus from an individual desire to be different, and thus is difficult to transform into co-ordinated opposition to authority.[10]

The women discussed by Jessica Mayer (Chapter 8), in a very different context, find themselves incorporated at close quarters into an 'ideology of masculine strength', which prior to the Australian government's intervention manifested itself in tribal warfare. The male warriors are metaphorically castrated by the official 'peace' in which they can no longer see themselves as protectors of women. In a sense what happens is a form of intrusion of warfare into the society, which initially causes disorder or – to use Jessica Mayer's own descriptive term – 'gender shock'. As we have noted, classificatory systems are not easily and permanently altered without some form of co-ordinated confrontation; and in the case of Ommura, the old ideology reasserts itself, though in a new guise. In the new state of affairs, the men protect the women from intangible 'enemies' which manifest themselves in illness. Interestingly, there is a suggestion that this new form of male protector role may even extend men's authority into the traditionally female domain of childbearing. It is tempting to make analogies here with the alleged 'male-takeover' of childbirth in Western culture. Although Helen Callaway has argued that 'the control structures of human reproduction . . . in most societies . . . have been male-dominated' (Callaway, 1978, p. 174), it might be suggested that *direct* management by men of fertility and childbirth is a symbolic statement of a specific sort. If male sexual identity is made insecure, by disruption of men's traditional domain of power (as might be said to have happened through equal opportunities legislation and such like in Western societies), gaining *direct* power over the most powerful aspects of women's sexuality would seem to be a clear restatement of male potency.

As we have seen, women's lives, and even their bodies, may act as ciphers for men's sexual and martial identities. Women's roles, and images of women, are not, therefore, *neutral* in the military scheme of things, but have a carefully defined structural relationship as *part of* that scheme. However, women do not necessarily passively accept the place allotted them, and may themselves use symbolism to order – or reorder – their lives.

Order, rebellion and body symbolism

The women internees discussed by Margaret Brooks (Chapter 9) managed to create their own social order out of a kind of *bricolage* of ceremonies and taxonomies from their previous experience. The need for order, as a means of classifying oneself 'civilised', or even as merely 'human' – even if it is created through such apparently 'unimportant' rituals as afternoon tea – is well illustrated here.

The women also created symbolic means of protecting themselves, and even rebelling to a limited extent. On one occasion recorded by Margaret Brooks, the women drew on their own bodies as part of their protective *bricolage*. In their 'bottoms-up' gesture to the guard who may have been contemplating rape, the women used a form of sexual insult whose cross-cultural significance has been discussed by Shirley Ardener (1975b; 1987). Tabitha Kanogo describes a similar phenomenon: Kikuyu women, furious with a male capitulation to the authorities, use a traditional sexual insult, involving the exposure of their genitals, as 'the strongest challenge the women could put to the men' (p. 82). Such 'insults' draw their power from the very fact that they are beyond the range of normally accepted behaviours (in much the same way as the 'immoral' component of Mau Mau oath ceremonies did), and in so being they affront the normal classificatory structures. That is, they are implicit expressions of 'disrespect, or the denial of dominance' (S. Ardener, 1975b, p. 43). However, because they are particularly intimate expressions, the person to whom they are directed cannot be regarded as wholly innocent in the matter: he himself feels shame or 'loses face'. Because the body – especially the sexual body – is so imbued with social meanings, it is a particularly effective tool with which to offend those meanings. The details of the meanings must themselves be understood in terms of the cultural significance with which particular natural features are imbued (though as we have noted, many cultures may build on nature in the same ways). When, in Irish mythology, King Conchobar orders the women of Emain to go out to confront their aggressor Cú Chulainn with their breasts bared (see Cormier, 1981), he draws also, it would seem, on the opposition between maternal and warlike characteristics, and makes a statement which is not so much a denial of dominance, as an assertion of peaceableness and a reminder of the world of women, mothers and fertility. It is not only *women's* bodies that may be used as symbolic operators, of course: witness, for example, the co-ordinated revelation of backsides by the servicemen inside the Greenham Common base (Blackwood, 1984, pp. 105–6). The action was clearly intended as an insult to the women outside the fence, though we might suggest that it was also a sign of the men's feeling of insecurity, for as Shirley Ardener's examples suggest, symbolic use of the body is more likely to come from those who lack an effective political voice. As sexual difference and sexuality are given semantic ramifications throughout the domain of peace and war, it is not surprising that the symbolic use of the body should find particular occurrence here.

Through the medium of the body, it is possible symbolically to articulate, and therefore in some circumstances question, attitudes and associations which are deeply embedded in the social life. When the women of Greenham smeared their naked bodies with ashes, on Nagasaki Day 1984, their action spoke both at the non-sexual level of nuclear victims, and also at that of 'challenge to [men's] stereotypes of naked women' (p. 201). It is not surprising that, on a previous occasion, a man expressed his fear of Greenham women in terms of the threat of nakedness (p. 187). As Lynne Jones shows in Chapter 10, there is a richness and density to the meanings that can be encompassed in symbolic action. In their actions, Greenham women often draw on traditional or 'natural' aspects of women's imagery or sexuality. The ways in which they do this, however, as we see in the following section, effects a transformation at the heart of the imagery of gender, peace and war.

Transforming gender, peace and war

'Peace' in Western culture is frequently associated with 'passivity', and is depicted as an *inactive* state, as a mere 'absence of war'.[11] In the structural network of concepts which underlies the imagery of gender, peace and war, there is a collocation of 'femininity', 'peace' and 'passivity', which is opposed in a delicate balance to a set comprising 'masculinity', 'war' and 'activity'. This is not a simple rigid grid of absolutely defined concepts: their sense and moral load may shift, but this occurs within the relational pattern. These interlinked concepts, which bring many other dualisms into their orbit, have become enshrined in imagery, text and social life, so that their relationships seem, reasonably enough, to be natural and inevitable.

The women who argue that women should be accepted into the armed forces on absolutely equal terms with men, believe that only this will fully disrupt the algebra. Their argument is also that if the military is seen as some sort of exemplar for society, or as the ultimate protector, then women's exclusion can be read only as an exclusion from full citizenship, and its attendant responsibilities and rights (see Segal, 1982). The examples of female fighters in the first half of this book suggest, however, that in entering the military domain, it is usually the definition of these *particular* women that alters, and more general ideas about women, and about masculinity and war are left intact. Even if these women were to come to be seen as representative of their gender, we must consider the nature of the transformation so effected, for the change would be one wholly towards previously 'male' values. The positive and negative markings of the categories 'peace' and 'war', 'masculine characteristics' and 'feminine characteristics', would not change, only their referents would.

A recurring problem for peace movements has been the accusation that they offer a weak, passive and negative alternative to war; they are imbued with supposedly 'feminine' characteristics. Thus, men involved in peace movements may be called 'effeminate': for example, Woodrow Wilson's reluctance for America to join the Great War was characterised by Roosevelt as a 'lack of manhood' (Wiltsher, 1985, p. 172). The association of women with the private and domestic, rather than the public political, sphere may also be built into a politically enfeebled picture of peace movements. Their vision is said to be limited or naive, and their concerns are depicted as those of individual rather than national security.[12]

Many women peace-protesters, however, as we see in Ruth Roach Pierson's study, stress their participation *as women*, explicitly leaving the link between women and peace intact, and using it as part of their argument. See, for example, the following (not untypical) lines from the manifesto of the Women's Peace Party (set up in the United States during the First World War):

> As women, we are especially the custodian of the life of the ages. We will no longer consent to its reckless destruction. (In Wiltsher, 1985, p. 218)

Their attempt is to alter the image of both women and peace, and to see both as positive, active and politically important. They steer a fine line here, for truly to disrupt the prevailing system of classifications, their activities must not be perceived and classified as either marginal and irrelevant, or as part of the discourse of war. The creativity and energy with which Greenham women steer this course, and the chronic reinterpretation and misrepresentation of their activities by wider society, are well documented by Lynne Jones who speaks from personal experience.

Images and actions

Although images can condense a whole range of meanings or possible interpretations (as in the case of Greenham women's use of symbolism), very often they mask a great deal of complexity on the ground (see especially Chapters 7 and 10 by McKechnie and Jones). Although the distinction is not absolute, it is useful perhaps to call the first 'open images' and the second 'closed images'. The distinction is similar to that between 'symbol' and 'ideal' or 'stereotype', though the latter terms do not quite express the sense of 'closed images' (perhaps because we have become too used to them, and so denied them some of their power). 'Open', unlike 'closed', images are to be interpreted, read and to an extent repopulated; and the form of condensation that they employ is not meant to reflect or define the social life itself, as is that of 'closed' images. The difference, then, between say, Greenham women's use of the image 'Greenham Woman' or 'Peace Woman', and the use of these images by the media, is that for the women themselves the image is 'open', whereas for the latter it is 'closed'. Maintaining 'open' images, as we see in many of the essays here, is a very difficult and energy-consuming process: it is an enterprise which requires almost constant action.

In this book we consider both 'open' and 'closed' images, and the more complicated reality which lies behind them. Imagery is by no means a purely superficial phenomenon: it is the means through which we articulate and define the social order and nature; and the concern here is not only with symbolism and imagery on the large and public scale, but also with the ways in which women's lives may be affected in their most intimate detail. Gender, peace and war, in Western culture, are intricately interlinked at many levels, and these links are firmly rooted in the social life. It is for this reason that images of women – and the definition of women's lives – are never irrelevant or neutral in the discourses of peace and war. And it is also for this reason that if women want to question or disrupt these definitions, they must take on, through both words and actions, the imagery itself.

Notes

1. For an excellent exploration and analysis of women's lives in situations of (sometimes violent) political conflict, and their responses to that conflict, see Ridd and Callaway (eds) (1986).
2. In using the term 'Western culture' I do not intend to imply that the ideological traditions of Western countries (by which I mean Western European and New World countries) are wholly homogeneous. There is always a problem in defining the scope of a particular 'world-view', and at almost any level inconsistencies will manifest themselves under a finer focus. The scope of this book, however, is broad, and the historical connections between the Western countries and the similarities of perspective on various issues, make 'Western culture' a suitable starting point for analysis.
3. For case-studies and analyses of these themes see, for example, the following compilations: S. Ardener (ed.) (1975, 1978, 1981) and MacCormack and Strathern (eds) (1980). We might note in particular Strathern's suggestion for the nature–culture dualism that 'a male–female distinction in Western thought systems plays a crucial role as symbolic operator in certain transformations between the terms nature–culture' (Strathern, 1980, p. 176).
4. In a paper given in the 'Women, Peace and War' seminar organised by the Oxford University Women's Studies Committee in Autumn 1983, Marina Warner argued that Athena (Nike) and Mrs Thatcher have been made to serve as allegories of female virtues. For a more extensive analysis of the ways in which the female form has acted as an embodiment of human qualities, see Warner (1985).
5. Although the colonial government's interpretation of events was that the Mau Mau rebellion had been put down, it has been argued that

Mau Mau laid the foundations for the creation of an independent Kenya (see, for example, O'Barr, 1985, p. 5). Not available at the time of the writing of Tabitha Kanogo's study, unfortunately, were Muthoni Likimani's moving short stories (1985) which express some aspects of women's experience of Mau Mau. Together with Jean O'Barr's introduction, they complement and support Tabitha Kanogo's analysis here.

6. For overviews of the position of women in liberation struggles and revolutions and their aftermath, see Berkin and Lovett (eds) (1980); Enloe (1983, Chapter 6); O'Barr (1985, pp. 23–9); and chapters by Griesse and Stites, Jancar and Amrane, together with the introduction in Goldman (ed.) (1982).

7. Menstrual blood, for example, is often an inherently ambiguous symbol of life and loss of life (for the individual or whole community); and the penis might represent strength, in war in particular, and control (submission to authority) or its lack.

8. British military nursing was set up during the Crimean war (see Summers, 1983) and the British Army Nursing Service was founded in 1881. In a paper given by Anne Summers at the Oxford University Women's Studies Committee 'Women, Peace and War' seminar, Autumn 1983, she described how war nursing between 1854 and 1884 was largely a philanthropic enterprise by well-to-do ladies, whose presence lent a respectability to the war.

9. We should note here that in both the Victorian army and the Foreign Legion today, a distinction is made between women associated with upper-ranking men, and those with lower or unranked men (in effect, between upper and middle, and lower class women). The former women in both armies are more readily incorporated.

10. Again there may be class/rank differences here. The women discussed by Rosemary McKechnie, and wives of lower ranks in at least some regiments in the British army seem to demonstrate little co-ordinated activity. Compare this, however, with the camaraderie and organised activities of the officers' wives discussed by Mona Macmillan (1984).

11. 'Peace' and 'passivity' are not from the same Latin root. 'Peace' is from '*pax pacis*', whereas 'passivity is from '*passivus*' which has the sense of suffering (as in 'passion').

12. For further debate on this subject see Pierson (ed.) (1987), and in particular the chapter by Carroll. This book also contains a broad historical and cross-cultural selection of descriptions of women's peace movements. Other historical accounts of women's peace campaigns are Liddington (1983) and Wiltsher (1985). Contemporary material on peace movements may be found in Jones (ed.) (1983), Cambridge Peace Collective (1984) and Thompson (ed.) (1983).

References

Ardener, E. (1975) 'Belief and the Problem of Women', and 'The "Problem" Revisited', in S. Ardener (ed.) (1975, pp. 1–28).

Ardener, S. (1975a) 'Introduction', in S. Ardener (ed.) (1975, pp. vii–xxii).

Ardener, S. (1975b) 'Sexual Insult and Female Militancy', in S. Ardener (ed.) (1975, pp. 29–54).

Ardener, S. (ed.) (1975) *Perceiving Women* (London: J. M. Dent).

Ardener, S. (1978) 'Introduction: The Nature of Women in Society', in S. Ardener (ed.) (1978, pp. 9–48).

Ardener, S. (ed.) (1978) *Defining Females* (London: Croom Helm).

Ardener, S. (ed.) (1981) *Women and Space* (London: Croom Helm).

Ardener, S. (1987) 'Gender Iconography: the Vagina', in P. Caplan (ed.), *The Cultural Construction of Sexuality* (London: Tavistock).

Barthes, R. (1973) *Mythologies* (orig. 1957, Paris) (London: Granada).

Berkin, C. and Lovett, C. (eds) (1980) *Women, War and Revolution* (New York and London: Holmes and Meier).

Blackwood, C. (1984) *On the Perimeter* (London: Heinemann).

Bloom, A. R. (1982) 'Israel: the Longest War', in N. L. Goldman (ed.) (1982, pp. 137–63).

Brownmiller, S. (1976) *Against Our Will* (London: Penguin).

Callaway, H. (1978) '"The Most Essentially Female Function of All": Giving Birth', in S. Ardener (ed.) (1978, pp. 163–85).

Cambridge Peace Collective (1984) *Our Country is the Whole World* (London: Pandora).

Cormier, R. J. (1981) 'Pagan Shame or Christian Modesty?', *Celtica*, XIV, pp. 43–6.

Douglas, M. (1966) *Purity and Danger* (London: Routledge and Kegan Paul).

Douglas, M. (1970) *Natural Symbols* (London: Barrie and Rockliff).

Enloe, C. (1983) *Does Khaki Become You? The Militarisation of Women's Lives* (London: Pluto Press).

Erika, S. (1984) 'Rape: Our Window of Vulnerability', *Social Alternatives*, 1, 3 (Sidney, Australia).

Goldman, N. L. (ed.) (1982) *Female Soldiers – Combatants or Noncombatants? Historical and Contemporary Perspectives* (Westport Conn. and London: Greenwood Press).

Goldman, N. L. and Stites, R. (1982) 'Great Britain and the World Wars', in N. L. Goldman (ed.) (1982, pp. 21–46).

Jones, L. (ed.) (1983) *Keeping the Peace* (London: The Women's Press).

Kimble J. and Unterhalter, E. (1982) '"We opened the road for you, you must go forward", ANC Women's Struggles, 1912–1982', *Feminists Review*, 12 pp. 11–35.

Liddington, J. (1983) 'The Women's Peace Crusade. The History of a Forgotten Campaign', in D. Thompson (ed.) (1983, pp. 180–98).

Likimani, M. (1985) *Passbook Number F.47927: Women and Mau Mau in Kenya* (London: Macmillan Education).

MacCormack, C. and Strathern, M. (eds) (1980) *Nature, Culture and Gender* (Cambridge: Cambridge University Press).

Macmillan, M. (1984) 'Camp Followers: A Note on Wives in the Armed Services', in H. Callan and S. Ardener (eds), *The Incorporated Wife* (1984, pp. 89–105) (London: Croom Helm).

Michalowski, H. (1982) 'The Army Will Make a "Man" Out of You', in P. McAllister (ed.), *Reweaving the Web of Life, Feminism and Nonviolence* (Philadelphia: New Society Publishers).

Needham, R. (ed.) (1973) *Right and Left* (Chicago and London: The Chicago University Press).

Nhiwatiwa, N. (1982) 'Women in the National Liberation Struggle in Zimbabwe', interview, introduction by Carole B. Thompson, in Judith Hicks Stiehm (ed.), *Women and Men's Wars, Women's Studies International Forum*, V, 3/4, pp. 247–52 (Oxford: Pergamon Press).

O'Barr, J. (1985) 'Introductory Essay', in Likimani (1985) pp. 1–32.

Pierson, R. R. (ed.) (1987) *Women and Peace: Theoretical, Historical and Practical Perspectives* (London: Croom Helm).

Randall, M. (1981) *Sandino's Daughters: Testimonies of Nicaraguan Women in Struggle* (Vancouver: New Star Books).

Ridd, R. (1986) 'Powers of the Powerless', in R. Ridd and H. Callaway (eds.) (1986 pp. 1–24).

Ridd, R. and Callaway, H. (eds) (1986) *Caught Up in Conflict. Women's Responses to Political Strife* (London: Macmillan Education).

Sayers, J. (1982) *Biological Politics* (London: Tavistock).

Segal, M. W. (1982) 'The Argument for Female Combatants', in Goldman (ed.) (1982, pp. 267–90).

Spender, D. (1980) *Man Made Language* (London: Routledge and Kegan Paul).

Spender, D. (1985) *For the Record. The Making and Meaning of Feminist Knowledge* (London: The Women's Press).

Stiehm, J. H. (1982) 'The Protected, the Protector, the Defender', in Judith Hicks Stiehm (ed.), *Women and Men's Wars, Women's Studies International Forum*, V, 3/4, pp. 367–75 (Oxford: Pergamon Press).

Strathern, M. (1980) 'No nature, no culture: the Hagen case', in C. MacCormack and M. Strathern (eds) (1980, pp. 174–222).

Summers, A. (1983) 'Pride and Prejudice: Ladies and Nurses in the Crimean War', *History Workshop*, 16.

Thompson, D. (ed.) (1983) *Over Our Dead Bodies. Women Against the Bomb* (London: Virago).

Trustram, M. (1984) *Women and the Regiment, Marriage and the Victorian Army* (Cambridge: Cambridge University Press).

Warner, M. (1985) *Monuments and Maidens. The Allegory of the Female Form* (London: Weidenfeld and Nicolson).

Warner, M. (1986) 'Images of Peace', in *Listener*, 24 April, p. 26.

Wiltsher, A, (1985) *Most Dangerous Women. Feminist Peace Campaigners of the Great War* (London, Boston and Henley: Pandora).

Yuval-Davis, N. (1981) 'The Israeli Example', in W. Chapkis (ed.), *Loaded Questions. Women in the Military* (Amsterdam and Washington, D.C.: Transnational Institute).

2

Images of Amazons: marriage and matriarchy

ILSE KIRK

Bachofen in the middle of the last century developed an evolutionary history[1] in which he claimed that social life had passed from a
state of primitive communal marriage (hetaerism) through mother-
right (*Mutterrecht*) to the patriarchy of his own time, which he
considered ideal. He presented an Amazonian stage of development as an extreme form of mother-right. During the twentieth
century the idea of an Amazonian way of life has been revived and
entwined with an idea of matriarchy,[2] mainly by feminists. This has
been part of the broader enterprise of 'discovering' powerful
women in history or in other cultures in order to prove that male
dominance is not an inevitable social order, but that there are
alternatives.

It is not the intention here to discuss whether Amazons or
matriarchal rule ever existed. Various scholars have given attention
to solving these problems, but without any convincing results, and it
seems that with our present knowledge it is impossible either to
prove or to disprove the existence of such societies. Rather, the aim
here is to explore the ways in which our contemporary images of the
Amazon differ from the Amazons of ancient Greece, and to trace
how and when certain elements in our contemporary images were
incorporated into accounts of Amazons in previous historical
periods.

Amazons in ancient Greece[3]

Many writers of antiquity in the Mediterranean area from the time
of Homer until the fall of Rome either refer briefly to or tell

27

elaborate stories about Amazons. From around 700 BC sculptors and painters depicted Amazons on vases and paintings. Here I confine myself to the Greek material, and by showing the role of the tales in Greek society I suggest a broader framework for understanding the interest in Amazons generally.

In the ancient stories Amazons were considered to be female warriors living in an all-female state somewhere on the border of the known world. The oldest stories seem to connect them with Thrace or western Anatolia (Homer, *Il*. III, 187; Arktinos[4]), and it is claimed that they founded many towns in these areas.[5] But the majority of ancient writers placed them somewhere in Asia Minor, south of the Black Sea along the Thermodon River, or further east near the Caucasus and the Scythians.[6]

Warfare was so institutionalised among the Amazons that they were said to remove a breast (usually the right one) by burning or cutting and searing in order to make it easier to use their weapons. Indeed the most common etymological explanation for the word 'Amazon' is 'breastless' (*a mazos*).[7] Amazons generally enter the stories as warring counterparts of Greek heroes, the names of the heroes changing according to current political conditions. In the earliest references to such a battle, Bellerophon and Achilles were the fighting heroes (Homer, *Il*. VI, 186; Arktinos). Through most of antiquity, however, Heracles was the hero fighting the Amazons, but in the classical period, when Athens was at the height of its powers, he was replaced for a time by Theseus.[8]

In all the battle accounts, the opponents of the Amazons are the Greeks. In the stories of Bellerophon, Heracles and Theseus, the hero makes an expedition to the Amazons' land to conquer them or to get the queen's girdle. In another tale it is recounted that the Amazons took part in the Trojan War on the Trojan side against the Greeks, and the Amazon queen, Penthesilea, was killed by the Greek warrior, Achilles. In later stories it is the Amazons themselves who go to Athens in order to reclaim their abducted queen.[9] While in all cases the Amazons are eventually defeated, they are nevertheless, in the classical tales, almost the equals of the Greek male warriors. Apollodorus calls them 'a people great in war, for they cultivated the manly virtues' (*Bibl*., 2, 5, 9) and vase painters depict both fallen Amazons and Greek warriors slain by Amazons. They are 'thought about . . . first as a warrior and then as a woman' (Tyrell, 1984, p. 22).

Marriage not war

Despite the emphasis on the Amazons as warriors, however, they are not necessarily described as hostile to men or to outsiders. We hear for instance from Apollodorus of how Heracles was well received by the Amazon queen Hippolyte when he arrived to fetch the Amazon girdle. She 'inquired why he was come, and promised to give him the belt' (*Bib.*, 2, 5, 9). The writer of the Hippocratic medical text *Airs Waters Places* called the Amazons 'man-loving' (mentioned in Tyrell, 1980, p. 1). Plutarch recounted another story told by an older writer, Bion, about Theseus's arrival in the land of the Amazons:

> The Amazons . . . were naturally friendly to men, and did not fly from Theseus when he touched upon their coasts, but actually sent him presents, and he invited the one who brought them to come on board his ship; she came on board, and he put out to sea. (Plut., *Thes.*, 26, 2)[10]

The Amazons were never said by the Greeks to be ugly; rather, they are described as beautiful – women to marry. Early stories tell of Achilles falling in love with Penthesilea (Arktinos); Heracles was married to a woman with an Amazon-sounding name (see duBois, 1982, p. 103); Theseus abducted the Amazon queen and married her (Plut., *Thes.*, 262; Diod., 4, 28, 4); and the Scythians in Herodotus's story gave up home and family to settle down with the Amazons (Hdt., 4, 114–17). Later writers describe the beauty of Queen Thalestris, the Amazon queen who visited Alexander the Great 'for the sake of offspring' (Strab., 11, 5, 4).[11]

Two recent studies of Amazons, by duBois (1982) and Tyrell (1984), bring our understanding of the Amazons in antiquity a great step forward by analysing the image of Amazons in classical Athens. They agree that marriage and the control of children are the key points. But while Tyrell sees the Amazons simply as reversals of the ideal marriage partner, duBois shows a develop-ment in the relations of the sexes over time from an analogous polarity to a hierarchical one. She places this change in the context of transformations in the Athenian political and social scene.

The status of the women of Athens has often been discussed, but the ambiguity in the available material has made it impossible to arrive at any simple conclusion on the question of whether the women of Classical Athens were *despised* or *respected*.[12] It seems to be agreed, however, that Athenian women lived very restricted lives and were more or less confined to the women's parts of the house.[13] As the famous 'funeral speech of Pericles' states:

> women are . . . to be neither seen, heard, nor spoken of, yet they reproduce the generations of warriors who constitute Athens. (Thuc., 2, 45, 2, in duBois, 1982, p.103)

Pericles here touched on the weak point in the Athenian patriarchy: the city's dependence on the women for providing sons. Male attitudes to women generally therefore,

> are marked by tension, anxiety and fear. Women are not part of, do not belong easily in, the male ordered world of the 'civilised' community; they have to be accounted for in other terms, and they threaten continually to overturn its stability or subvert its continuity, to break out of the place assigned to them by their partial incorporation within it. Yet they are essential to it: they are producers and bestowers of wealth and children, the guarantors of due succession. (Gould, 1980, p.57)

Women started their lives conceptually 'outside' society, but were taken 'inside' by marriage (King, 1983, p.111). An Athenian woman like Pandora was considered 'a necessary evil' (Hes., *Th.*, v. 585): a threat to the social order and a being who had to be *tamed* by men.

This ambivalence towards Athenian women is expressed more forcibly in myths of the Amazons:

> Whether we are talking about the Amazons or the Lycians, it is the Greek *polis*, that male club, which is being defined by its historians and its 'ethnographers' in terms of its opposite. (Vidal-Naquet, 1981, p.190)

The Amazons were the opposites of the *ideal* Athenian women: they did not marry, they controlled their own offspring, they were warriors, and they lived 'outside'.

At the same time, the Amazons were *liminal*: they were

androgyne, (females and warriors); they lived on the borders of the known world; they were neither virgins nor married; they desired men but did not want male babies – they were like initiates, who

> exist in limbo, a state of marginality where they are without social status and are outside ordinary time and space. (Tyrell, 1984, p. 66)

Marginal and ambiguous, Amazons were either killed or made into proper women through marriage.

The image of the Athenian woman changed over time. For the Mycenaean period we do not know anything about the women of Athens, but at other times and in other places:

> The message of the myth had to be repeated and heard again and again because the problems of women and marriage could never be solved once and for all. (Tyrell, 1984, p. 113)

Marriage ideals also changed over time. In the Archaic period between about 700 and 500 BC marriages with foreigners were favoured, since allies could be acquired and war avoided (duBois, 1979, p. 39). In the Classical period, however, endogamous marriages became the ideal, and in 451 BC a law was passed stating that an Athenian citizen had to have both an Athenian mother and an Athenian father.

But towards the end of the 5th century – when the Peloponesian War broke out – ideals were falling apart, and the 'Woman Question' came under discussion among the intelligentsia at Athens (Tyrell, 1984, p. 33; duBois, 1982, p. 112). Also Athenian women themselves were voicing dissatisfaction with the established pattern of gender relations, as suggested by Medea's famous speech in Euripides's tragedy of the same name:

> Of all things which are living and can form a judgement
> We women are the most unfortunate creatures
> Firstly, with an excess of wealth it is required
> For us to buy a husband and take for our bodies
> A master; for not to take is even worse.
> And now the question is serious whether we take
> A good or a bad one; for there is no easy escape

> For a woman, nor can she say no to her marriage . . .
> What they say of us is that we have a peaceful time
> Living at home, while they do the fighting in war.
> How wrong they are! I would very much rather stand
> Three times in the front of battle than bear one child.
> (Euripides: *Medea*, vv. 230–8, vv. 248–51, quoted from
> duBois, 1982, p. 126)

Boundaries were breaking down: Greeks fought Greeks; distinction between men and women was no longer clear-cut; and the Amazons therefore were no longer a danger; they represent, 'within the comedy, an alternative to the destruction of internal war'. (duBois, 1982, p. 121)

In Aristophanes's comedy *Lysistrata*, the Amazons[14] have indeed invaded the Athenian Acropolis and turned the world upside down; they are now insiders. That this really was the case can be witnessed in the Mausoleum in Halicarnassus in 353 BC, which

> bore an Amazonomachy which was a celebration of the female warriors, . . . The Amazons are no longer the enemies of the city; they are the ancestors of the Halicarnassian plutocrat. (duBois, 1982, p. 131)

Bachofen and matriarchy

Towards the end of the period of antiquity there was a slight mixing up of Amazon stories with gynaecocracies. This is a tendency which Bachofen in the middle of the nineteenth century developed fully. In his work *Die Mutterrecht*, published in 1861, he argued that there had been a separate phase in the evolution of mankind, in which Amazons held the reins of power.

> Amazonism arose out of an earlier warlike life. Amazonism was only an unnatural exaggerated matriarchy. . . . brought about by a corresponding degeneration of the male sex. (Bachofen, 1967, p. 153)

As the men were killed in battle the women took up arms themselves. Later they founded a state, 'if one may apply the word "state" to a nation of women' (Bachofen, 1967, p. 162). Amazonism was a primitive stage in our evolution, argued Bachofen, but nevertheless,

> in it lies the first germ of the matriarchy which founded the political civilization of peoples. (Bachofen, 1967, p. 105)

When matriarchy had been achieved it might degenerate in some places into Amazonism again, although this was not common. For Bachofen, Amazonism was a preparation for matriarchy.

In the matriarchy, women by definition held power in both political and private life. One thing which this entailed was the ability to defend themselves:

> the exercise of arms was never wholly relinquished by the women of matriarchal states, who could not but regard it as indispensable for the defense of their position at the head of warlike peoples. (Bachofen, 1967, p. 107)

Contemporary views of Amazons

The association of Amazons, matriarchy and fighting women has coloured images of Amazons in the twentieth century. In ancient Greece, as we have seen, Amazons were described as living apart from men in an all-female state. Such a social order would be at odds, of course, with that of a matriarchy (defined as rule over men). Further, matriarchies are believed to attach much importance to motherhood, while Amazons reject sons. Today, as in the ancient Greek case, however, Amazons not only represent an alternative social system, but also an alternative *type* of woman – a woman flouting feminine ideals.

Just as Amazon myths acted as cautionary tales for Athenian women, the contemporary Amazon has at times had a similar function in our own society. Boslooper and Hayes describe the negative caricature of the Amazon:

> The popular image of an Amazon is hardly flattering: a big, burly, single-breasted female; hostile, unattractive, a woman who has chosen to act like a man. (Boslooper and Hayes, 1973, p. 116)

The use of the term 'Amazon' to apply to 'unnatural' women is not new, however. Simon Shepherd describes in his interesting study of seventeenth century drama how the image of the Amazon at that time was applied to the supposedly sexually frustrated or overly independent woman:

> the loading of the name Amazon is pejorative; it can indicate aggressive lust, unbridled will, disobedience. On the stage it is frequently used as an insult, applied to women who fight and drink, especially wives who are aggressive and women who refuse traditional submission to men. (Shepherd, 1981, p. 14)

The once heroic women have also been turned into sexually titillating curiosities. Sobol recounts how

> Visitors to the New York World's Fair of 1939–40 had a once-in-a-lifetime opportunity to buy admission to *The Amazons*, an extravaganza in which showgirls armored in scanty cardboard dueled with wooden swords and for an energetic encore played at badminton. The huge, broad-shouldered star of the attraction graduated to nightclubs and burlesque houses, titling herself as 'Queen of the Amazons'. A strip-tease by a six-foot-two heavy-weight had its effect, but it was other than to inculcate in onlookers a feeling for history. (Sobol, 1972, p. 11)

Amazons have entered popular culture in this century in a variety of guises. The ever-popular 'Wonder Woman' devised in a comic strip of the 1940s was modelled on an Amazon princess (Steinem, 1982; Boslooper and Hayes, 1973, p. 126). Amazons have appeared in science fiction pulp magazines, under such names as 'The Golden Amazon' and 'The Black Amazon of Mars' (Sobol, 1972, pp. 11–12); and Mary Renault's novel *The Bull from the Sea* concerns the love affair between Theseus and the Amazon Antiope. These are but a few cases of the popular and varied use of Amazon imagery in the twentieth century.[15] No clear-cut picture emerges, however, of a consistent underlying political theme.

Some feminists, however, have revived a positive image of the Amazons. Helen Diner's *Mothers and Amazons*, which first appeared in the 1930s, was the first of such analyses, and served as sourcebook for various later incorporations of Amazons into

feminist imagery. Diner considers Amazonism as a kind of matriarchy, and indeed sees the Amazons themselves as champions of
matriarchy in the war against patriarchy:

> In the Amazon war, the issue was which of the two forms of life
> was to shape European civilisation in its image. (Diner, 1973,
> p. 105)

Phyllis Chesler, who draws on Diner's work, describes Amazonism
as 'the universal male nightmare' (Chesler, 1982, p. 97) which men
have 'exorcized by ridicule or disbelief'; though she also considers
the Amazon war still not finally concluded. Matriarchy is what is at
issue:

> The ancients were closer . . . to such matriarchal phenomena as
> female ownership and inheritance of land and crops, female
> 'ownership' of children, and female control of reproduction and
> religion. (Chesler, 1982, p. 98)

In some ways paradoxically, the comparatively peaceful Amazons
of Greek mythology are often described today in more warlike
terms. Hrdy states that the Amazons ('prototypical matriarchs')
were 'aggressive and warlike – masculine spirits in drag' (Hrdy,
1983, p. 11). Chesler claims that the main theme of the Amazon
myth is 'women sacrificing and killing men' (Chesler, 1982, p. 97).
Davis quotes Bachofen's description of the Amazons' 'bloody
vengeance against the male sex' (Davis, 1978, p. 114), and talks of
Amazon 'savagery' and of how the Amazons of Thrace 'lived
entirely without men, murdering any man who dared approach
their boundaries' (Davis, 1978, p. 49).

Not all women have been happy to accept this aggressive image,
however. Some try to explain it. Brantenberg, for example, claims:

> the Amazons' culture has been created by its enemies, and
> [therefore] gives a rather prejudiced picture of a warrior people
> consisting of women with cruel habits. (Brantenberg, 1980, my
> translation)

A cause for such denigration is suggested by Tyrell. In ancient
Athens, marriage and the next generation of warriors was the

overriding concern. Accordingly, as the Amazons do not marry, dispose of male offspring and act as warriors, they are considered a threat to existing conditions, and therefore they were 'developed by men in charge of the media' (Tyrell, 1984, p. 22).

Boslooper and Hayes explain Amazon acts of aggression as simply the consequence of having to protect this ideal way of life:

> [The Amazons] were fierce and hostile only in reaction to the barbarians who sought to oppress them. (Boslooper and Hayes, 1973, p. 120)

If Athenian men emphasised the negative image of Amazon society in order to contrast it with their alternative ideal social order, and to promote conventional Athenian marriage patterns, some feminists have used the model of Amazon rule as a positive social ideal. Thus, alongside the imagery of war, an image of an ideal peaceful harmonious society is drawn out.

The main points in the stories today are not *marriage* but *independence*, not *offspring* but *power*. The stories are now used by women against the male-dominated society – the Amazon myth is still serving its turn in society but the implications are reversed: it is now women who are using the Amazons as a bogey towards men. The imagery through which women were once put in the place men allotted to them (marriage and the production of sons) is reversed to express women's independence and power. However, the new feminist ideal would not simply replicate a patriarchal society turned upside down, as we see in Phyllis Chesler's idealisation of women's rule as

> a more securely ordered, fruitful, lawful, ethical, and spiritual way of life . . . [S]uch female rule may have been kinder to both men and women than male rule has been to either of the sexes. (Chesler, 1982, p. 101)

Conclusion

As we have seen, the image of the Amazons has changed completely since antiquity. The role of the Amazon stories as far as the Athenian woman was concerned seems likely to have been as that of a cautionary tale. Far from glamourising female independence and escape from male dominance, the message in the myths was that marriage was desirable.

Through the centuries, the image of the Amazons has changed, and they have in many cases been depicted as ridiculous figures. Today feminists have seriously taken up the idea of the ancient warrior women. But the all-female state is now bound up with ideas of matriarchy even though, strictly speaking, the two principles are in fact incompatible, as the Amazon state is recounted as a one-sex system, while matriarchy implies sexual stratification. Nevertheless the notion of the Amazons as matriarchs is more embedded in the positive image employed by feminists themselves than in the image used against them.

Notes

Translations from classical Greek texts taken from Loeb editions unless otherwise specified. The abbreviations of ancient writers and their works are those used in the *Oxford Classical Dictionary* (1964 edn).

1. Man's origin and evolution were sources of great debate and speculation at this time. Darwin's *The Descent of Man* was published in 1871.
2. Bachofen used the words *Mutterrecht* (Mother-right) and *Gynaikokratie* (rule of women) and not *Matriarchie* (Matriarchy).
3. The ancient Greeks called themselves *Hellenes*, a name which was generally acknowledged by 600 BC (*Oxford Classical Dictionary*, 1964 edn, p. 411).
4. To Arktinos of Miletus, who is supposed to have lived in the eighth–seventh century BC, is ascribed the epic *The Aithiopus*. This is only in part handed down in later works, see Proclus, *Chrestomathia*, 175–180. Homer is generally said to have lived earlier, in the eighth century BC.
5. Sources which connect the Amazons with the Thermodon and Themiscyra are, for instance: Hdt., 9, 27; Pherec., FGrH, I, 64; Aesch., *PV* 721–5 and Lys., II, 4. These all lived in the fifth century BC. Later Ap.Rhod., 2,370; 2,995 (third century BC); Diod., 2, 45; 3, 52, 1–2 and Strab., 11, 5, 4; 12, 3, 21 (both first century BC).
6. Writers who place the Amazons north of the Black Sea are: Hdt., 4, 116; Eur., *HF*, 408–10 (late fifth century BC), and in the Caucasus area: Strab., 11, 5, 1–2; Diod., 17, 77, both living in the fifth century BC. Strabo is claimed by a few modern writers to have placed the Amazons in Europe, but the ancient Albania, as he mentions, is actually situated in the Caucasus area (see Chesler, 1982, p. 105). Aesch., *Suppl.*, 287–9 and Diod., 3, 52, place Amazons in North Africa.

7. This explanation was also given in ancient Greece, see Diod., 2, 45, 3. For other explanations see Diner, 1973, pp. 101–2; Chesler, 1982, p. 103.
8. The story of Heracles's fight against the Amazons is mentioned by Pind., *Nem.*, 3, 38 and Eur., *HF*, 408–18; Eur., *Ion*, 1144–5 – both fifth century BC; Ap.Rhod., 2, 966–9; Apollod., *Bibl.*, 2, 5, 9, 7–8 (first century BC); Diod., 2, 46; 4, 16; Paus., 1, 2, 1 (second century AD). Theseus's fight is to be found in Pind., fr., 175; Pherec., FGrH, I, 64; Isoc., 12 (*Panathenaicus*), 193 (fifth century BC); Diod., 4, 16, 4; Plut., *Thes.*, 26–7.
9. This story is known towards the end of the fifth century (Lys., II, 4; Isoc., 4 (*Paneg.*), 68, who both refer only briefly to an already well known story. Later sources are Apollod., *Epit.*, 1, 15–16; Plut., *Thes.*, 27; Diod., 4. 28.) See Merck, 1978, pp. 100–2.
10. Other writers who tell about the Amazons' kindness are for instance Aesch, *PV.*, 727; Diod., 2, 46, 2; 4, 16; Plut., *Thes.*, 26, 2; Strab., 11, 5, 4; and Hdt., 4, 110–17.
11. See also Diod., 77, 1; Plut., *Alex.*, 46, 1; Tyrell, 1984, p. 24.
12. See for instance, Just, 1975, pp. 154–7; Pomeroy, 1975, pp. 58–60; Gould, 1980, pp. 39–42; Williams, 1983, pp. 92–106.
13. Just, 1975, pp. 160–3; Gould, 1980, pp. 46–50.
14. The women are compared with Amazons in this play.
15. In 1986, the Oxford University Students' Union issued a new women's paper – and called it 'Amazon'.

References

Bachofen, J. J. (1967) *Myth, Religion, and Mother Right* (London: Routledge and Kegan Paul) (orig. *Die Mutterrecht*, Basle, 1861).

Boslooper, T. and Hayes, M. (1973) *The Femininity Game* (New York: Stein and Day).

Brantenberg, G. (1980) 'Amazone', in *Pax Lexicon* (Oslo: Pax Farlag A/S).

Chesler, P. (1982) 'The Amazon Legacy', in Charlene Spretnek (ed.), *The Politics of Women's Spirituality* (New York: Doubleday).

Davis, E. G. (1978) *The First Sex* (Harmondsworth: Penguin).

Diner, H. (1973) *Mothers and Amazons. The First Feminine History of Culture* (New York: Anchor Books) (orig. 'Mütter and Amazonen', published in the 1930s under the pseudonym of 'Sir Galahad').

duBois, P. (1979) 'One Horse/Men, Amazons, and Endogamy', in *Arethusa*, 12.

duBois, P. (1982) *Centaurs and Amazons: Women in the Pre-History of The Great Chain of Being* (Ann Arbor: University of Michigan Press).

Gould, J. P. (1980) 'Law, Custom and Myth: aspects of the social position of women in Classical Athens', *JHS*, 100.

Hrdy, S. B. (1983) *The Woman That Never Evolved* (Cambridge, Mass., and London: Harvard University Press).

Just, R. (1975) 'Conceptions of Women in Classical Athens', *Journal of the Anthropological Society of Oxford*, 6, 1.

King, H. (1983) 'Bound to Bleed: Artemis and Greek Women', in Averil Cameron and Amelie Kuhrt (eds), *Images of Women in Antiquity* (London: Croom Helm).

Merck, M. (1978) 'The City's Achievements', in Susan Lipshitz (ed.), *Tearing the Veil* (London: Routledge and Kegan Paul).

Pomeroy, S. B. (1975) *Goddesses, Whores, Wives, and Slaves. Women in Classical Antiquity* (New York: Schocken Books).

Shepherd, S. (1981) *Amazons and Warrior Women. Varieties of Feminism in Seventeenth-Century Drama* (Brighton: Harvester Press).

Sobol, D. J. (1972) *The Amazons of Greek Mythology* (London: Thomas Yoseloff).

Steinem, G. (1982) 'Tales of a Reincarnated Amazon Princess: The Invincible Wonder Woman!', in Charlene Spretnek (ed.) *The Politics of Women's Spirituality* (New York: Doubleday).

Tyrell, W. B. (1980) 'A View of the Amazons' in *The Classical Bulletin*, 57, 1.

Tyrell, W. B. (1984) *Amazons. A Study in Athenian Mythmaking* (Baltimore and London: Johns Hopkins University Press).

Vidal-Naquet, P. (1981) 'Slavery and the Rule of Women in tradition, myth and Utopia', in R. L. Gordon (ed.), *Myth, Religion & Society* (Cambridge: Cambridge University Press).

Williams, D. (1983) 'Women on Athenian Vases: Problems of Interpretation', in Averil Cameron and Amelie Kuhrt (eds), *Images of Women in Antiquity* (London: Croom Helm).

3

Boadicea: warrior, mother and myth

SHARON MACDONALD

An historical puzzle

Boadicea, as national legend has it, was a great British queen who led her people to battle against the Roman invaders. Her scythed chariots and rearing stallions, together with a sense of victory and patriotism, are embedded in our national memory. In fact, however, she was not queen of Britain, and our vision of her is greatly distorted. Indeed, the more closely we look at what is actually known about Boadicea, the more puzzling appears the fact that she is so famous a figure of British history now, nearly 2000 years after her death.

We have very little actual evidence about Boadicea,[1] and that evidence we have is hardly the most appropriate for a national heroine. Boadicea was not a national monarch: there was no unified nation that could be called Britain[2] or England in the first century AD. The island was divided among various tribes and Roman colonies; and Boadicea was the leader, after her husband's death, of one Celtic tribe, the Iceni. The Iceni were not the only ones involved in the rebellion against the Romans in 60 AD; this was not the first or indeed the last rebellion; and it did not succeed in ousting the Romans from Britain. Yet in the transformation of Boadicea into a national figurehead these features are often forgotten and we are left only with the barest bones of her story persisting through history. This skeleton story is fleshed out in different ways in different historical periods, and the details of the ways in which this is done can be fully understood only in their social and political

40

contexts, a task which is unfortunately beyond the scope of the present study. Here my main concern is simply to show the nature of the 'template' that Boadicea provides, for it is in the equivocal nature of this multi-faceted template that we find the key to her historical resilience and resurgence.[3]

Sexual anomaly

One feature of Boadicea which remains constant in the accounts of her is that she was a woman who led her people to battle. This association of a woman with war appears to be both fascinating and problematic for those who have written about Boadicea. The reason for this, I suggest, is that for our culture the woman warrior is an anomaly: she is transgressing the normal bounds of her sex, and as such, she both excites our interest and disturbs us. Mary Douglas has argued that marginal anomalous figures become hedged around with ritual and taboo which makes us more heedful of the boundaries that our society has laid down. The witch, for example, in being external to normal social categories, becomes a focus for normative social mores (Douglas, 1970). So too, the gender anomaly becomes a focus for explicit and implicit comment on sexual roles. Gender deviations, we should note, are probably the most powerful or 'dangerous' of all slips from designated social roles. Accusation of sexual misconduct may be the clinching conjunct to a more general accusation: the sexual misdeeds of witches, for instance, are well documented.

Before looking at the ways in which the anomaly of a woman warrior is 'resolved' in the different accounts of Boadicea, I want to give a short account of her story as we find it in Tacitus. This is likely to be our most accurate source, though even this was not written until fifty years after the rebellion, and was not from first-hand observation.[4] Later historians are unlikely to have any further sources than Tacitus's brief account, though it has been claimed that Hector Boece, writing in the sixteenth century, may have had access to an indigenous narrative (Spence, 1937, p. 158). Boece had, in any case, read Tacitus's version.

Boadicea's story

The Romans began their concerted invasion of Britain in 43 AD, in the reign of Claudius. By the mid-50s AD they were well established in the South of Britain and had set up several client kingdoms, that of the Iceni being one. A client kingdom bore allegiance to Rome, though the British tribal leader remained partly in charge. There was some resistance to the Romans, led principally by Caratacus, but by the mid-50s AD he and his supporters had been pushed back into Wales and were pursuing their raids against the Romans from Anglesey, which appears to have been the centre of Druidic power at that time.

Tacitus tells us that when Boadicea's husband, Prasutagus, died (c. 60 AD), he tried to appease the Romans by making his daughters and the emperor co-heirs to the Kingdom. However, his gesture was ignored and the 'kingdom was plundered . . . his wife Boadicea was scourged, and his daughters outraged' (*Annals*, XIV, §31). It was these events that roused the Iceni and their neighbours, the Trinobantes, to action. They marched first on the Roman colony of Camulodunum (Colchester), where a great statue of the Roman Goddess Victory 'fell prostrate . . . as though it fled, before them' (*Annals*, XIV, §32). The town was thoroughly plundered.[5]

Next they sacked London, and then Verulamium (St Albans). Tacitus writes that about 70000 citizens and allies were massacred in the three towns. Meanwhile, the Roman Governor of Britain, Suetonius Paulinus, was amassing troops to face the Britons; and it is at the scene of the battle that we first hear mention of Boadicea's leadership. Tacitus credits Boadicea with a brave and rousing battle speech (*Annals*, XIV, §35), but the Britons are beaten, and Boadicea poisons herself (*Annals*, XIV, §37).

A Celtic anomaly?

It is unclear to what extent a woman's leadership would have been exceptional among first century Brittonic tribes. In Tacitus there is a discrepancy between Boadicea *persuading* the tribes that she should lead, and her 'protest . . . that it was indeed usual for Britons to fight under the leadership of women' (*Annals*, XIV, §35). Other details in Tacitus fail to resolve the matter. He describes, for example, how the Icenian and Trinobantian wives were kept well out of the way of the fighting, and records that they were present at the battle-scene only to *witness* the victory that the Britons expected, and not to participate in it (*Annals*, XIV, §34). Elsewhere, however, he mentions women with a magico-religious role dashing between the ranks in the Celtic resistance (*Annals*, XIV,

§30); and he also tells of how Cartimandua, Queen of the Brigantes, waged war against her husband (*Annals*, XII, §36).[6]

Altogether in classical histories we find a number of examples of women warriors in the Northern Gallic and Celtic peoples, and in Celtic mythology women frequently influence battles either magically or by participating on the battle-field. Some Celtic scholars have even suggested that women warriors were an institutionalised part of Celtic life (for example, Chadwick, 1970, p. 136). The position of women in Celtic life is shadowy, however, and we should not assume that all Celtic peoples necessarily followed the same tradition. Nevertheless, it should be noted that although a woman battle-leader may be an anomaly for classical historians, and for those historians who followed them in writing about Boadicea, she was not necessarily extraordinary in her own culture.

Sexual symbolism in the classical texts

Tacitus

The way in which Boadicea's femaleness is used in her speech in Tacitus is worth comment, for there are themes here which recur in later accounts. It was standard practice in classical histories to attribute battle-leaders with speeches, so we must understand that the words are not her own. There are several dimensions or levels to the use of Boadicea's gender in the speech, and this possibility of several interwoven readings is characteristic of her anomalous potentiality.

Firstly, there is the contrast between Boadicea's sense of dignity and the crude aggression of the Romans. This contrast is made in sexual terms, though this may be seen in literal as well as metaphoric terms, since her daughters had been raped. She proclaims:

> I am avenging . . . my scourged body, the outraged chastity of my daughters. Roman lust has gone so far that not our very persons, nor even age or virginity, are left unpolluted. (*Annals*, XIV, §35)

On one level, violations of the female body are acting as particularly graphic representation of the wrongs done to the society as a whole. The sense of violation is further heightened by the fact that the female victims are from sexually ambiguous categories of women: the virgin and the 'old woman'.[7] This also strengthens the idea of wrong done to *society* rather than to women as such, for women categorised as sexually inactive may well be classified as sexually 'unspecified' or 'desexualised' (Hastrup, 1978, p. 59). In this respect, Boadicea herself, as a widow and representative of 'age', is made atypical of women in general; and thus it is as 'one of the people' (*Annals*, XIV, §35) that she enters the arena of warfare.

On another level, however, Boadicea is classified as a woman, and her role as battle-leader is shown to be exceptional by the focus on wrongs against women. It is under force of circumstance that she goes to battle, and she goes as honourable mother, and upholds the female virtues of virginity and chastity.

Dio's inventions and inversions

Writing nearly a century later than Tacitus, and almost certainly from no additional sources, Dio Cassius also uses Boadicea's femaleness, though to different effect. Unlike Tacitus, Dio gives us a description of Boadicea's appearance:

> In stature she was very tall, in appearance most terrifying, in the glance of her eye most fierce, and her voice was harsh; a great mass of the tawniest hair fell to her hips; around her neck was a large golden necklace; and she wore a tunic of divers colours over which was a thick mantle fastened with a brooch . . . She now grasped a spear to aid her in terrifying all beholders. (Dio, LXII, p. 85)

Boadicea is no longer merely the politician and potential battle-leader she was in Tacitus: here she has become an actual warrior. We later see her in her own chariot 'at the head of an army of about 230 000 men' (Dio, LXII, p. 97).

There is no mention in Dio's account of the Roman outrages against Boadicea, and no mention of her daughters at all. Boadicea's femaleness is never used to highlight a Roman/male aggressiveness, as it is in Tacitus, but instead it illuminates the Romans' ignominy at being beaten: 'all this ruin was brought upon the Romans by a woman, a fact which in itself caused the greatest shame' (Dio, LXII, p. 83). The speech Dio invents for Boadicea illustrates a remarkable inversion of the structure we found in Tacitus, for in Dio it is the *Romans* who become the 'women'. They are not, however, women with the positive qualities that Tacitus attributed to Boadicea. The Roman emperor Nero, she is reported as saying, 'though in name a man, is in fact a woman, as is proved by his singing, lyre-playing and beautification of his person' (Dio, LXII, p. 94). And in prayer to her goddess before the battle Boadicea asks for

> preservation of life, and liberty against men insolent, unjust, insatiable, impious, – if, indeed, we ought to term those people men who bathe in warm water, eat artificial dainties, drink unmixed wine, anoint themselves with myrrh, sleep on soft couches with boys for bedfellows, – boys past their prime at that, – and are slaves to a lyre-player and poor one too. Wherefore may this Mistress Domitia – Nero reign no longer over me or over you men; let the wench sing and lord it over Romans, for they surely deserve to be the slaves of such a woman after having submitted to her so long. (Dio, LXII, pp. 94–5)

Such remarks surely ring strange coming from a woman, though of course the speech is Dio's, and the words could have been put into the mouth of a male warrior. However, it isn't quite the case that Boadicea becomes an 'honorary man'; it is rather that she loses the problematic *content* of her gender (her motherhood, the crimes against her as a woman), but her femaleness remains as symbol. It is important to point out too that Boadicea is not presented as a *typical* woman: she is 'possessed of greater intelligence than often belongs to women' (Dio, LXII, p. 85). Her gender stands, however, as a marker to illustrate the perversity of the sexual roles in general in Dio's narrative.

Again diverging from Tacitus, Dio Cassius gives us a detailed description of the barbarous treatment of the Romans by the Britons:

> They hung up naked the noblest and most distinguished women and then cut off their breasts and sewed them to their mouths, in order to make the victims appear to be eating them; afterwards they impaled the women on sharp skewers run lengthwise through the entire body. (Dio, LXII, p. 95)

In these horrible tortures it is women's sexuality (their reproductive and nourishing capabilities) that is destroyed, so graphically displaying the sexual distortion of the whole story.

These acts are carried out 'particularly in the grove of Andate'. Andate is the goddess to whom Boadicea prays, and she is, according to Dio, the Briton's version of the goddess Victory (Dio, LXII, p. 95). Although we should not assume that the Celtic goddess was identical to that of the Romans, scholars suggest that Andate was a goddess of war among other things (see Ross, 1967, p. 218). The recurrence of Victory in Dio's account – the falling Victory statue, the ritual invocation of Victory, the sacrifices to Victory – further indicates a preoccupation with gender and war.

Honourable matron and virgin queen

The manuscripts of Tacitus and Dio were largely unknown to medieval historians, and it isn't until the sixteenth century that Boadicea again appears in histories. She was first incorporated into what was at the time a somewhat shocking 'new' version of national history by Polydore Vergil in his *English History* (probably written c. 1512–13). The account of Boadicea ('Voadicia') is, apart from cartographical errors, a fairly accurate summary of Tacitus (Vergil, [1846], pp. 71ff).

Upholding the honour of British ladies

A second rather different account of Boadicea also appeared in the sixteenth century: in Boece's *Chronicles of Scotland* (1531). Boadicea, called Voada by Boece, is situated in northern Britain, and said to be sister of Caratak (Caratacus) and Corbreid, Kings of Scotland.[8] Her husband is keen to make alliance with the Romans, and at one stage even imprisons her in order to go adultering with a Roman woman. After various battles between the Romans and Britons, Voada's husband dies, and as in the classical versions he has made his daughters and the Emperor heirs to the kingdom. This is given a new slant here, however, for he also has a son who he has been trying to disinherit, to the boy's uncles' annoyance. As in Tacitus, however, the Romans overrun the kingdom, publicy thrash

Voada, and rape the daughters. Her brother Corbreid, after unsuccessfully demanding compensation from Rome, assembles a confederation of kings to avenge the crimes. Voada declares that she will join the men, not to lead them, but with her own band of dishonoured women:

> The proud Romans may know what vassalage ladies may do when extreme danger occurs. And though I may no wise devoid me of wifely image, I shall not lack men's hardiness, but armed foremost in the brunt, where most danger appears, with 5000 British ladies who were all sworn to vindicate their injuries, we shall proceed foremost in battle, not regarding fear of death, or bloody wounds or terrible slaughter of ourselves or enemies; for I can have no commiseration with those who pursued my tender friends with such cruelties, deflowering so many virgins and matrons by effeminate lust, putting so many rich cities and towns to subversion, and innocent people to murder. (My rendering of Bellenden's 1551 translation, Boece, [1938], p. 113)

Her words stress her womanliness; and it is made clear that it is wrongs against *women* that she is principally avenging. She says, 'Had the Gods given me the fortune to be a man I might not have sustained so many unbearable injuries done by Romans' (Boece, [1938], p. 113). The 5000 women accompanying Voada to battle are a striking addition to the classical versions of the story. We are reminded, however, that warring women are out of the ordinary: the women who were not maltreated by the Romans remain in carts on the edge of the battle-field (Boece, [1938], p. 146).

Voada kills herself rather than fall into the hands of her enemies. Her daughters, however, are captured, and their stories make an interesting continuation of the playing out of sexual themes. The eldest daughter is given in marriage to the Roman who raped her. For a society where chastity is to be upheld at all costs this is one acceptable solution.

The younger daughter, Vodicia, decides to 'revenge the pollution of her body, and injuries done to her mother' (Boece, [1938], p. 155), and so she assembles an army and continues to attack the Romans with 'manly courage'. Finally, she is captured and brought before her Roman adversary who asks her 'why she dares pretend such things about the spirit and courage of women' (Boece, [1938],

p. 156). She gives no answer and is slain. Vodicia dies, not a virgin, but nevertheless chastely celibate.

Boadicea and Elizabeth I

During Elizabeth I's reign and the evaluation of it that continued after her death, stories of Boadicea and the rebellion flourished. In many cases previous accounts were used selectively and 'reinterpreted' to provide comment on contemporary politics. It was as though the inherent problem of a powerful woman in a patriarchal society could be dealt with most safely through the intermediary of a figure from the past. The first volume of Holinshed's *Chronicles* (1577) included a description of Boadicea (here called 'Voadicia, alias Bunduica'), with elements from all previous accounts (Holinshed, 1577, pp. 60–4). The *Chronicles* were a source of inspiration for many Elizabethan writers, and several of Shakespeare's contemporaries made use of the Boadicea tale.

The first to use this newly discovered history for Elizabeth's glory was Spenser in his *Faerie Queene* (1589). The poem is a celebration of Elizabeth with Gloriane as a representation of her. 'Bunduca' – 'O famous monument of women's prayse' (Spenser, Canto X, v. 56, 1.l) – provides an edifying parallel, with many lines equally appropriate to Elizabeth (v. 54–6).

Two of the Boadicea myths – namely that she was Queen of England, and that she was victorious – were both prevalent in literature at this time. For example, Ben Jonson writes that in Boadicea's history 'is express'd all magnitude of a spirit, breathing to the liberty, and redemption of her Countrey' ([1914], ll.11. 606–7), and Newstead points out the historical continuity: 'most of their [the Britaines] prosperous battels were when women did lead them' (in Shepherd, 1981, p. 145). Boadicea's fight against Romans was also given a contemporary religious slant, and used to Protestant ends.

Other potential ingredients of the myth, notably Boadicea's motherhood, and her daughters and their rape, are ignored in these indirect praises of the Virgin Queen. Daniel Tuvil even refers to '*princely* Voadicea [my emphasis] . . . who with her warlike *Amazoneans* maintained the reputation of her State' (in Shepherd, 1981, p. 145). It is only devoid of womanliness, as 'prince' or 'virgin', that Boadicea can stand unproblematically as a leader and warrior.[9]

Unnatural woman

The political uses of Boadicea in the seventeenth century were not all positive and complimentary, however, as *Bonduca*, a play by John Fletcher, illustrates. The play was first performed in 1610, seven years into James I's reign. In *Bonduca*, in contrast to literature praising Elizabeth, sexuality is made a central issue.

The hero of the play is Caratacke (Caractacus) who represents James. Unlike Bonduca and her daughters, he is keen to be reconciled with the Romans, providing all is done in a manly way. The different attitudes of Bonduca and Caratacke to the Romans are frequently expressed using sexual imagery. While Bonduca refers to them as 'girles' (Fletcher, [1951], 1.15), Caratacke expresses their virility in powerfully homoerotic language. He talks of making a mistress of the soldier who 'bend[s] my manly body with his sword' (l. 68); and says that he is 'married to the man that wounds me' (l. 71). At several points in the play, war is presented as a preferable alternative to marriage for men.

Although the women in the play try to participate in the battle, they do not conduct themselves as men: they are neither chivalrous nor effective, as Caratacke constantly points out. Bonduca is accused of 'meddl[ing] in mans affairs' (l. 1642) and ordered back to a suitable womanly role:

> Caratacke: home and spinne woeman spinne. goe spinne you
> trifle. (Fletcher, [1951], l. 1647)[10]

In trying to lead her people, Bonduca is, as the Roman Governor puts it, an 'unnaturall woeman' (l. 2271). Bonduca's daughters twice capture Roman soldiers and on both occasions Caratacke frees the men. In both cases we are reminded of the women's sexuality. In the first the captured soldiers joke bawdily that they would like to be tortured in bed (ll. 899–902). In the second, Caratacke reprimands the daughters for taking the Romans by treachery (the soldiers were lured by a love-letter):

> Younger Daughter: I vowe uncle
>   wee will have vengance for our rapes
>   Caratacke: good cozen
>   you should have kept yor legs close then.
> (ll. 1552–9)

Rape, unlike love-letters, is an accepted part of the male arena of warfare, and one which the victims were better able to resist according to Caratacke. One message of the play is clearly that warfare is for men only.

In a play a century and a half later, *Boadicia* by Richard Glover, these sexual themes are expressed even more forcefully. Here the unnaturalness of Boadicea's desire to lead and fight is represented in an exaggerated 'bloody disposition' (Glover, 1753, p. 12). She looks forward to 'Lead[ing] rout and slaughter thro' a tide of gore' (II, 2), and even hopes to ruin her ally, Dumnorix, the leader of the Trinobantes. Dumnorix is the epitome of reasonable manliness, and his wife the ideal of gentle, merciful womanliness. All attempts by this female paragon to appeal to Boadicea as wife and mother are spurned, and we are left in no doubt at the end of the play, as all die and Britain falls to the Romans, of the potentially devastating consequences of giving women authority:

> Dumnorix: I find a woman cursed with pow'r
>   To blast a nation's welfare. (Glover, 1753, III, 4)

Boadicea was also an 'unnatural' woman for Milton. He located the faults, however, not in Boadicea herself, but in the way that she (and by implication Britain) had been presented by the biased classical writers, particularly Dio Cassius ('the Greek Historian'). He is particularly horrified that Boadicea is made immodest enough to 'speak of her own lashing and her daughters' rapes – these are 'things worthier Silence, Retirement, and a Vail, than for a woman to repeat as don to her own Person, or to hear repeated before an Host of Men' (1698, p. 28). Milton is well aware of the political power of sexual inversion, and he feels that a literary coup has been effected against Britain through this means. The Roman historians hoped to

> embellish and set out thir History with the strangeness of our manners, not caring in the mean while to brand us with the rankest note of Barbarism, as if in *Britain* Women were Men, and Men Women (1698, p. 28)

Even war itself was rendered to 'impotence' and 'the wild hurrey of a distracted Woeman, with as mad a crew at her heeles' (1698,

p. 29). Milton himself attempts to set the record of the British Nation and British women straight; and he does this partly through Boadicea. He repudiates her lack of modesty and shame, her 'loose-bodied gown' and the superstitious 'hare in her bosom'; and gives us instead a tempered version of Dio's description that denies her warlike attributes. Milton's Boadicea has a face that is 'grim and stern', she wears a 'thick robe', and does not carry a spear (1698, p. 28).

The tension between Boadicea's womanliness and her status as warrior is mediated in the various versions of her story by portraying as exceptional either her participation in warfare, or else the nature of her sexuality. Yet the tension is not absolved completely – partly for the tautological reason that the very attempts at resolution make it more conspicuous. There is another logical alternative, however, and that is to argue that womanliness is not incompatible with war, and that Boadicea is not exceptional in being a powerful woman leader. Again, of course, having to make such an argument shows the issue to be contentious. It is an argument that scarcely figures in our history, however, although in the relatively hidden history of women we do occasionally find Boadicea mentioned as both a fighter and a representative of women in general, as we shall see below.

National and feminist symbol

Interest in Boadicea has been sporadic, and the reasons for this lie in her suitability as a symbol at different points in history. She once again became a focus of literary endeavour and patriotic sentiment in the latter half of the eighteenth century. As the British Empire expanded, early British resistance movements were idealised as prognostic of the day when the Roman Empire would give way to that of the British. The Roman element in contemporary British-ness was ignored, and Boadicea and the Britons were depicted as victorious. The fact that Boadicea was a woman was scarcely mentioned, and her maternity was forgotten. Cowper's *Boadicea: An Ode* (1780), learnt by thousands of schoolchildren in the twentieth century, fostered this triumphant asexual image. Most of the poem consists of a rousing patriotic speech by a Druid chief, and

Boadicea's own part is but briefly mentioned in her reaction to his words:

> She, with all a monarch's pride,
> Felt them in her bosom glow,
> Rush'd to battle, fought and died;
> Dying hurl'd them at the foe. (Cowper, [1967], p. 310)

Boadicea's gender here has no reference to contemporary women, she is simply a single exceptional and virtually genderless figure from Britain's distant past.

The two 'Victorias'

A century later, in the reign of Queen Victoria, reference to Boadicea again flourished, and did so to an extent matched only by that in Elizabethan times. It was no doubt felt that homage could be paid to one powerful queen by reference to another, though perhaps also there was an underlying uncertainty over women leaders that made the problematic figure of Boadicea an image of the times once again.

We should make a caveat here, however: there is no necessary link between a particular description of Boadicea and the times in which it was written. We can only make such links where they are hinted at in the literature itself. It has always been possible for an artist to simply pick up a book, come across a description of Boadicea, and feel intrigued or horrified enough to make his own literary comment. For example, we cannot, I think, make any suggestion that the Poet Laureate, Tennyson, had his monarch in mind at all when he wrote of an excessively cruel and barbaric Boadicea in 1859.[11] As in previous accounts, however, there is an expressly sexual content to Boadicea's savagery:

> Cut the Roman boy to pieces in his lust and voluptuousness,
> Lash the maiden into swooning, me they lash'd and humiliated,
> Chop the breasts from off the mother, dash the
> brains of the little one out. (Tennyson, [1969], ll. 68–8)

The analogy at work here, through the figure of Boadicea, is that a warring woman, who by definition flouts sexual conventions, also flouts conventional morality. This is demonstrated particularly directly through a sexual dimension to that immorality; and we might also note this as a device for distinguishing (decent, moral) 'war' from 'savagery'. In this case, as in its inspiration, Dio (above), the savagery is clearly and significantly anti-maternal. Tennyson's poem was written in an unusual metre and was never popular (though it remained one of his personal favourites). Perhaps part of the reason for its lack of success was that it was not in keeping with the general line of opinion on Boadicea and Britain's primitive past.

From the Victorian era the image that has been most resilient is that created by Thomas Thornycroft, sculptor to the royal family. Thornycroft's massive statue of a charioted Boadicea and daughters which now stands on Westminster Bridge, opposite the Houses of Parliament, was built with the Prince Consort's encouragement.[12] He lent his own horses as models, and according to Thornycroft had said, 'You must make . . . the throne upon wheels' (Manning, 1982, p. 38). Thornycroft's interpretation of this was what he saw as a poetic rather than realistic image of regality – a wild and powerful warrior woman. Although Boadicea's daughters crouch fearfully by her side, they are merely, in Thornycroft's words, 'young barbarians who would regard their violation simply as an insult to be avenged' (Manning, 1982, p. 38); and there is no evocation of Boadicea's maternal role. She stands, arms upraised, spear in hand, in a heavy Roman-style chariot with long sharpened scythes on the wheel axles, and two rearing stallions in the shafts. This is the first mention of the graphic and gory detail of the rotating knives. Archaeological remains and classical descriptions give no suggestion of them for this part of the world, and the Britons' chariot seems to have been in reality a lightweight wicker affair (Webster, 1978, p. 29).

It is interesting to compare Thornycroft's bronze with the marble Boadicea and daughters by another Victorian sculptor, James Harvard Thomas.[13] Whether he was making any conscious reference to his monarch we cannot know, but if he was, he drew upon another side to Victoria – her motherhood. In Thomas's sculpture there is no chariot, no spear in Boadicea's grasp, no sign of war whatever. Her breasts are full and maternal, her arms encircle her daughters' shoulders. The daughters themselves are soft-eyed innocents, with pure childlike faces; yet their bodies are fully developed. There is none of the wild warrior's fury of Thornycroft's

Boadicea here, only the suffering and stoicism of a mother. The image, unlike Thornycroft's, could be of any mother with her daughters.

As representative of women

In the accounts of Boadicea we have considered so far, it is only in her maternal aspect that she has been used as a role model for women in general. We might just illustrate this further by the following comments from a semi-scholarly book on Boadicea, which contains summaries of the classical texts and their archaeological corroboration. As we see, the author couldn't resist adding (at some length) his own patriotic interpolations:

> Boadicea's disdain of Roman immorality is typical of the British woman. . . . She was wounded in that part of her which was most vulnerable, her maternal affection, that sense of modesty and decency . . . those self-same qualities which the great majority of British wives and mothers, even in these latter days are known to possess. (Spence, 1937, p. 155)

Boadicea also possesses the potentiality of being used, in her guise of fighter or leader, as a model for women's strength and willingness to fight for what they believe. Sporadically through history women have indeed used her in such a way.

In a petition by women Levellers (1649), she is said to have freed Britain from the Danes, and is so used as a symbol for the freedom from oppression, though ironically not the oppression of women (see Fraser, 1984, p. 260). In reply to a scurrilous pamphlet on women, another seventeenth century woman, Ester Sowernam, used Boadicea as a representative of women's bravery and valour. Boadicea is listed as a heroic woman

> that defended the liberty of her Countrey, against the strength of Romans, when they were at the greatest, and made them feele that a woman could conquer them who had conquered almost all the men of the then known world. (Sowernam, 1617, p. 19. See also Shepherd, 1981, p. 150)

We might note that these women using Boadicea as an example do not seem to feel the need to explore and explicate the nature of her sexuality, or to dissociate her nature from that of ordinary women.

Boadicea was also used by the Suffragists. The Artists' Suffrage League designed banners 'to celebrate the memory of the great women of all ages'.[14] The Boadicea banner showed a gold silk scythed wheel, and the points of spears. Boadicea also appeared, along with Joan of Arc, Agnes of Dunbar, Florence Nightingale and many more, as one of the Warriors in Cecily Hamilton's *Pageant of Great Women* (1910), which was first produced at the Scala theatre in London in 1909.

Suffragists, however, were by no means insensitive to the ambiguous potentiality of Boadicea as a symbol; and the possibilities were drawn out in consciously divergent ways by the constitutionalist and militant suffragists. Dora Montefiore, writing about a Women's Social and Political Union meeting held under Thornycroft's statue of Boadicea, saw Boadicea in her chariot as advancing threateningly on the Houses of Parliament, and said 'she was therefore a symbol of the attitude of us militant women' (Montefiore, 1927, p. 109). At a dinner presided over by Millicent Garrett Fawcett, leader of the constitutionalist National Union of Women's Suffrage Societies, to welcome released prisoners of the militant Women's Social and Political Union, each guest was presented with a redrawing of Thornycroft's statue (see Plate 1).[15] In the borders of the drawing are inset two cameos: one of a madonna-like mother and baby, the other of a mother and child perusing a book together. The female figures in the chariot itself are not so wild as Thornycroft's originals, and Boadicea's spear is transformed into a banner reading 'Votes for Women'. In Boadicea's other hand are scales of justice, and an angel presents her with a laurel crown (a symbol of victory). The message to the militants was conveyed very clearly through this image of Boadicea.

Conclusion

Boadicea has found various niches in history, and she has been portrayed in widely divergent, even opposed, ways. She has been seen as a cruel, bloodthirsty savage, who would happily torture and

56

Plate 1 *Boadicea as champion of women's suffrage*

Source: Mary Evans/Fawcett Library

kill men, women and children; and also as a decent and honourable British lady, whose righteous actions stem from her motherly sense of propriety. She has been shown to possess the worst of female failings, immodesty and the repudiation of her femininity; and also to be the epitome of respectable womanhood. It is the ambiguous and problematic nature of the warrior woman – and in particular the warrior mother – that gives rise to such distinct alternatives. These alternatives supply – positively or negatively – a focus for the proper behaviour of women. British patriotism has also taken Boadicea as an example of the exceptional and historically specific category of women leaders, and in particular our most virginly and most matronly of queens. Devoid of her sexual specificity, she has represented the more general and abstract ideas of Britain and national struggle.

Boadicea's participation in battle has almost invariably been attributed either to exceptional and limited circumstances, or else to savage perversity, thus casting the female warrior and battle leader as abnormal and historically specific. In the fleeting appearances of Boadicea in women's writing and art, however, we do find something which we have seen in the work of no male historian: Boadicea both as warrior and as a symbol for all women. Yet Boadicea also presents problems for women wishing to 'rent' her as a symbol for their own determination in struggle – should they stress or forget her motherhood, and should they forget the Britons' savagery and their ultimate defeat? Perhaps it is an unnecessary scholarly nicety at this stage in the mythification of Boadicea to point out possible discrepancies with the original details of her story. Histories of Boadicea have rarely been 'objective', but have been embellished and elaborated on the flimsiest of evidence. Indeed, it is because of the brevity of the oldest historical account that Boadicea has been such an effective cipher for so much moralistic and patriotic comment (cf. Warner, 1981).[16]

Warrior or mother? For male commentators, it is only as representing the latter in all its propriety that Boadicea could be an appropriate role model for Britain's women. As warrior, Boadicea could only be presented as unnatural, exceptional, and often almost genderless. I say 'almost' because, of course, her gender is never quite forgotten: it is the very anomaly of a woman warrior in our culture which has thrust Boadicea into our national history and made her such a tantalising and provocative figure.

Notes

1. I use the name 'Boadicea' throughout this essay, except where I am specifically referring to a particular variant, as it is with the popular image of Boadicea rather than some supposed real person that I am concerned. 'Boadicea' is not itself a Celtic name, though it is usually thought to be a Romanised version of the Celtic form 'Boudica'. Through the texts we find many variants of the name due to translation and transcription errors: for example, Bonduca, Boundouika, Voadicia and Voada. The name 'Boudica' is derived from reconstructed Brittonic *'bouda'*, meaning 'victory', so rendering 'Boudica' an equivalent of 'Victoria' (Jackson, 1962, p. 143). The Romans may have known the meaning of her name, although this isn't mentioned. If not the instances of 'Victory' and 'Victoria' in Boadicea's historiography would seem to be rather wonderful coincidences.
2. The term *'Britannia'*, 'Britain', was used by Romans, though not to refer to an area congruent with what we would today call Britain. The Britons were a Celtic group of peoples occupying South-Eastern Britain. It is in the sense of 'Brittonic' that Boadicea can properly be called 'British'.
3. Although this essay treats accounts of Boadicea roughly chronologically, it is not meant to be an exhaustive survey of references to her, and only those works which deal with her particularly fully or originally are mentioned here.
4. As senator and consul, Tacitus would have had access to Imperial archives. Also he was probably told of the events by his father-in-law, Agricola, who was in Britain at the time of the rebellion, though probably not involved with it (see Lloyd-Jones, 1964, p. xvii).
5. Archaeologists have found 'thick destruction layers, covering burnt timber buildings' in London, Colchester and St Albans (Webster, 1978, p. 20). King's Cross was long thought to be the site of the battle, and was called 'Battle Bridge' for this reason.
6. Tacitus is the only Roman historian who mentions Cartimandua, the other woman leader at the time of the rebellion. Caractacus, fleeing from the Romans, goes to Cartimandua and her husband Venutius, but they turn him over to the Romans (the responsibility lying with Venutius, as he is leader at this stage). The split between Cartimandua and Venutius, in which Ventutius turns against the Romans, is subsequent to this. In all later histories this order of events is reversed, making Cartimandua solely responsible for betraying Caractacus. In Boece, for example, her act is made even more reprehensible by making her Caractacus' mother (Boece, 1983, p. 129); and in Holinshed, her lust for power is equated with sexual lust by making her adulterous (Holinshed, 1577, p. 58). Cartimandua remains through history a villain, standing as Boadicea's complementary opposite in those cases where Boadicea represents respectable womanhood. She is used, it seems, as a reminder of the dangers of powerful womanhood.

7. For a full discussion of the symbolic significance of these categories see Hastrup (1978) and Ardener (1978, pp. 35–43).
8. The cartography and relationships in Boece's account are not congruent with those in classical descriptions. Tacitus, for example, situates Caratacus in the South-West of Britain.
9. The symbolic importance of Elizabeth's virginal status has been discussed in Heisch (1980) and mentioned in Ardener (1978, p. 41). We may perhaps note in advance that it is also pointed out in the latter that Queen Victoria was more popular in her youth and old age than during her actively maternal years (Ardener, 1978, p. 42). For the importance of virginal status in another female warrior, Joan of Arc, see Warner (1981); and for further discussion of virginity and female warriors see Warner (1985, Chapter 8).
10. This is a parody of a famous occasion in James I's court when a highly academically accomplished woman was brought before him, and he merely asked 'but can she spin?' (see Shepherd, 1981, p. 148).
11. Tennyson's *Boädicea* can be understood perhaps as an embodiment of the cruel and savage nature (in opposition to civilised morality) that Tennyson saw Darwinian evolutionism as presenting.
12. Photographs of the sculpture may be found in Read, 1982 Plate 55; and Manning 1982, Plate 25. I would like to thank Julie Macdonald for help in ferretting out these and other visual representations of Boadicea, as well as a number of references, not all of which I have been able to include here.
13. The sculpture is in the City Hall, Cardiff (see Webster, 1978, Plate 1).
14. Quote from the *Sunday Times* in National Union of Women's Suffrage Societies' Press Reports of the Banners (Fawcett Library, London). The Boadicea banner is in the Fawcett Library, London.
15. With thanks to Liza Tickner for this information, and references to the suffragists' material. This dinner was held just before relations between these two suffragist groups became strained. The drawing is by J. Blake Wirgman.
16. In recent years, it is Boadicea's warrior role that has been predominant. She has been used on several occasions to refer to the the 'warmongering' characteristics of Mrs Thatcher – 'a bargain basement Boadicea' (Denis Healey), and 'a cross between Boadicea and the girl-next-door' (Godfrey Smith *Sunday Times*, 10 February 1985). For an excellent discussion of how the public image of Mrs Thatcher is more than just that of 'a battle-axe like Boadicea', see Warner (1985, Chapter 3).

   The singer Toyah Wilcox has attempted to use the warrior image as a positive symbol for women's insurrection and sexuality. In one of her videos she is shown wildly charging around in a chariot, brandishing a whip. Of this she has said, 'In my naivety, I've seen Boadicea as the most magnificently sexual woman there is going' (*Imaginary Women*, film made for Channel 4, shown in 1986). As she perceptively observes, however, this is not the real rebellion of everyday life: real rebellion 'is flicking his dirty underpants back in his face' (*Imaginary Women*).

References

Ardener, S. (1978) 'Introduction: The Nature of Women in Society', in S. Ardener (ed.), *Defining Females*, pp. 9–48 (London: Croom Helm).

Boece, H. [1938] *The Chronicles of Scotland*, trans (into Scots) J. Bellenden, 1551 (Edinburgh and London: Chambers and Batho).

Chadwick, N. (1970) *The Celts* (London: Penguin).

Cowper, W. [1967] 'Boadicea: An Ode', in H. S. Milford (ed.), *Cowper Poetical Works*, p. 310–11 (Oxford: Oxford University Press).

Dio, Cassius [1955] *Dio's Roman History*, VIII, trans (London: Loeb Classical Library).

Douglas, M. (1970) 'Introduction', in M. Douglas (ed.), *Witchcraft, Confessions and Accusations* (London: Tavistock).

Fletcher, J. [1951] *Bonduca*, prepared by W. Wilson Greg (The Malone Society Reprints).

Fraser, A. (1984) *The Weaker Vessel* (London: Methuen).

Glover, R. (1753) *Boadicea. A Tragedy* (Dublin).

Hamilton, C. (1910) *Pageant of Great Women* (London: The Suffrage Shop).

Hastrup, K. (1978) 'The Semantics of Biology: Virginity', in S. Ardener (ed.), *Defining Females*, pp. 49–65 (London: Croom Helm).

Heisch, A. (1980) 'Queen Elizabeth I and the Persistance of Patriarchy', *Feminist Review*, 4, pp. 45–56.

Holinshed, R. (1577) *The firste volume of the Chronicles of England, Scotland and Irelande* (London: George Bishop).

Jackson, K. H. (1962) 'The name Boudicca', in D. R. Dudley and G. Webster (eds), *The Rebellion of Boudicca*, Appendix II (London: Routledge & Kegan Paul).

Jonson, B. [1914] 'The Masque of Queens', 1609, in Hereford and Simpson (eds), *Ben Johnson*, VII (Oxford: Clarendon Press).

Lloyd-Jones, H. (1964) *Tacitus' Annals and Histories* (Chalfont St Giles: Richard Sadler and Brown).

Manning, E. (1982) *Marble and Bronze: The Art and Life of Hamo Thornycroft* (London: Trefoil).

Milton, J. (1698) *The History of England* Book 2 (Amsterdam).

Montefiore, D. (1927) *From a Victorian to a Modern* (London: E. Archer).

Piggott, S. (1968) *The Druids* (London: Penguin).

Read, B. (1982) *Victorian Sculpture* (Newhaven: Yale University Press).

Ross, A. (1967) *Pagan Celtic Britain* (London: Routledge & Kegan Paul).

Shepherd, S. (1981) *Amazons and Warrior Women: Varieties of Feminism in Seventeenth-Century Drama* (Brighton: Harvester Press).

Sowernam, E. (1617) *Esther hath hang'd Haman* (London: Nicholas Bourne).

Spence, L. (1937) *Boadicea, Warrior Queen of the Britons* (London: Robert Hale).

Spenser, E. [1912] *The Faerie Queene*, J. C. Smith and E. de Selincourt (eds), (Oxford: Oxford University Press).

Tacitus [1891] *The Annals*, trans A. J. Church and W. J. Broadribb (London: Macmillan).

Tennyson, A. [1967] 'Boädicea', in C. Ricks (ed.), *The Poems of Tennyson*, pp.1118–23 (London: Longmans).

Vergil, P. [1846] *English History*, I, H. Ellis (ed.) (London: Camden Society).

Warner, M. (1981) *Joan of Arc. The Image of Female Heroism* (London: Penguin).

Warner, M. (1985) *Monuments and Maidens. The Allegory of the Female Form* (London: Weidenfeld and Nicolson).

Webster, G. (1978) *Boudica* (London: Batsford).

4

Women and ritual conflict in Inka society[1]

PENNY DRANSART

The European world first encountered the Inka empire of Tawantinsuyu[2] when a band of invaders led by Francisco Pizarro disembarked at Tumbes in 1531. Writing later of the battles with the Inka, Spanish historians made frequent mention of women on or near the battlefields, and even of Inka women fighting with weapons. However, the *conquistadores* changed the very notion of 'war' for the Inka people; and although women were indeed present at 'battles' in traditional Inka society, both the roles of the women and the roles of the conflict itself were significantly different from those envisaged by the Spanish. Our information on pre-conquest Inka society is unfortunately limited, and the description here is built up from scattered records of Inka society and rituals; traditional Inka art; some insights glimpsed through the Spanish accounts; and various post-conquest sources, including comparative ethnographic material. The intention here is not only to give some indication of women's involvement in conflict in traditional Inka society, but also to show how this society and its values were, sometimes wilfully, misinterpreted by the Spanish.

The Spanish conquest

The conquest and its aftermath have been described as a clash of two conflicting and irreconcilable forms of society (Livermore, 1966). Inka society has been seen as a collectivist one in which there was no need for individual conscience. The maintenance of order and the hierarchy was of paramount importance, this being the duty and responsibility of the privileged Inka classes. The Spanish, on the other hand, lived by a faith in which the individual conscience was accountable before the Christian God. The invaders were particularly lacking in an ordered collectivist ethic:

> the unruly soldiers who came to Peru [were not] the choicest specimens of Spanish culture. The very history of the civil wars shows that they would only combine in the face of a dire threat to their interests and when the threat was removed they fell into disorder. (Livermore, 1966, p. xxix)

Not only was the conquest brutal and violent, the arrival of the white soldiers and the overthrow of Andean deities induced long lasting psychological shock, followed by madness and mourning. This is well described by Nathan Wachtel in what he calls the 'vision of the vanquished', where he shows how the trauma of the conquest persists in present day folklore (Wachtel, 1977). The resulting disintegration of native societies is evident in what he calls 'destructuration', or the partial survival of ancient structures no longer contained within the relatively coherent context in which they previously existed. Not only were Christian religion and a market economy imposed on Andean societies, but the brutality continued long after the conquest, becoming by its permanence a structural factor of colonial society. It is true that conflict and a readjusting of the hierarchical status of groups of people had taken place before the conquest, witness Inka dominance, but now the Spanish sector survived by draining its subsistence from the Indian sector, through domination by violent means (Wachtel, 1977, pp. 85, 86). There was a demographic collapse resulting from civil wars, newly introduced epidemics to which the people had no resistance, and a marked drop in the birth rate. From the census figures, it seems that there were fewer children born in the 1560s and 1590s. Also, there was an imbalance in the sex ratio; more men than women died or fled the censuses. Census findings dated 1562 of the Chupachu people of the Huánuco region indicate that polygamy was practised, though it was no longer the exclusive privilege of the *kuraka* (leader) class. Under the influence of Christian missions, polygamy ceased and the balance betwen the sexes was gradually restored over the years (Wachtel, 1977, pp. 91, 92).

Understanding the consequences of the conquest for women from the point of view of the defeated is not easy, as most of the sixteenth and seventeenth century histories were written by men representing the conquering class. Thus our view of women's roles is doubly distorted, since much of the information we have at our disposal was written by outsiders, men who interpreted what they saw according to their perception of male/female roles in their own society. Moreover, much of their information was obtained from their dealings with *kuraka* men – that is, the ruling lords. Historical accounts often show little understanding of the nature of the high status achieved by some women in Inka society. However, Felipe Guaman Poma, who was of Inka descent and the author of an illustrated manuscript letter to the Spanish monarch dated 1615, tells us that Chinbo Mama Caua, sister/wife of the fifth Inka Emperor, was unable to 'govern the land' due to the onset of epilepsy after marriage. Guaman states that after her reign, her younger sister, Cuci Chinbo Mama Micay Coya (queen), ruled as second wife of the Emperor (Guaman Poma, [1980], pp. 101, 128, 129).

The Spanish historians tended to raise women's issues when they wished to be critical of either Inka or Spanish actions. For example, Pedro Pizarro relates how the Marqués don Francisco Pizarro had Asarpay, the sister/wife of the Ataw Wallpa (the Inka chief), garroted. Pedro Pizarro comments that Asarpay, as *coya* (queen), was held greatly in awe and esteem, but he adds that she, and the wife of Ataw Wallpa's brother, Manco Inka, were killed without regard to the fact that they were women, implying that women were necessarily innocent (Pizarro, [1978], pp. 200, 201). This statement is intended to be critical of the Marqués, but it also denies women any part in the maintenance of Inka society and preservation of its values. Yet, there are indications that women acted bravely in the attempted defence of those values.

Inka women on the battlefield

In his history of the discovery and conquest of Peru, Agustín de Zárate mentions that when Diego de Almagro was returning from Cuzco back to Quito with a band of men, they passed through the province of Liribamba where they encountered a great number of

Indians waiting for battle. The Spanish only won with difficulty as women were also fighting, using slings very skilfully (Zárate, [1862], p. 482). Although the Spanish fought with arquebuses and wore armour, the sling was capable of inflicting great injury and was one of the main weapons used by highland peoples and the Inka army.

The circumstances of war observed by the Europeans were unusual; their very presence disrupted normal Andean practices, and we do not know if it was usual for women to fight as soldiers. The fact that the women of Liribamba were skilled in using slings probably reflects the usefulness of this piece of equipment. Slings were, and are, used by herders of the altiplano while herding animals, and it should be noted that among Andean pastoralists, everyday herding tasks do not imply a marked division of labour on the basis of either sex or age (Celestino-Husson, 1985, p. 89). Slings were also used by agriculturalists to scare birds away from ripening crops. Today the making of slings is a male activity and a non-utilitarian dance sling is also made by men, but used by women (Cahlander, 1980, pp. 5–9). It would, therefore, not be unexpected for women to use slings very effectively even if warfare was not the usual use to which they were put.

The nature of war in Inka society

Murra (1965) regards war in the Andes during pre-hispanic times as a magico-religious matter. Llamas were sacrificed and their entrails examined for military omens. Besides being beasts of burden, llamas were also used in ceremonies greeting the new moon, which involved the temporary cessation of military operations, something the Europeans did not respect. The type of military encounter with the Spanish was of a sort previously unknown in the Andes – a desperate fight for survival – and women's participation should be understood in this context.

Zárate tells us that, after the execution of Ataw Wallpa, one of his generals fielded an army of 12 000 Indian soldiers. In the main body of this force were women and servants, as well as many llamas. When Quizquiz, the general, had to withdraw suddenly by night to the sierra, the Indians burned all the clothing they could not take with them. They left more than 4000 men and women and more than 15 000 llamas (Zárate, [1862], p. 483; Murra, [1965], p. 207).

Zárate regarded the women in this force as prisoners taken by Quizquiz. However, this may not be the explanation for their presence at the scene of battle. Zárate's history is not an eye-witness account: he arrived in South America in 1544, after the events he described, and he wrote his history after returning to Europe.

From Pedro Pizarro's account of the conquest, written forty years after his landing at Tumbes with the first group of Spanish invaders, it is clear that women's participation in the rituals accompanying war was essential. He relates how unmarried noble women, the daughters of Inka lords and local rulers, went to the field of battle with their relatives. Here, Pizarro adds that no value was attached to remaining a virgin, nor were the women reprimanded for not being chaste until after marriage. Every night, men and women went out to the battlefield, forming many circles, singing and dancing. Then each Indian took the woman he was holding by the hand away from the circle and, to quote Pizarro, 'he threw himself on her, and fulfilling his desire, returned to the dance' (Pizarro, [1978], pp. 201, 202). This ritual was accompanied by the drinking of *chicha*, fermented maize drink, which was supplied by the *accllacona*, the chosen women who served the Sun, Moon, Stars and the holy shrines, and who led chaste lives. Also in connection with war, Pizarro adds that great repositories were kept by the Inkas full of clothes and food for this purpose. Much of this must have seemed incomprehensible to a newly arrived European soldier such as Pizarro, but the implications of the religious nature of ritualised conflict and its interconnections with fertility are present in Pizzarro's account. That it was institutionalised is also evident from the fact that the *accllacona* provided the *chicha*.

The complementary roles of women

The Spanish historians of the early colonial period did not – and perhaps could not have – understood the nature of women's participation in war as an essential complement to male war activities. Nor did they question whether war meant the same thing to European and Andean peoples. Soldiers in both Andean and European societies were rewarded with culturally relevant prizes. For the Inkas, the wearing of certain types of clothing was a royal privilege and grants of highly valued cloth enhanced one's status and prestige. Murra has suggested that feather-ornamented cloth was particularly associated with soldiers and war, both feather garments and armour being prepared for military operations (Murra, 1962, p. 718). (For an illustration of a feather garment of Inka date see Ubbelohde-Doering, 1952, Plate 51).

It is clear that warriors were expected to show valour in war, and that this valour was recognised by Inka society. Guaman Poma illustrates a series of Inka captains and the accompanying text repeatedly describes these captains of noble birth as '*ualerso*', or valiant (Guaman Poma, [1980], pp. 145–74). In the section of his letter concerning the general inspection of the tax-paying commoners who were now subject to the Spanish crown, Guaman portrays a warrior, *avec camaioc*, with the accompanying text indicating that this represents a '*balente moso*', or valient bachelor (Guaman Poma [1980], pp. 217, 218), whose status seems to be marked by his dress.[3] Guaman illustrates different categories and age-grades of people whose duties included weaving for the state. One of these categories is that of married women and widows called *auca camayocpa uarmin*, meaning wives of soldiers. They held the office of weaving 'exquisite clothing' for the Inka nobility and for soldiers as war attire (Guaman Poma [1980], pp. 217, 218). The known standardisation of certain tunics and the organisation of the weavers lends further support to the theory that through the demonstration of military valour, men received social recognition in the form of valued clothing. Women played an essential role in the production of this very important cloth. Guaman's letter shows that the weaving of different categories of cloth was itself organised on an hierarchical basis, but he does not inform us of the social recognition awarded to weavers of prestige textiles.

Whereas the warriors are conventionally described as 'valiant' by Guaman, it would seem that the ideal attributes of women of the realm were associated with the adjectives '*muy bizarra y hermosa*' (Guaman Poma, [1980], pp. 176, 178, 180, 182). The adjective *hermosa* may be translated as 'goodly' rather than 'beautiful', since he describes the Colla lady as *hermosa* and ugly in the same sentence (Guaman Poma [1980], p. 180). The adjective '*bizarra*' can be translated as either 'gallant, brave, high spirited', or as 'general, liberal, high-minded' (Velazquez, 1971, p. 106). This implies that male and female roles in Inka society were different, but complementary.

Women, fertility and war

However, the question remains: what was the reason for women's presence at the scene of battle as observed by Pizarro? This does not seem to be a subject directly tackled by the historians of the period and I know of no Inka visual representation which might help clarify the issue. The Inka art style is refined, but primarily abstract. It does not provide iconographic detail equivalent to that of some of the pre-Inkaic cultures. But a pair of Nasca-style ceramic beakers in the Royal Museum of Scotland, Edinburgh[4] (illustrated in Plate 2) sheds some light on the nature of war in Andean societies. The Nasca culture of the south coast of Peru has been dated AD 100–800. These orange-pink pottery beakers have two rows of mammiform protuberances, and on the tall, flaring neck are painted a warrior and a vanquished, naked enemy. The warrior appears to be in the process of taking a trophy head. What is of interest are the two rows of flesh-coloured 'breasts' and the painted representations of slings. Apparently, breasts, warfare and the taking of a trophy head have been conceptually linked and expressed in visual form.

During an earlier period, the trophy head was an important component of Paracas-style iconography, best known from its embroidered textiles found on the Paracas Peninsula and the south coast of Peru. This art style flourished in the latter part of the first millennium BC. Dwyer (1979) has analysed the nature of the Paracas visual forms and their underlying concepts, and the trophy head seems to be at the core of this symbolic system with connotations of death and rebirth. She concludes that trophy headhunters take other lives in order to go on living, providing the graphic allegory of the necessity of death to sustain the living (Dwyer, [1979], p. 127).

The paradox of the taking of a trophy head to help maintain life-giving sustenance, represented by breasts, is implicit in the Nasca-style beakers. Trophy heads are also depicted in the hands of warriors, woven in textiles and painted on ceramics, in the highland Wari style of the latter part of the first millennium AD.[5] Depictions of trophy heads are rare in the predominantly abstract Inka art style, although Guaman Poma drew the fifth in his series of noble captains and the previously mentioned valiant warrior holding trophy heads (Guaman Poma, [1980], pp. 153, 196).

An interesting post-conquest panel painting by an anonymous

69

Plate 2 *Inka vase*

Source: The Trustees of the National Museum of Scotland

artist in the Museo Arqueologico in Cuzco, portrays the Ñusta (princess) Chanan Cori Coca presenting a severed head to an Inka monarch. She stands on a headless corpse, and in the background is a rainbow coming out of the mouth of a puma, representing a pre-hispanic motif. (This picture is illustrated in Gisbert, 1980 Figure 162.) In general, most of the Inka women in early Seventeenth century portraits, for example those by Guaman Poma and Martín de Morúa, are shown carrying flowers and birds. However, both the Ñusta and the Inka monarch are shown with warlike attributes; she is carrying the staff usually depicted in male hands and he is wearing the Inka helmet, and not the triple crown, as one of the insignias of royalty.

Female deities

It might be expected that we would find the themes of women, fertility and war bound together in Inka religion. As with other aspects of traditional Inka culture, however, we have only indirect information. Christian saints were 'mapped onto' pre-hispanic deities, altering various features in the transitional process, leaving us with a complex sequence of substitutions in many instances.

In the case of Pachamama, the earth goddess, there are only a few images from the viceregal period which represent the explicit substitution of the Virgin Mary for Pachamama. However, Mary was used as a synthetic principle whose worship encompassed many pre-hispanic holy sites and deities, and whose enthronement began a process of disassociation (Gisbert, 1980, pp. 17, 22). It is clear that the church had to suppress those facets of Andean deities which were not compatible with Christianity. The identification of a saint with a pre-hispanic mythical being relegated to neglect the least Christian aspects. Male deities have probably been more likely to survive as saints in a new guise than have female divinities. Also, given that war was intimately connected with religious beliefs, it is likely that warlike attributes were suppressed.

Patricia Lyon has examined the iconographic and literary evidence for female supernaturals in prehispanic Peru (Lyon, 1978). Pachamama was, and is, a major Andean deity. She is independent and without a male consort. Revered by both pastoralists and agriculturalists, she has her own self-sufficient and creative power to maintain life on this earth, whether in the farmers' fields or in the pastures of the herders. Although she is beneficient to humans, she also has the power to withhold those benefits. The nature of some female supernaturals, however, would seem to have been awesome and fearful. They include the warlike Mama Guaco, who was one of the founding mothers of Inka society (Lyon, 1978, p. 117), though it should be pointed out that the description of the horrible and inhuman Mama Guaco comes from an historical account written to discredit the Inkas (Sarmiento, [1942], see below). There were important female divinities of whom no clear description has survived. That some of them made gruesome demands is clear from Pizarro's account of an oracle he saw in Apurimac, which contained an upright tree trunk with golden belt and breasts, dressed with very fine women's clothes. She was flanked with smaller, similar idols and all were covered with blood offerings (Pizarro, [1978], p. 82). We do not know, however, whether the warlike attributes of these female deities were emphasised, while other features were minimised, by the Spaniards at the time of the conquest.

Ritual conflict

The essential presence of women at the scene of battle is a persistent Andean theme. In the highlands of Peru and Bolivia, ritual battles are still fought between neighbouring communities, and as recently as the first half of this century, a chance killing was regarded as enhancing the fertility of the soil. From her recent fieldwork with the Laymi Indians of the central Bolivian highlands, Olivia Harris has made the following observations:

> While she is unmarried, a girl will sing, dance, get drunk. She will fight against other girls in the ritual fights, *tinku*, that take place at big fiestas. In particular, the presence of unmarried girls is essential for the success of the group of male warriors who go together to the *tinku*. This same group of warriors and unmarried girls, known as *wayli*, has an important ritual function for the community, since it is they who intercede with the sun-god for protection and pardon, especially if epidemic or disaster strikes. (Harris, 1980, pp. 74, 75)

Harris notes that the members of the *wayli* group have ritualised roles; the girls act as standard bearers in the troop, carrying flags and sacred images; and they also help the 'majors' maintain discipline in the ranks.

The fundamental Andean concept of *tinku* is of social, political and economic importance. In both the Quechua and Aymara languages, it is significant, and van Kessel lists the following meanings:

1. The territorial limit between two farmsteads or communities; this limit separates and unites at the same time.
2. Ritual combat between two parts of a community, or between two communities, constituting a mechanism for the redistribution of community lands between contending groups.
3. The balance between two equal parts, for example, the load on a llama.
4. The point of confluence of two rivers.
5. The verb *tincuy* signifies to pair, to balance two equal parts which are opposed and complementary, the bringing together of which constitutes a dynamic balance. It brings about a fertile union which is tense and mobile, such as that between masculine and feminine principles. This concept is usually translated as 'reciprocity' and is a structural principle of Andean economy and society (van Kessel, 1980, p. 355).

That this concept was valid in Inka society can be seen from the number of entries in connection with it listed in the Quechua dictionary compiled by Gonçalez Holguin and published in 1608 (Gonçalez Holguin, [1952]).

It is also clear that in Inka society, warfare did not only involve the taking of individual lives. One of the important functions of warfare was to wage war against illness and plagues. For example, *Coya Raymi*, the festival of the queen, was celebrated every September. The festivities included preparing warriors for war, equipping them with slings, and ordering all Inkas with illness and plague to leave the realm (Cobo, [1956], pp. 217–19; Guaman Poma, [1980], pp. 254, 255). Guaman Poma makes it clear that this was the great festival of the Moon, considered to be wife of the Sun, and women especially celebrated this feast, inviting men to participate.

War was also waged against eclipses of the moon. During the reign of Manco Capac Yupanqui two eclipses occurred. The people wept and shouted, while the warriors made ready for war against the two comets which they regarded as a lion (probably a puma) and a serpent which they thought were about to tear the moon to pieces. This action was taken to prevent permanent darkness and to stop the instrument of men and women from turning into lions and reptiles. The spindles of the women were especially feared to turn into serpents, and their looms into bears, 'tigers' and ferocious animals (Montesinos, [1920], pp. 36, 37). Bernabe Cobo reported that when a lion or serpent threatened to destroy the moon during an eclipse the people shouted and cried, and they whipped dogs to make them howl. The men prepared for war, sounding trumpets and drums (Cobo, [1956), pp. 158, 159).

Women's participation in magico-religious ritual conflict was assured since women's roles and symbolic significance were essential complements to those of the men. Pre-eminence and greater prestige was accorded to men, but their dominance has been regarded in the nature of 'first among equals' (van Kessel, 1980, p. 142). The complexity of Inka cosmology, and of gender and conflict ideology within it, was not understood by the Spanish invaders and so the essential ritual participation of Inka women in conflict has been overlooked. The burial of Inka women's importance in history was also helped by more active attempts by the Spanish to alter the historical record.

Historical misrepresentation

When Andean people first met Europeans, they encountered soldiers and military aspects of Spanish society, but with the governorship of Viceroy Francisco de Toledo (1567–81), the Andes entered a new phase in colonial rule. The Viceroy instigated an enquiry in Cuzco which included the commission of a history from Pedro Sarmiento de Gamboa, part of which has survived, and a series of paintings (Sarmiento [1942]; Gisbert, 1980, p. 117). These pictures included portraits showing the descent of the Inka monarchs. Coya Cusi Huarque, widow of Inka Sairi Tupac (who was the son of Manco Inca and nephew of Waskhar and Ataw Wallpa, and who ruled the independent state of Vilcabamba which had survived since the conquest), protested against the Viceroy's version of Inka history, since he showed the collaborator Don Carlos Inka in a more prestigious place than her own lineage (Livermore, 1966, p. xxvii). Spanish rule recognised the danger to its authority represented by the prestigious position of the noble women of Cuzco and their support for Inka values. In an attempt to silence them, the Viceroy married Coya Cusi Huarque to a common soldier (Garcilaso, [1966], pp. 619, 1444, 1445; Guaman Poma, [1980], pp. 409, 445). The aristocratic mother of the Inka chronicler Garcilaso de la Vega, El Inka, suffered a similar humiliation. She was Ñusta Chimpu Ocllo, second cousin and granddaughter of Inka emperors. Garcilaso's father, governor of Cuzco, had her married as a concubine to a Juan del Pedroche, apparently a soldier or a trader. He may have contributed to her dowry (Livermore, 1966, p. xx).

The year 1572 saw the defeat of the Vilcabamba with the execution of Inka Tupac Amaru. A month previously, there had been a public reading of Sarmiento's history, which presented the Inkas as conquerors, like the Spanish themselves, and often as cruel and despotic rulers. The Viceroy made forty-two Indians declare that this history accorded with tradition. On 1 March 1572 the history and paintings were sent to Felipe II of Spain.

Conclusion

The royally accepted version of Inka history is unreliable, for it was written and distorted to serve the colonists' political ends. Even where the intention was only to describe however, the Spanish could often only offer incomplete accounts as Inka society differed so considerably from their own. Andean societies had achieved a sophisticated sociocultural adaptation in some very hostile environments, both in desert coastal valleys and at altitudes at and beyond the upper limits of cultivation, and their whole notion of warfare was unlike that of the conquistadores.

Actual or ritualised war played an important role in the maintenance of the hierarchical order both within Inka society and in its relations with other Andean societies. War was part of the annual cycle of events and warriors received social recognition. It was a complex affair, integrated with religious beliefs and economic practices, as is the evident from the fundamental Andean concept of *tinku*. The taking of some human lives was thought necessary to sustain life for the whole of the community, though war was not only fought against other people, but also against illness and disaster. Although women do not seem to have fought as warriors in the normal course of events, the presence of unmarried women at the scene of battle was essential. Male and female roles in Andean society were (and are) complementary, but also in opposition, in a tense but reciprocal balance.

War for the Inkas was a magico-religious phenomenon which played a part in controlling the cosmic and social orders. Being a warrior was part of the masculine career, and a means through which men could obtain social recognition. Women played important practical roles in this prestige system, and acted as complementary opposites to the male roles. Women were also vitally important symbolically in the ideology and rituals of war and fertility, which were based on the paradox of taking an individual's life to sustain life for the whole community.

Notes

1. The modern orthography 'Inka' is used throughout in preference to the more traditional but less accurate rendering 'Inca'.
2. The Empire of Tawantinsuyu, meaning 'land of the four quarters', had reached its greatest extent at the time of the conquest, incorporating many peoples from north of Ecuador to as far south as the River Maule in central Chile. The Inkas themselves were a highland people and their empire was oriented around Cuzco, which they regarded as the navel of the world. We should not take for granted the nature of their 'empire', however: Gonzalo Aguirre Beltran has stated emphatically that there were no nations in the modern sense of the word in Central and South America at that time, instead there were ethnic groups organised as separate and segregated communities. These groups formed confederations which enabled each community to maintain its independence, or for one of them to dominate the rest in a form of tribal *imperio* which, on occasions, could achieve prolonged stability (Aguirre Beltran, 1967, p. 159). The control imposed by the tribal *imperio* maintained a situation whereby each native community considered itself different or even hostile to the rest, even though culturally the communities may have had much in common. The Empire of Tawantinsuyu, which is conventionally dated from 1430–1532, should be understood in this context.

3. The warrior is wearing what is called a *q'asana* pattern tunic, which is similar to at least one known museum specimen (Rowe, 1979, p. 261). The standardisation in the design of certain Inka tapestry tunics and the categories of people who wore them has been analysed by John Howland Rowe (1979).
4. Royal Museum of Scotland, accession numbers 1962 855 and 1962 856.
5. For an example in pottery, see Idiens, 1971: (no. 1962/860).

References

Aguirre Beltran, Gonzalo (1967) *Regiones de refugio* (Mexico: Instituto Ingidenista Interamericano).

Cahlander, Adele (1980) *Sling braiding in the Andes* (with Elayne Zorn and Ann Pollard Rowe), *Weavers Journal Monograph, IV* (Colorado Fiber Center, Boulder, Col.).

Celestino-Husson, Olinda (1985) 'Eleveurs Aymaras des punas de Puno', *Production pastorale et société*, 16 (Spring) pp. 85–94 (Paris).

Cobo, Bernabe [1956] 'Historia del Nuevo Mundo', 1653, in *Obras*, II, Biblioteca de Autores Espanoles, 92, P. Francisco Mateos (ed.) (Madrid).

Duviols, Pierre (1973) 'Huari y Llacuaz. Agricultores y pastores, un dualismo prehispanico de oposicion y complementaridad', *Revista del Museo Nacional*, 39, pp. 153–91 (Lima).

Dwyer, Jane P. (1979) 'The chronology and iconography of Paracas-style textiles', in Ann Pollard Rowe, Elizabeth P. Benson and Anne-Louise Schaffer (eds), *The Junius B. Bird Pre-Columbian Textile Conference* (Washington, D.C.: The Textile Museum and Dumbarton Oaks).

Garcilaso de la Vega, El Inca [1966] *Royal commentaries of the Incas and general history of Peru, 1609*, trans and introduced Harold V. Livermore (Austin and London: University of Texas Press).

Gisbert, Teresa (1980) *Iconografia y mitos indigenas en el arte* (La Paz: Gisbert y CIA SA).

Goncalez Holguin, Diego [1952] *Vocabulario de la lengua general de todo el Peru llamada lengua Qquichua o del Inca*, 1608 (Lima: Edicion del Instituto de Historia).

Guaman Poma de Ayala, Felipe [1980] *El primer nueva coronica y buen gobierno*, 1615, Edicion critica de John V. Murra y Rolena Adorno (Seiglo Veintiuno, America Nuestra, and Instituto de Estudios Peruanos).

Harris, Olivia (1980) 'The power of signs: gender, culture and the wild in the Bolivian Andes', in Carol MacCormack and Marilyn Strathern (eds), *Nature, culture and gender* (Cambridge: Cambridge University Press).

Idiens, Dale (1971) *Ancient American Art* (Edinburgh: Royal Scottish Museum).

Kessel J. J. M. M. van (1980) *Holocausto al progreso: los Aymaras de Tarapaca*, Centro de Estudios y Documentacion de America Latina publication, 16, (Amsterdam).

Livermore, Harold V. (1966) 'Introduction', in Garcilaso [1966].

Lyon, Patricia J. (1978). 'Female supernaturals in ancient Peru', in *Nawpa Pacha*, 16, pp. 95–140, (Berkeley, Cal.).

Montesinos, Fernando [1920] *Memorias antiquas historiales del Peru*, 1644, trans Philip Ainsworth Means (London: Hakluyt Society).

Murra, John V. (1962) 'Cloth and its function in the Inca State', *American Anthropologist*, 64, 4, pp. 710–28.

Murra John V. (1965) 'Herds and herders in the Inca State', *Man, culture and animals: the role of animals in human ecological adjustments*, pp. 185–216, publication 78 of the American Association for the Advancement of Science (Washington, D.C.).

Pizarro, Pedro [1978] *Relacion del descubrimiento y conquista del Peru*, Guillermo Lohman Villena, 1572 Pontificia Universidad Catolica del Peru (Lima).

Rowe, John Howland (1979) 'Standardization in Inca tapestry tunics', in Ann Pollard Rowe, Elizabeth P. Benson and Anne-Louise Schaffer (eds), *The Junius B. Bird Pre-Columbian Textil Conference*, pp. 239–64 (Washington D.C., The Textile Museum and Dumbarton Oaks).

Sarmiento de Gamboa, Pedro, (1942) 'Historia Indica', in *Don Francisco de Toledo. Supremo Organizador del Peru*, 1572, 3, pp. 1–159 (Buenos Aires: Espasa-Calpe SA).

Ubbelohde-Doering, Heinrich (1952) *The art of ancient Peru* (London: Zwemmer).

Velazquez de la Cadena, Mariano (1971) *New revised Velazquez Spanish and English Dictionary* (London: Heinemann Educational).

Wachtel, Nathan (1977) *The vision of the vanquished. The Spanish conquest of Peru through Indian eyes 1530–1570* (Brighton: Harvester Press).

Zárate, Agustin de [1862] *Historia del descubrimiento y conquista de la provincia del Peru*, 1555 in Enrique de Vedia (ed.) 26, pp. 259–74 (Madrid: Biblioteca de Autores Espanoles).

5

Kikuyu women and the politics of protest: Mau Mau

TABITHA KANOGO

This study aims to examine the roles and images of women in the Mau Mau war of liberation in Kenya. It is hoped to depict the prevailing male stereotypes of women; how men manipulated these; and the way in which women conformed to – and in some cases overcame – such stereotypes by creating new female images and by adopting new roles during the struggle.

Since the Second World War, Mau Mau has been the only major war that the British had to fight in Africa. In its open form, this conflict largely took place in the Mount Kenya and Aberdare Forests and lasted from 1952 to 1957 (see Clayton, 1976). There were thousands of forest guerrillas, most of them Kikuyu. Significantly, up to about 5 per cent of the guerrillas were women; by joining the men in warfare they subverted their traditional role-status and challenged formal and traditional political authority in Kikuyu society where political power and decision-making were customarily dominated by men (Kenyatta, [1953], pp. 194–5).

The transition from being the guardians of the domestic front to becoming partners in a political and military struggle was a slow and painful process for the women involved. Kikuyu men resented and strongly opposed the presence of women in the forest and initially relegated them to familiar domestic chores (Barnett and Njama, [1966], p. 226). The forest women objected to this assignment and proved themselves capable of executing 'male' tasks.

Meanwhile, thousands of women who did not go into the forest comprised the vital civilian wing of the struggle, the lifeline without which the forest guerrillas would not have survived for as long as they did.[1] These women also took up new roles, modified the old ones, and grappled with extensive social reorganisation to accommodate their new dual politico–domestic identity. This study seeks to portray the conflicts and contradictions that characterised the male–female 'alliance' in the liberation struggle as women were co-opted to such roles as warrior, political decision-maker and judge. Because the cases of women's protest and participation examined in this study took place in a colonial past riddled with tradition, women are depicted as struggling against traditional socio-political structures and stereotypes on the one hand, and colonialism on the other.

Kikuyu women before Mau Mau

The colonial background

The Mau Mau war was a nationalist struggle born of the agrarian and political frustrations of Kenyan peasants, the urban proletariat and squatter labourers in the White Highlands (see Rosberg and Nottingham, [1966], pp. 234–319). The decision to base the economy of the country on an alien European settler community created a racially structured society in which the Europeans occupied a dominant and privileged position.

As well as reserving about seven million acres of the most fertile land for European agriculture, the government concentrated infrastructure, capital, agricultural and veterinary services in the settler sector (see Brett, [1973], Chapters 1–6). The government also enacted a whole range of legislation, both financial and political, to coerce the reluctant Africans into the labour market, since settlers needed cheap and abundant labour. Taxation (Hut and Poll Tax, 1901 and 1911 respectively), the Masters and Servants Ordinance (1906, 1924), and the infamous *Kipande* – a pass registration certificate (similar to one in use in South Africa) – were among measures introduced to force Africans into the labour market and to curb desertion (Rosberg and Nottingham, [1966], pp. 45–6). To ensure that Africans did not become self-sufficient and so avoid wage labour they were denied the right to grow cash-crops, and wages were kept low for the benefit of the settlers.

In urban areas living conditions were particularly poor and social services, especially education, were extremely inadequate. In the African reserves, especially among the Kikuyu, land shortage was rife and over-grazing and over-cultivation resulted in soil erosion. The Africans had no electoral rights and their interests were 'represented' by various Europeans in the Legislative Council. The colonial period was thus characterised by a deep sense of grievance among the Africans. However, between 1920 and 1946 many political parties were founded, which sought reforms within the colonial state by constitutional means. These included the Young Kikuyu Association (YKA), the Kikuyu Central Association (KCA) and the Kenya African Union (KAU).

By the late 1940s people were becoming impatient with the constitutional approach to the problems of the day. This was particularly evident among the young members of KCA which in the late 1940s launched an oath-based membership-drive committing the partakers to the campaign for the recovery of the 'stolen lands' through an armed struggle. By 1949 the oaths sworn by the KCA and KAU membership had come to have much in common. The practice, traditionally used as a tool of unity, was radicalised to include and unite most Kikuyu, regardless of sex or age, against colonialism. By 1951 a *'Batuni'* (platoon) oath[2] was being administered symbolising the anticipation of a military confrontation (RH Mss Afr. S. 424, 1954, p. 343). Acts of intimidation and violence against Kikuyu opposed to the oaths, and against settlers who reported subversive Kikuyu or who had weapons that the Kikuyu needed, became widespread on settler farms, in urban areas and in the Central Province, the Kikuyu homeland. By 1950 the term '*Mau Mau*' had gained currency and the escalating breakdown in law and order forced the colonial government to declare a 'State of Emergency' on 20 December 1952. In the ensuing months thousands of men and women fled to the forests from where they waged attacks against British and loyalist troops, settlers and uncooperative Africans.

Women's traditional roles

Among the Kikuyu, women were primarily perceived as the custodians of the domestic welfare of the community. They were responsible for reproduction and production, ensuring that there was adequate food for the family and extra for the various social functions on which the status of the homestead depended (Kenyatta, [1953], p. 63). Men broke the land, and women planted, weeded, harvested and oversaw the disposal of the food-crops. To cope with these tasks women evolved the *Ngwatio* system under which members' farms were worked in rotation. An *Ngwatio* comprised women married to men of the same lineage.

There were several women's councils which dictated behaviour patterns for their members and enforced sanctions as necessary. Although these councils could be said to have provided women with a forum for participating in socio-economic matters which could challenge male authority, they were restricted to matters pertaining to domestic affairs, agricultural matters (but not the ownership of land), discipline (Lambert, [1956], pp. 95–6) and the regulation of the social life of girls and women.

Formal political power was invested in exclusively male councils (Lambert, [1956], p. 100). Because women could not affect the wider political decision-making process, they were perceived as subordinate members of the community; a viewpoint which the colonial government strengthened by excluding women from any alliances or consultation. However, all this did not prevent women from protesting. Prior to the Mau Mau war, there were a few cases of women's revolts, two cases of which are examined below.

Women's protest

The Harry Thuku riot (1922)

Harry Thuku was a young Kikuyu proto-élite who co-founded the East African Association (see Rosberg and Nottingham, 1966, p. 36). This party championed various African grievances including increased taxation, the *Kipande*, the lack of title deeds for African lands and forced labour. Thuku, among others, was opposed to the forcible removal of young girls for employment in settler plantations. Some of these women underwent all manner of sexual harassment including sexual abuse (Ross, 1968, pp. 225–6).

To curb Thuku's increasing support, the colonial government arrested him on 14 March 1922. A crowd of between 7000 and 8000 people, including 150 women, gathered outside the Police Station where Thuku was held to demand his release (Rosberg and

Nottingham, 1966, p. 51). Negotiations between the Colonial Secretary and some African male leaders were not successful and the latters' attempt to disperse the crowd proved futile.

The women were enraged by this male compromise, they jeered at the men and taunted them. To emphasise the extent of female displeasure with male leadership, one of the women, Mary Nyanjiru, resorted to a traditional insult, *Guturama* (Rosberg and Nottingham, 1966, pp. 51–2). This act, which entailed the exposure of a women's genitals to an offending party, was the ultimate recourse of those consumed by feelings of anger, frustration, humiliation or revenge.[3] Here, it symbolised the strongest challenge the women could put to the men. Nyanjiru rebuked the men thus:

> You take my dress and give me your trousers.
> You men are cowards. What are you waiting for?
> Our leader is in there, let us get him. (Rosberg and Nottingham, 1966, p. 51)

By challenging men to give her their trousers – a symbol of manhood – Nyanjiru implied that men had proved incapable of dealing with the situation, and so women would take over and free Thuku. As a result of their action, leadership for the next few moments passed to the women. Nyanjiru's challenge and the sound of the women's ululations in her support stopped the crowd from dispersing. In the ensuing agitation, the crowd lunged forward, the police opened fire and 21 people, four of them women, were killed, and many people were injured.

Although short-lived and not successful in releasing Thuku, this incident was a strong testimony to the hidden political dynamism of women. They had used a ritual practice to score a political point. An exclusively female institution had challenged both the traditional male monopoly of political power, and the colonial authority. The bravery and ingenuity of these women was enshrined in the Kanyegenyuri song that inspired later female militancy.

The revolts of 1947, 1948 and 1951

By the mid-1930s land in Central Province was badly eroded (Sorrenson, 1967, pp. 3–96). The colonial government enforced soil conservation measures including terracing, intercropping and the planting of trees on steep slopes, all of which increased the work-load (Kitching, 1980, pp. 101–4). It also enforced measures to improve stock by vaccination and culling. Because up to 50 per cent of Kikuyu men were short-term migrant labourers, and so not always available to work on family plots, the bulk of the additional labour fell on women, and women's labour hours were dramatically increased (KNA: DC/FHI/26, 1947, p. 1). Since the women were not allowed to grow cash crops, they had no inducement for the additional work which was to be performed under the very harsh local Native Authority regulations (KNA: MAA/2/3/16/iv, 1948). They also resented the authority of the chiefs and agricultural officers who constantly interrupted their work. By July 1947, about 2400 acres had been terraced in Muranga. Women were breaking their backs trying to combine their domestic and 'official' duties. Following a KAU meeting on 20 July 1947, where it was decided that women should abandon terracing work, they began to defy agricultural regulations. On 14 April 1948:

> 2500 [women] arrived in the station from Chief Paterson's location and danced and sang and informed everyone that they would not take part in soil conservation measures mainly because they felt they had enough work to do at home. (KNA: DC/FHI/ 27/1948, p. 1)

Attempts to incorporate women into the colonial structure had not paid due regard to their reproductive and productive labour and this elicited strong objections from the women. Their defiance, however, was seen as a direct and personal attack on the colonial chiefs and the colonial administrators feared that this might cause 'a landslide in government authority' (KNA: DC/FHI/27/1948, p. 1). The women had also defied traditional authority as embodied in clan heads, to whom government had given the power to fine any women who did not complete their tasks.

While the District Commissioner sympathised with the burdens the women had to shoulder, he retorted that 'the soil could not wait for a few men to terrace it' (KNA: DC/FHI/27/1948, p. 1). However, the women did not take up their tools and on 4 May 1948 the DC ordered the arrest of these recalcitrant women. However, they 'were quickly released by a large crowd of their own sex brandishing sticks and shouting Amazonian war-cries' (KNA: DC/

FHI/27/1948, p. 2). The emulation of a battle scene, although it did not escalate to actual fighting, was indicative of the extent of the women's anger and their determination to fight the system. In this protest, women symbolically threatened to engage men in a fight, thus challenging traditional male authority. Because the men involved represented the colonial government too, the action also threatened the latter.

The DC served all the women with summonses to appear before the Native Tribunal in Fort Hall on 7 May for hearing on 8 May. To forestall further disruption, the DC warned the sympathisers not to go to the station or create disturbances. A fine of ten shillings was imposed on each arrested woman and no sooner had this been made known than 'a large crowd of angry females descended on the offices' (KNA: DC/FHI/27).

The DC grew impatient with what (quoting from John Knox) he called 'the monstrous regiment of women' and ordered the police to drive the women out of the towns. Although the women did not succeed in achieving a complete change of the colonial government's agricultural policy, the revolt was referred to as 'probably the biggest . . . social event of importance during the year' (KNA: DC/FHI/27). The women managed to wrest some concessions, such as individual as opposed to communal terracing, but more importantly they demonstrated that they would challenge the abrogation of their rights.

In adjacent Kiambu District, women's protest took a different form. Here, in October 1947, women stopped picking coffee in the areas between rivers Chania and Ndarugu because they wanted the prices per measure (the *debbie*) to be put up by 50 cents. Roads were picketed and a number of the leaders were apprehended for questioning. To ensure solidarity amongst the women, their leaders threatened to apply a traditional sanction of 'put[ting] a curse on anyone going to pick coffee' (KNA: MAA/2/3/16/iv, 1947, p. 3).

Female rebellion took a more violent turn in Muranga in 1951. To control rinderpest, the government had ordered wholesale innoculation of animals in the area. At the same time, the cattle began to die *en masse* and anti-innoculation demonstrations followed. Hundreds of women from Muranga 'stormed the innoculation centres – they burned down the cattle crushes and pens and chased away the innoculation inspectors'. Over 500 women were arrested while others were injured in the scuffle and needed medical treatment. The women's view of this riot is well captured in the following song:

> We women of Muranga were arrested for refusing
> To have our cattle poisoned. And because we
> Rejected such colonial laws we were thrown into
> Prison cells and our children were wailing because
> They had no milk to drink.

Chorus

> We beseech you, our *Ngai* [God]
> Take us away from this slavery

> We were taken to Nairobi after being finger-printed
> And on our way they kept asking us,
> Do you belong to this conspiracy,
> Fighting for Liberation?
> And our children continued wailing because
> They had no milk to drink. (Maina-wa-Kinyatti, 1980, p. 60)

A seemingly innocent colonial regulation had interfered with the domestic and productive domains of women – the children had no milk to drink – and women could not sit back as the government 'destroyed' their cattle. The DC's observation that the year 1947 'came like a lamb but went out like a lion' (KNA: MAA/2/3/16/iv, 1947, p. 3), could well symbolise the changes evident in women as they emerged from their domestic cloisters and entered 'a world of men': the political arena. Women had awakened to the fact that they could use their collective labour power as a pawn in the shifting socio-economic relations. The use of ritualistic threats ensured some degree of unity among the women as they challenged male political authority both in its traditional and colonial forms. However, it was in the Mau Mau war of liberation that women made their greatest impact.

Mau Mau women: the oath

Mau Mau was preceded by an intensive campaign of oath-taking to ensure unity among the Kikuyu (RH.Mss.Afr.S.424, 1954).

Although there were no female oath administrators, women were highly involved in oath-taking ceremonies and performed such tasks as arranging candidates by sex, and beating and intimidating them to ensure that they did not betray the struggle (Nyamarutu, 1984).

All of the oaths incorporated features relating to female sexuality, and women were required for the performance of the rites. Menstrual blood was an ingredient in some oath concoctions, and various higher oaths included sexual acts, such as placing a dog's or ram's penis into the woman's vulva, and/or the initiate inserting his penis into the woman's vulva for a specified number of times. Such higher oaths bound the partakers to greater violence, more secrecy, and deeper commitment to the struggle. The following is a description, by a male initiate, of the ceremony for the fourth oath:

> I found a circle of banana leaves potatoed [*sic*] and sugar cane leaves and sorghum leaves . . . The whole front of the ram had been cut off including the penis; I was made to squat on the ground in the circle. The meat was placed on my penis and chest, I held it in place and ate one end of the meat. The girl stood on one side, the meat and the penis of the ram were then placed in her vagina, who was at that time having her 'monthlies'. It was given back to me and I was made to eat parts of it, including the penis and the testacles . . . The girl's name is Waithera. I hear she has taken five oaths. *She was not a whore*, but she is one [*sic*]. There are ten girls, and they are used when they have their 'monthlies' if the fourth oath is given. This is part of their job. (RH. Mss. Afr. S. 424, 1954)

To have taken five oaths, Waithera must have been a staunch supporter of the movement, and like other Mau Mau women she only allowed herself to be subjected to unnatural sexual acts, which were a breach of all normal Kikuyu sexual mores, for the sake of the movement. The reason for such an inversion of the traditional sexual code is difficult to determine, and I can only suggest that the Mau Mau leaders believed that the bizarre nature of the rites would invoke a greater sense of commitment and dissuade initiates from divulging details of the oath.

It is notable that in the quote, the informant alludes to prostitution. Prostitutes were involved in the struggle in various ways, but their contribution was nearly always denigrated by being portrayed in the context of their sexual flexibility rather than their political commitment. There is evidence, however, to suggest that their image was unfair and that prostitutes made an active political contribution.[4]

Women of the forest

While some women went to the forest voluntarily to join other freedom fighters, some did so to escape harassment and torture by loyalists and British troops (Wachira, 1984; Gitahi, 1984). Those who went to the forest were generally young and single or otherwise free from domestic duties (e.g., widows or women with older children). However, a married woman who supported Mau Mau activities in the village, in urban areas, or on settler farms, could flee to the forest if she learnt, or suspected, that the government was after her (Gitahi, 1984). After a while, a forest council would meet and free such women from their forest duties so that they could rejoin their families and continue to support the movement from the homestead. Some women, especially younger ones, were abducted to the forest as porters or as 'wives' of freedom fighters (Barnett and Njama, 1966, p. 243).

As noted above, men initially resisted the entry of women into the forest on various grounds. They argued that women could neither withstand the harsh forest conditions of torrential rains and bitter cold, nor could they defend themselves against enemies. As well as being a security risk, women would be extra mouths to feed, but would do nothing useful in return (Barnett and Njama, 1966, p. 226). It was also feared that women could cause tension and conflict among male guerillas as the men competed for sexual favours from the small number of women. Although sex was historically taboo for active warriors, the protraction of the Mau Mau war resulted in the violation of the taboo and the establishment of forest liaisons (Barnett and Njama, 1966).

Roles and stereotypes

Since traditionally women did not participate in warfare, their status and roles in the forest were initially 'highly ambiguous and tended to shift as the battle lengthened' (Barnett and Njama, 1966). At the beginning, they were allocated domestic chores including fetching firewood, cooking, washing and cleaning. In certain camps, male leaders were each allowed to choose a woman, derogatorily referred to as *Kabatuni* (literally meaning a small platoon to be commanded by the man), who as well as seeing to the other needs of the leader was also expected to meet his sexual needs (Barnett and Njama, 1966, p. 242). Women were induced to fulfil such 'tasks' 'for the good of the cause' as can be seen from the following comment by one involved:

> Generally, I would think of sleeping with a man as an individual concern. Here, it seems to me that the leaders consider this as part of the women's duty in the society [Mau Mau]. I believe that since I could not do any other better service to my people, I would then willingly accept it as my contribution to the society. (Barnett and Njama, 1966, p. 243)

These forests liaisons were contrary to Kikuyu customs, and by the end of 1953 it was ruled that they should be declared and publicised as marriages.

Women warriors

Some women combined domestic tasks with minor military duties like cleaning guns and helping in the making of weapons and ammunition, while others became fully-fledged warriors fighting alongside men. In August 1953 a meeting of all the Aberdare forest leaders decided that women would be commissioned up to the rank of 'Colonel', depending on military competence (Barnett and Njama, 1966, p. 227).

However, if such a woman soldier fell pregnant, she would 'lose the rifle' that is: lose her honour and position in the army, while the man involved would be subjected to punitive chores (Ndungi, 1984). An expectant woman was generally escorted to the nearest government post for safe return to the village, though if security militated against this, she would be attended to by a nurse or 'doctor' resident in the forest. Gakonyo Ndungi was one such forest 'doctor' during her two and a half years stay in the forest (Ndungi, 1984).

Political roles

As noted earlier, Kikuyu political institutions were exclusively male. The same was initially true of guerilla councils, but as women continued to prove themselves trustworthy and capable of executing Mau Mau tasks, some of them were co-opted into the political arena through the creation of dual-sex councils. As Ruth Gathoni, a former freedom fighter, said:

> Mau Mau created joint men and women councils. Women's voices were heard during Mau Mau. Earlier women only heard what had been decided. They did not help to make decisions. (Gitahi, 1984)

Leadership ceased to be a male preserve and there was seen to be 'no difference between a male or female leader and Mau Mau would not oppose a woman leader' (Gitahi, 1984). Women's political abilities were recognised, and some women – for example Muthoni Ngatha – even rose to the senior position of Field Marshal.

A symbolic acknowledgement by men of female political competence was the crowning of Wagiri Njoroge in June 1953 as the Queen of Mau Mau. This was a symbolic counterpart to the coronation of Queen Elizabeth II. According to *The Courier* (2 February 1954):

> Wagiri 'ruled' for seven months in the Thompson's Falls District, an area rife with Mau Mau activities including some bizarre murders of Europeans.

Mau Mau women on the domestic front

Operating from villages, urban townships and European settler farms, thousands of women played diverse and vital roles in their support of the struggle. The authorities allowed women greater freedom of movement than men during the emergency and they were subjected to less harassment by the security forces (RH Mss Afr.S.596 Box 38A, 1953). They acted as go-betweens and carriers of food and firearms, and generally provided a system of intelligence (RH Mss Afr.S.596 Box 38(A), 1953).

Provision of food

The government considered that if it could 'weaken the morale and resistance of gangs by a complete denial of food' (RH Mss Afr.S1676, 1953–1963, p. 32), then a major part of the battle against forest fighters would have been won. The government therefore imposed measures to ensure that all livestock and grain were to be enclosed and guarded while rations to labourers on settler farms were to be issued 'frequently in limited amounts and not in bulk' (RH Mss Afr.S1676, 1953–1963). Also, all Kikuyu, Embu and Meru labourers were to be concentrated in labour camps which were to be inspected regularly for strangers. Despite these restrictions, women utilised firewood gathering sessions as opportunities for passing vital information, food and other supplies to freedom fighters. Once this tactic became known to the authorities, settlers were urged to ensure that the collection of firewood was confined to certain days 'when farm guards can accompany the wood gatherers and keep them under observation' (RH Mss Afr.S1676, 1953–1963). In the reserves, people were concentrated in villages and at the height of the emergency women were allowed to go to their gardens for only one hour, and that was under the supervision of loyalist guards (Mbutu, 1984).

The collection of food and its delivery to freedom fighters was a major logistical operation necessitating centralised organisation. A woman leader would gather information about the guerrillas' requirements either directly from the guerillas at pre-arranged meetings (Mbutu, 1984; Nyamarutu, 1984, Gitahi, 1984) or from her 'field workers'. With the help of assistants, the leader would mobilise women, who had taken the oath to collect food. Uninitiated women did not participate and 'did not know that this was happening' (Gitahi, 1984).

After preparation, the food would be put in Kikuyu baskets (*Ciondo*) and water pots (*Ndigithu*) and despatched at prearranged times by appointed women. The delivery trip to the forest edges, or to other venues such as river banks or garden plots, required each woman to avoid being suspected by loyalist Home Guards:

> One would conceal the food by covering it with goat manure. On your way back you would bring vegetables – a little amount – to create the impression that you had been to pick vegetables. (Mbutu, 1984)

Talking of the dilemmas involved, one woman said:

> It was difficult. If you were found by the government giving them [guerillas] food, you would be beaten and taken to detention. You could not avoid feeding the Mau Mau either because the Mau Mau would beat you and half-throttle you and let you loose again. (Mbutu, 1984)

Children

Women also contributed the services of their children. From the age of ten children took the oath, while younger ones were 'sealed' with the sign of the cross dedicating them to the struggle. For the most part unsuspected, the children acted as members of vigilante committees, errand boys and girls and informers. As Gakonyo remembered:

> If you saw my young son Hinga on the road with his toy-wheel – *mubara* – you would think he was playing. But he was really on duty . . . [children] knew what to do. (Ndungi, 1984)

Some of these children were killed in the struggle and the news was broken to their parents with great mockery by the loyalist soldiers:

> Come and see your child who has independence in the shamba. (Ndungi, 1984)

To identify a corpse of one killed in Mau Mau action was dangerous, hence Mau Mau supporters were expected to exercise great restraint. For women who had lost their children in the struggle the experience was horrendous.

New roles for women

Domestic strife and social reorganisation

The Mau Mau movement often instigated cold war in the home. This was particularly acute where only one of the spouses supported

Mau Mau, as an initiate was expected to execute Mau Mau tasks without informing or consulting the spouse. Even money was considered unclean if it had come from somebody who had not taken the oath (Gitahi, 1984).

Where a woman had risen to such a position of authority that the movement's activities interfered with her domestic duties, or where a mother had fled to the forest, other Mau Mau women would help in her home as much as possible, beyond which her husband had to cope as best he could. If a man objected to his wife's involvement, he risked being regarded as an enemy of the movement, a crime which carried a death penalty (Gitahi, 1984; Wachira, 1984). In this regard, it could be argued that female membership of Mau Mau to some extent resulted in the subordination of domestic subservience to the liberation struggle.

The demands of the movement entailed extensive social reorganisation: women had to adopt new roles, form new social networks and develop new bases of group control as dictated by the movement. The collective care of the homesteads of women who had fled to the forest was one new feature, and it was said that, 'if you were a Mau Mau woman going for Mau Mau journeys other women would dig your *shamba* co-operatively' (Ndungi, 1984). The Mau Mau woman in the villages would perform all the necessary tasks and where necessary raise money to keep the family well supplied. A homestead would only 'get lost' if it belonged to an anti-Mau Mau women who had died at the hands of Mau Mau or was unable to cope with the tasks because of illness or some other reason (Gitahi, 1984). During the liberation struggle this exclusive Mau Mau women's collective replaced the traditional *Ngwatio* system.

Mau Mau imposed a new social code for all its adherents. Women were forbidden from getting involved with non-Kikuyu men, *Nduriri*, or with unsworn Kikuyu who were considered enemies of the struggle (Gichure, 1984).[5] However, women were allowed to (and might even be asked to) flirt with 'enemies' to gather vital information, weapons and other resources. For example, in Gakenia's village in Nanyuki, four girls lured four loyalist African soldiers to Kaarage Forest where the soldiers were killed and their rifles taken. On learning about the disappearance of the four soldiers, the government ransacked the farm, confiscated livestock and sought to arrest all the youths that were present, though 130 young people including Gakenia and 25 young women managed to flee to the forest (Wachira, 1984; see also Itote, 1967, p. 149).

An evaluation of women's involvement in Mau Mau political militancy: the case of Wanjiru Nyamarutu

A brief examination of Wanjiru Nyamaratu's contribution to Mau Mau will illustrate how important and extensive women's participation in the struggle could be.[6] An active member of the KAU in the 1940s, Wanjiru's political career predated Mau Mau. As treasurer of the party's local branch in the Njoro, she collected money to be relayed to the party's headquarters in Githunguri. During the 1940–50 Olenguruone crisis, in which residents of the Olenguruone scheme rose in defiance against agricultural regulations, Wanjiru oversaw the administration of the Olenguruone oath in 1947–8 to squatter labourers in Njoro and Nakuru. Here, thousands of Kikuyu took the oath (1947–9) against 'the slavery of the White Highlands' (Rosberg and Nottingham, 1966, pp. 248–59; Kanogo, 1977, p. 245).

Wanjiru belonged to a militant category of freedom fighters who discarded 'western clothes' and wore stitched pieces of cloth wrapped in the traditional Kikuyu style. As a symbolic way of demonstrating allegiance to Mau Mau, young and newly married initiates might have their upper ear lobes pierced, *Gukaywo Nyori*, and their heads shaved clean as a sign of being pure Kikuyu.

For a long period Wanjiru was responsible for the collection and despatch of food to guerillas in the Ndothua, Nessuit, Gichobo and Menegai hill forests in Njoro and Nakuru areas and for her services she was accorded the rank of *Genero-wa-Rigu* – General-in-Charge-of-Food. With the help of female and male supporters she raised money and collected clothes, medicine, scrap metal for making rifles, and bottles for making ammunition. Trench coats, rifles and ammunition were solicited from sypathetic auxiliary staff at Nakuru District Hospital. While delivering the consignments, the Mau Mau women would also pass important logistical data about the movement of government troops, official raids, and the whereabouts of possible informers, to help the freedom fighters map out their next move.

Because of her extensive involvement in militant politics, Wanjiru was forced to flee from Njoro to Nakuru. Here she continued to oversee the administration of the oath, however, and remained very active helping to recruit and despatch new guerillas to the various regiments where additional manpower was needed. As the moving spirit behind the team undertaking this task, Wanjiru became known as *Nyina-wa-Anake* – the Mother of Senior Warriors.

Women and killing

Even the colonial government acknowledged that many women held 'influential positions' in the Mau Mau cells (RH Mss Afr.S.1676, 1953–1963). Wanjiru was appointed judge in Nakuru's Mau Mau Courts which passed sentences on anti-Mau Mau crimes, some of which carried death sentences. Mau Mau rule No. 19 stated that women should not be informed about killings, though Wanjiru's position as judge indicates that with the changing roles of women this was no longer strictly observed, thus illustrating a shift in the male perspective of women.

These changes are graphically illustrated by the emergence of a small number of women who acted as executioners. Those women, such as Wambui (referred to as *Kamuirigo*), were seen to represent a new category of women who having undergone the worst of the hair-raising ordeals of Mau Mau could not revert to domestic subservience. Wambui had been an ardent forest guerilla and when her husband was killed she refused to remarry. I was told, 'She could not be ruled. She knew everything. Her hands had become very light and she could easily kill a useless husband' (Gitahi, 1984).

Continuing the struggle

With each Mau Mau errand, supporters at worst risked being killed by the government troops, or, if they escaped death, being arrested and detained or repatriated. Neither were they safe from Mau Mau if they contravened any of the many regulations. Wanjiru for example, was repatriated to Muguga (her parents' place of origin). This did not kill her spirit however, and she joined the local Mau Mau support groups which recruited new guerillas for the Ndeiya Forest.

Although by 1956 the freedom fighters had been militarily

defeated, they were undaunted in their quest for independence. At the end of the Emergency (1960) Wanjiru returned to Nakuru and took a new oath, the Kenya Land Freedom Army (KLFA) oath. KLFA was an exclusive vigilante organisation consisting of Mau Mau diehards in the White Highlands and the Central Province (see Tamarkin, 1973; Kanogo, 1980, pp. 392–423), who swore to revive the forest struggle should the decolonisation process undermine Mau Mau ideals. They were especially concerned with the retrieval of the stolen lands which they hoped to redistribute to ex-freedom fighters, ex-squatters and other landless people.

While keeping a close watch on political developments, KLFA continued to conduct selective oath ceremonies and to accumulate more rifles and ammunition. Wanjiru was in charge of the safe-keeping of some of these weapons and ammunition, though once again she was caught and this time she was detained in Lamu – a far-off island where dangerous political prisoners were held.

Wanjiru's contribution to the struggle was outstanding, but other women also sacrificed long hours and suffered extreme hardship in the struggle for the country's liberation. Many were killed, others maimed and families were neglected while women performed the movement's work.

Examined against the background of the traditional status-roles of women, the above cases reveal the evolution of women as they moved from their exclusively domestic and subordinate positions to the forefront of political bargaining. This development involved the contravention of established societal patterns of behaviour and male-supported stereotypes of female roles. Women seized the opportunity to fight both their own traditions and colonialism, forces which hitherto relegated them to an inferior and exploited position. Using traditional symbolic rituals coupled with sheer determination and commitment, women made a breakthrough in the political arena. Although elements of historical stereotypes remained strong, in some areas women made drastic breaks with tradition, especially in their military participation. As forest guerillas and as civilian supporters of Mau Mau, women proved to be dedicated and competent, and men were obliged to acknowledge the contribution of women in the liberation struggle.

What, then, is the significance of all this to the Kenyan woman today? Does she seek to emulate the female guerillas, does the spirit of the Mau Mau women inspire her?

The impact of Mau Mau on the Kenyan woman today

Because Mau Mau was largely a grass roots Kikuyu movement that drew its supporters from poor peasants, urban proletariats, squatters and the unemployed, its achievements seem to be more widely acknowledged among the same category of people. The bravery of the Mau Mau women, idealised and eulogised in the various Mau Mau songs (Maina-wa-Kinyatti, 1980), is a great inspiration to village women and the struggling urban poor, especially among those Kikuyu who lived through the Mau Mau ordeal. Various women's collectives–especially those involving self-help, business or financial projects – are inspired by the tenacity of the Mau Mau women. Wanjiru is a leader among the Nyakinyua women's group which plays a political-cum-commercial role in Nakuru, influencing the purchase of land and the acquisition of property among its members.

Although the modern woman struggles to combine her domestic tasks with formal employment, it is evident that she models herself – especially her aspirations – on the Western woman. Her inspiration is to a large extent an emulation of the achievements of the latter, especially in the academic, career, and (to some limited extent) business worlds. The achievements of the Mau Mau women are dwarfed by the contemporary strides of the Western women on whom the educated Kenyans model themselves. However, the Kenyan educated woman is in the minority. On a general level, the extent of the ordinary women's entry into traditionally male roles as heads of families, business women, political brokers and other roles are testimony to the landmark of Mau Mau women.

Notes

1. As go-betweens, these women delivered food, medicine, weapons and ammunition, clothing and logistic information to the guerillas. [Women's roles in Mau Mau are also described in Muthoni Likimani's collection of short stories *Passbook Number F.47927: Women and Mau Mau in Kenya* (1985), introduced by Jean O'Barr, which was unfortunately unavailable at the time this study was written. The stories convey the impact of Mau Mau and the Emergency on women's daily lives; and also – particularly in the story 'Unforgotten Flames' – depict women's participation in the fight for freedom (Eds).]

2. The Batuni oath committed the initiates to greater violence and included swearing to kill one's father, mother, brother or sister should they 'refuse Mau Mau in any way'. See RH Mss Afr.S.424, 1954, p. 3430

3. See also Ardener (1975) for comparison and general remarks on sexual insults. Audrey Wipper's study, which examines three incidents of female militancy in Kenya, Nigeria and Cameroon, provides an insight into common themes characteristic of the three incidents. See Whipper, A. (1982).

4. Mau Mau leaders had ambivalent attitudes towards prostitutes involved in the struggle. Male members were barred from socialising with prostitutes who on the one hand were seen as prospective informers since they had liaisons with enemies. On the other hand, Mau Mau leaders did not hesitate to 'use' prostitutes to get information and other resources from enemies. The prostitutes were seen in the context of their sexual flexibility and not political commitment. There is evidence to prove that this male stereotype of the prostitute was ill-informed and biased. Some prostitutes were committed to the cause (Kanyoi Muita, 1984). They were not always apolitical. A colonial administrator observed that:

> Many prostitutes incite their clients and even withhold their favours until action [for Mau Mau] has been taken. (RH Mss Afr.S.596 Box 38(A) 1953)

In the same manner, an ex-guerilla observed:

> We had convinced some prostitutes so that if a man went to a prostitute he would be distracted by her when he was at his house because he had the gun around. The prostitute would hide a Mau Mau man who would steal that gun and kill that man or he would leave them but take the gun with him (Kanyoi Muita, 1984).

5. If on trial by a Mau Mau High Court, a woman was found to be 'friendly with an enemy', the penalty was death (see RH Mss Afr.S1676, 1953–1963, p. 17).

6. The reconstruction of Wanjiru's political career is largely based on interviews conducted by the author with Wanjiru on 11 November 1976, 18 December 1976, 15 and 16 January 1984 and supplemented by data from other interviewees who worked with, or in the same area as, Wanjiru during Mau Mau.

References

Ardener, S. (1975) 'Sexual Insult and Female Militancy', in S. Ardener (ed.), *Perceiving Women* (London: J. M. Dent).

Barnett, D., and Njama, K. (1966) *Mau Mau from Within* (London: MacGibbon and Kee).

Brett, E. A. (1973) *The Politics of Economic Change, 1919–1939* (London: Heinemann).

Clayton, A. (1976) *Counter-Insurgency in Kenya, 1952–1960* (Nairobi: Trans Africa Publishers).

Dilley, M. R. (1966) *British Policy in Kenya Colony* (1st edn 1937) (New York: Cass).

Gichure, S. (1984) Interview 6 January 1984.

Gitahi, R. G. (1984) Interviews 21 January and 29 January 1984.

Itote, W. (1967) *Mau Mau General* (Nairobi: East African Publishing House).

Kanogo, T. M. J. (1977) 'Rift Valley Squatter and Mau Mau', in J. Karim and W. R. Ochieng (eds), *Kenya Historical Review*, 5, 2 (Nairobi Kenya Literature Bureau).

Kanogo, (1980) 'The Historical Process of Kikuyu Movement into the Nakuru District of the Kenya White Highlands: 1900–1963' Ph.D. thesis, University of Nairobi. See also *Squatters and the Roots of Mau Mau, 1905–1963* (London: James Curry, 1987).

Kenyatta, J. [1953] *Facing Mount Kenya: The Tribal Life of the Kikuyu* (1st edn 1938), (London: Secker and Warburg).

Kitching, G. (1980). *Class and Economic Change in Kenya: The Making of an African Petite Bourgeoise* (London: Yale University Press).

KNA (Kenya National Archives) DC/FHI/26 (1947) Fort Hall Annual Report.

KNA: DC/FHI/27 (1948) Fort Hall Annual Report.

KNA: MAA/2/3/16/iv (1948) Intelligence Report for Fort Hall, April.

Lambert, H. E. (1956) *Kikuyu Social and Political Institutions* (London: Oxford University Press).

Likimani, M. (1985) *Passbook Number F.47927: Women and Mau Mau in Kenya*, with an introductory essay by Jean O'Barr (London: Macmillan Education).

Maina-wa-Kinyatti (1980) *Thunder from the Mountains: Mau Mau Patriotic Songs* (London: Zed Press).

Mathu, D. (1973) *The Urban Guerilla. The story of Mohammed Mathu*, (Richmond Canada): LSM Information Centre, Life Histories from the Revolution series.

Mbutu, W. (1984) Interview November 1984, Granada Copyright.

Mwangi-wa-Githumo (1981) *Land and Nationalism: The Impact of Land Appropriation and Land Grievances upon the Rise and Development of Nationalist Movements in Kenya, 1895–1939* (Washington D.C.: University Press of America).

Ndungi, G. (1984) Interview 2 January 1984.

Nyamarutu, W. (1976) Interview 11 January and 18 December 1976.

Nyamarutu, (1984) Interview 15 and 16 January 1984.

RH (Rhodes House) Mss Afr. S.424 (1954) 'Mau Mau Oaths and Ceremonies As Described by Participants'.

RH Mss. Afr. S.596 Box 38(A) (1953) 'A Review of the Present Emergency in Kenya, August'.

RH Mss. Afr. S.1676 (1953–1963) 'Mau Mau Miscellaneous Reports, Emergency Controls, etc.'.

Rosberg, C. G. and Nottingham, J. (1966) *The Myth of Mau Mau: Nationalism in Kenya* (Nairobi: East African Publishing House).

Ross, W. M. (1968) *Kenya From Within: A Short Political History* (1st edn. 1927) (London: Cass).

Sorrenson, M. P. K. (1967) *Land Reform in Kikuyu Country* (Nairobi: Oxford University Press).

Sorrenson, M. P. K. (1968) *Origins of European Settlement in Kenya* (Nairobi: Oxford University Press).

Tamarkin, M. (1973) 'Social and Political Change in a Twentieth Century African Community in Kenya', unpublished Ph.D. thesis, University of London.

Wachira, G. (1984) Interview 21 and 26 January 1984.

Wipper, A. (1982) 'Riot and Rebellion among African women: three examples of women's political clout', in J. O' Barr (ed.) *Perspectives on Power* (Durham, USA: Duke University Press).

6

Women soldiers and white unity in apartheid South Africa

ELAINE UNTERHALTER[1]

White society in apartheid South Africa is characterised by marked racism and sexism. Nonetheless, despite the legal and economic barriers to women's equality and a highly developed ideology of the inferiority of women, white women have served in the military for more than fifteen years. This study examines some of the ambiguities that have resulted from the recruitment of white women for white South Africa in general and the South African Defence Force (SADF) in particular.

In summary my argument is that the ideological need to unify the white race around the military policy of the regime in support of minority white rule has been of paramount importance in recruiting white women. The increasing military mobilisation of white society against the black majority and the growing problem the SADF faced in staffing its permanent force, led to white women beginning to perform some important back-up roles for the military. But when the economic climate changed, and recession and unemployment meant that more white men took jobs with the military, the pressures to recruit white women purely for their labour were reduced. To date, the actual role of white women in the SADF in no way matches the grandiose claims made for their participation. Their mobilisation seems most important in terms of their white race. However, the actual presence of white women members of the SADF itself poses questions about their gender identity, and a whole barrage of popular ideological representations have been forged to maintain a 'feminine identity' for women doing somewhat similar jobs to men in a society in which sexism is deeply entrenched.

The defence force and South African society

Before examining the recruitment of women into the SADF it is necessary to locate the changing nature of the defence force within South African society. Until 1957 the SADF was a conventional military force oriented primarily to external defence, organised on the British model. The Nationalist Party (NP) election victory of 1948, which intensified apartheid rule in South Africa, initially brought no major changes in the SADF bar the purge of some senior officers who did not support NP policies. The 1957 Defence Act, however, did lead to a change in the form of recruitment and mobilisation. The new SADF, partly modelled on the Swiss and Israeli armies, consisted of a small regular permanent force, a large part-time citizen force and localised militia groups called commandos. All white males between eighteen and sixty-five were eligible for military service, although a ballot system was in force and at that time only a small proportion of men were actually called up for a period of national service. However, from 1967 the ballot system was abandoned and all physically fit white males were called up for national service in the year that they turned eighteen; initially this was for a period of nine months, extended to two years in 1982 (Davies, O'Meara and Dlamini, 1984, pp. 180–1).

Until the early 1970s the SADF was largely oriented towards defending South Africa against military attack, widely perceived to come from outside Africa. However, a series of events in the early 1970s led to a new strategy being developed. Firstly, a mass popular uprising against apartheid which, after some quiescence through the repressive years of the 1960s re-emerged in 1973 with a wave of popularly-supported strikes, continued to gain momentum in the period 1976–7, when police attacks on student demonstrations in Soweto sparked off countrywide demonstrations and courageous acts of defiance against the regime. The police were frequently unable to control these. Secondly, in 1974, the collapse of the Portuguese dictatorship meant an end of colonial rule in Angola and Mozambique. South Africa hoped through its invasion of

Angola in 1975 that it might prevent the national liberation movement MPLA from forming the government there. But the SADF troops were ignominiously defeated and forced to withdraw in March 1976.

The disintegration of the political buffers with which the regime had protected itself through the 1960s led to a new military policy being formulated. This was articulated most coherently in the 1977 defence White Paper, in which the then Minister of Defence, P. W. Botha, elaborated what he described as the 'total strategy' to counter the 'total onslaught' facing South Africa. In terms of the 'total strategy' the SADF was responsible for maintaining and enforcing the regime's political policies, together with the police force and other supporters of the regime drawn from a wide range of South Africans. As Botha put it in the 1977 White Paper:

> The principle of the right of self-determination of the White nation must not be regarded as being negotiable. The defence of the Republic of South Africa is not solely the responsibility of the Department of Defence. On the contrary the maintenance of the sovereignty of the RSA is the combined responsibility of all government departments. This can be taken further – it is the responsibility of the entire population, the nation and every population group. (Quoted in Cawthra, 1986, p. 27)

It can be seen that the 'total strategy' equated the maintenance of white rule with the defence of South Africa and broadened responsibility for these two tasks from the SADF to the whole society.

The 'total strategy' gained political momentum after an internal power struggle within the NP led to P. W. Botha being promoted from Minister of Defence to Prime Minister in 1979 and then President in 1984. One of the consequences of this and of the reformulation of apartheid in this period was increased stress on the need to recruit black South Africans into the SADF. The major black SADF battalions mobilised during both the World Wars had been demobilised when the wars ended, but small numbers of black servicemen were recruited in 1963 when the Cape Coloured Corps was revived as part of the permanent force. From 1975 small numbers of Africans have again been recruited into the permanent force and the SADF has helped train and arm the armies of the

Bantustans which Pretoria has declared 'independent' (Grundy, 1983, pp. 158, 199). The most recent Defence White Paper (1986) envisages national service for Coloureds and Indians in the same form as that for whites, although this is a highly charged political issue in the present climate of intense black activism and demands for political rights (*Star*, 28 April 1986).

The expanded role for the SADF has been accompanied by a huge increase in its numbers and in the military budget. In 1960 military spending amounted to R40 million, some 0.75 per cent of GNP; this increased to R1654 million in 1977–8 and R2688 million in 1982–3, which represents 5 per cent of GNP (Davies, O'Meara and Dlamini, 1984, p. 179). According to the International Institute for Strategic Studies, in 1960 the SADF numbered 10000, while in 1982 the permanent force was 16000; further, there were 60000 national servicemen and 400000 men and women who could be mobilised through the citizen force and local commandos (*Cape Times*, 16 February 1982). Cawthra, using calculations based on parliamentary papers, estimates that the permanent force numbered between 36000 and 40000 in 1983, and that the most recent figures for the size of the military at the end of December 1985 are a permanent force of 43000, 67000 national servicemen, 265000 in the citizen force and 200000 in the commandos. He estimates the total size of the military, including Bantustan units and the South West Africa Territory Force, as 639000 (Cawthra, 1986, Tables 5 and 6). These figures indicate a seventy-fold increase in military recruitment and military expenditure over twenty-five years.

The early recruitment of women

White women served in the South African armed forces in the Second World War; there were 25000 women recruited into the permanent force and 65000 women in temporary positions, but they were all demobilised at the end of the war. In 1963 the Transvaal Congress of the NP voted for military training to be made available for white women and this form of political pressure culminated in 1971 when, largely through the initiative of the Minister of Defence P. W. Botha, the Civil Defence Army Women's College, a military training college, was opened at George in the Cape, Botha's own constituency, to train white women for the civil defence structure of the commandos and the citizens' force. The significance of the location of the College appears to be primarily as an act of local patronage. At the opening ceremony of the George College P. W. Botha described this recruitment of white women as

> an act of faith in the women of South Africa and a manifestation of faith that the civilian population was preparing, in an organised way, a national 'wall' against military threats as well as emergencies and national disasters. (*Sunday Times*, 12 April 1971)

Linking the recruitment of white women to acts of faith appears almost an elevation to religious heights; at the same time white women are identified as representing *all* South African women and, indeed, the civilian population as a whole, while South Africa itself is presented as a country facing imminent military attack.

Both this speech and this initial mobilisation pose several problems of interpretation. In 1971 the external military threats to white rule in South Africa in the immediate future seemed negligible. Portugal, militarily supported by NATO, appeared firmly in control of her southern African colonies despite many years of guerrilla war; Ian Smith and his Rhodesian Front also appeared well able to withstand the efforts of the liberation armies to end white domination in Zimbabwe; the newly-independent countries of Botswana, Lesotho and Swaziland were economically dependent on South Africa with no armed forces of any note. In 1973 a prominent military journal in South Africa, assessing this situation, concluded:

> South Africa faces no real threat from its immediate neighbours. None of these are likely to launch an attack against South Africa or even countenance harbouring an 'Army of Liberation' within their borders. (Quoted in Davies, O'Meara and Dlamini, 1984, p. 182)

Within South Africa too it appeared that the massive repression imposed during the 1960s, combined with an economic boom, had crushed the popular militancy and mass mobilisation of the liberation movement that had been so evident during the 1950s. Thus, at the time of the initial military mobilisation of white women, it appears there was no internal or external threat to the South African regime, and it is difficult to identify the 'military threats' against which the women in civil defence were meant to erect their physical 'wall'. I believe this mobilisation can be understood only if the recruitment of white women is seen not so much as a search to provide the SADF with new recruits because of labour shortages or pressing military need, but as a move to foster and reinforce white political unity portrayed (as P. W. Botha put it) as 'an act of faith in the women of South Africa'.

The early 1970s was a period of conflict and realignment within white politics. One of the consequences of the repression and the boom was that some political differences between whites became less marked and a consensus over white political interest began to emerge amongst all the white parties represented in parliament. But this involved some *Realpolitik* on the part of the ruling NP on the direction apartheid was to take which its own right wing could not stomach. Although at the beginning of the decade the Prime Minister, B. J. Vorster, was able to preserve his power base within the NP, and only a small minority of extreme right-wingers left the NP to form the Herstigte Nasionale Party (HNP), the struggle within the NP revealed deep divisions within the ruling party, divisions that were further to fragment the party at the end of the decade and cost Vorster his premiership. In this political climate of division and realignment amongst white South Africans, it appears that Botha raised the spectre of external military threat to alarm and unite white society 'to create a national wall'. The call for the recruitment of women into the SADF had been associated with the Transvaal wing of the NP, known for its extreme conservatism, while Botha himself had risen through the ranks of the Cape NP which had a somewhat more pragmatic approach to apartheid. In the creation of the College at George and the early military mobilisation of white women Botha was able to fuse both a long-standing demand of the *verkramptes* (reactionaries) with a project of the *verligte* (enlightened) Cape wing of the NP. White women were to be recruited to help foster white political unity and to stress the need for national security, even though at the time this was not under threat. Indeed the recruitment of white women appears an early instance of 'total strategy'. This suggests that the military strategy enunciated by Botha and the defence chiefs in 1977 had a longer intellectual and political history than has hitherto been thought the case.

The expansion of women's deployment

From 1974 white women began to be recruited into the permanent force as well as the citizen force and commandos (see Plate 3), and an increasing number of job categories within the SADF opened to women. This expansion of women's deployment took place against changing strategic conceptions of the SADF, but, as I will show, the need for women's labour remained overshadowed by the greater desire to use the recruitment of white women to foster and preserve a sense of white political unity.

In 1974 leaflets giving details of the career opportunities the permanent force offered white women were delivered to every house in the white residential areas of South Africa. The leaflets were aimed at women aged between eighteen and thirty with a minimum of Standard 8 education (minimum school leaving qualification). An army career was portrayed as providing:

> belongingness, thoughtfulness, recognition, security, fairness and opportunity. (*Cape Times*, 25 November 1974)

At the same time considerable publicity was given to the first commissions for women in the Air Force and the Navy since the Second World War, and the promotion of a small number of women in the Army. In 1974 the SADF as a whole boasted two women colonels, one commandant, five majors, ten captains, eight lieutenants, and thirteen second lieutenants (*South African Digest*, 12 April 1974).

In 1976 P. W. Botha announced that women would be trained for a range of new jobs in the permanent force. Women would also be recruited into the commandos and trained in the use of weapons (*Rand Daily Mail*, 17 December 1976). At the end of 1976 there were 300 women in the permanent force and seventeen job categories open to them. Botha's changes involved opening eleven new job categories to women in the permanent force while eighteen administrative, stores and clerical posts became available to women in the commandos. The Civil Defence College at George was renamed the Army Women's College and it was enlarged to take 500 recruits a year (*Cape Times*, 17 December 1976). These changes appear to be the first serious attempt to use white women's labour in the SADF, even though on a very small scale.

Plate 3 *Women members of the South African Defence Force (SADF)*

Source: IDAF (South Africa)

The trend of slight increases in recruitment and small expansions in the job categories open to women continued in subsequent years. This was the period of huge growth in the size of the SADF and continued discussion about a white skilled labour shortage. In 1978 the courses on offer at George College were expanded. In an attempt to attract more women to military service a new twelve-month course was introduced which involved seventeen weeks' basic training at George and seventeen weeks' work at a military base near the women's homes. All women volunteering for the Citizen's Force or entering the permanent force were sent to George on nine weeks' basic training (*Star*, 24 May 1978; *SA Digest*, 10 February 1978). For the first time, white women were encouraged to volunteer for national service in the South African Medical Corps, which provided facilities for 500 women a year to be trained as medical orderlies.

This drive to recruit white women volunteers into the SADF did have results. In 1973 women made up only 0.6 per cent of the permanent force; in 1977 this had increased to 5.9 per cent and in 1978 7 per cent. By 1981 women made up 12.5 per cent of the permanent force (*Star*, 12 July 1979; *Cape Times* 16 February 1982). According to the most recent figures there are 3500 white women in the permanent force (some 9 per cent of the total), with 10 000 women serving with the commandos out of a total of 26 000 volunteers, in a commando force totalling 200 000. If one includes 500 women in training at George College the total number of women in the SADF is 14 000. Cawthra calculates the total armed strength of the SADF as 639 000 in 1985, which makes women recruits 2.19 per cent of the total (Cawthra, 1986, Table 6). While women are numerically significant in the commandos, their numbers in the permanent force appear to have declined; their overall small numerical representation in the SADF is a function of the large numbers of national servicemen who make up the great bulk of SADF recruits.

The expansion of women's deployment took place in the decade which saw the SADF mount attacks on the neighbouring states of Botswana, Lesotho, Mozambique, Angola and Swaziland in search of African National Congress (ANC) members and supporters, as well as in efforts to destabilise the governments of the front-line states and militarily undermine them. At the same time the SADF built up and maintained a huge force in Namibia to fight the South

West Africa Peoples Organisation (SWAPO), the national liberation movement. Increasingly within South Africa the SADF takes
on the role, formerly played by the police, of breaking up
demonstrations, carrying out house-to-house searches in black
townships, manning roadblocks around townships, surrounding
and searching black schools, forcing students into classes and
attacking and killing black South Africans on the streets. With
white minority rule in South Africa and Namibia increasingly under
threat Botha's 'total strategy' is being put into effect, but what is
striking is (commandos aside) the small role that white women play
in the SADF, despite the rhetoric of 'total onslaught'. With the
recession of the 1980s the number of women in the permanent force
has declined, and attempts to recruit women have become low key.
The exclusion of white women in plans for the expansion of national
service bears this out.

In 1982 a White Paper laid out the expanded needs of the SADF
in funds and manpower. Before the publication of the paper there
had been much speculation that it would contain recommendations
for compulsory national service for white women. But this did not
prove to be the case. Instead the White Paper called for an
increased period of national service for white men, and an
elimination of the loopholes through which immigrants were able to
escape national service. In introducing the White Paper in Parliament, the Minister of Defence said it was in the 'national' interest
that white men should no longer be utilised as the SADF's only
manpower source:

> the SADF will be more and more dependent on other sources of
> manpower, such as white females and members of other popu-
> lation groups, and to involve these people in a meaningful
> manner their utilisation is already being based on programmed
> manpower development plans which extend to 1990. (*Rand Daily
> Mail*, 3 April 1982)

He went on to spell out his perspective on the mobilisation of white
women through national service:

> As regards white females, efforts in the short term will be
> directed at expanding the permanent force. It is envisaged in the
> medium term to increase the intake of female recruits for

voluntary national service. A large scale increase in the number of female recruits cannot however take place until the permanent force has been expanded to such an extent that the larger numbers can be accommodated. (*Cape Times*, 3 April 1982)

Thus, although it appears that there is some labour shortage in the SADF which some increase of white women in the permanent force will help to alleviate, there is no pressing need to extend national service to women. The minister's speech seems to suggest that national service for women might even undermine their usefulness, as there has not been adequate preparation for such an increase in conscripts.

It has been claimed that the importance of white women in the SADF is to relieve men from administrative tasks. According to the *Cape Times* defence correspondent women are important in the SADF because in their roles as:

air traffic controllers, nursing aides, radar operators and pilots of light aircraft, [they] release a lot of men from administrative work for fighting. (*Cape Times*, 16 April 1982)

In recent years considerable numbers of women have taken over administrative posts within the SADF. The personal assistant to the present head of the army is a woman. But I consider it still needs to be proved that white women provide labour for the SADF that cannot be found from any other group. At the time of rapid military expansion, which coincided with fears about a white skilled labour shortage, relatively large numbers of women were recruited, but as the labour shortage has become less pressing, with unemployed white men joining the permanent force, white women have not been conscripted as white men have been. Yet white women volunteers continue to be recruited and deployed even though they are not, at present, a crucial source of labour. I believe that the fact that women's presence in the SADF has been maintained at a fairly low level (the commandos aside), and that plans for national service for women have not been given high priority, indicates that in the mid-1980s as in the early 1970s political and ideological motives supersede labour requirements in the recruitment of women.

The period of the recruitment of white women in the SADF is

both the period of the rapid growth in armed forces and military spending and of the reformulation of military strategy in South Africa. But it is noteworthy that the recruitment of women into the permanent force preceded both the *débâcle* of the defeat of the South African invasion of Angola in 1975–6 and the Soweto uprising of 1976–7, both of which are cited as the chief reasons for the formulation of the 'total strategy'. It seems to me that the fact that white women were being recruited into the permanent force indicates the thinking that contributed to the 'total strategy'. The recruitment of white women was based on ideas about white political unity which preceded it and which informed the publication of the 'total strategy'. The expansion of women's deployment should be seen primarily in terms of 'total strategy' and only secondarily in terms of filling labour requirements.

The ideological dimensions of the expansion of women's deployment seem particularly important here. The 1974 recruiting leaflet portrays life in the SADF as a cross between a chummy boarding school and a girl guide troupe. Botha's 1971 speech exalts the nature of women's recruitment, seeing it as an act of 'faith'. In neither of these portrayals is there any hint that the defence force is involved in *war* or that, in consequence, the reality of the work might be a lot less cosy and exalted than it was portrayed. There is one projection of the SADF for women – where 'feminine' values are stressed; and there is another depiction for men – such as that which appears in the SADF's magazine and newspaper which stresses grit, grime, sporting prowess, cunning and malevolent enemies, military hardware, alongside semi-naked and apparently available young women.

Attitudes to women soldiers in South Africa as a whole are complex and sometimes patronising (see below). The SADF's gender images are a double-sided image of the female, both the 'thoughtful, belonging' fellow-worker and the passive sexual object. It seems to me that if the presence of white women in the SADF was of critical strategic significance, these stereotyped images – absorbed untransformed from white society as a whole – would have been reformulated. It is the very mirror they hold up to certain images of white women in white society that underlines my belief that women are more important in the SADF because they are white than because of the labour they perform.

The socio-economic background of women recruits

Women in the permanent force of the SADF are almost exclusively from Africaans-speaking families. One highly publicised career at the George College was that of the daughter of P. W. Botha, who spent a year in military training before going on to study at the elite Stellenbosch University. With her upper middle-class background and academic aspirations she was an atypical recruit. Most women who pass through the George College seem to come from rural areas or small towns and to have no aspirations to further education. Many appear to be the daughters of small farmers, skilled workers, and policemen, and there is some evidence that a significant proportion of the women come from permanent force families, mainly the lower ranks of the military. Religious services at the George College are conducted by a local Dutch Reformed Church minister, suggesting this is the religious background of the bulk of women recruits.

The narrow basis of recruitment into the permanent force through the George College suggests a further dimension to Botha's total strategy and the recruitment of white women. The social base of the *verkrampte* wing of the NP has always been small-scale farmers, skilled and semi-skilled white workers, low-ranking civil servants, and the police force. It may be argued that the recruitment of women of this background into the SADF represents an attempt by Botha and the *verligtes* to use the SADF and the job opportunities offered by the military as modernising forces to direct these women away from their traditional political allegiances. As members of the SADF they might be located within the *verligte* camp, and so be more likely to accept the reformulations of apartheid entailed by the total strategy. This may explain some of the hostility with which women in the services are viewed by women of the far right (see below).

White women serving with the commandos, on the other hand, show more diversity in language, religion and class background, reflecting the local character of commando units. In newspaper accounts of the activities of this section of the SADF there is mention of English and Afrikaans speakers, women from Anglican, Catholic and Jewish backgrounds; and in rural areas the wives of large landowners serve together with the wives of foremen. While the recruitment of white women into the permanent force may represent an attempt to create white political unity in the face of class and language differences, the deployment of women in the commandos is an example of that unity in practice.

Women's roles in the military

Despite the argument set out here so far giving reasons for the recruitment of women, it would be misleading to suggest that the role of white women in the SADF was merely symbolic and decorative. The job categories open to women in the services have expanded since the early 1970s and the SADF does offer white women certain unique experience in work. In 1974 the Air Force began training women as radar operators, fighter aircraft controllers, and telecommuncation officers, in addition to the tasks they had performed before as clerks and typists; they also formed a squadron of women pilots to fly communication flights and undertake the evacuation of casualties (*SA Digest*, 12 April 1974 and 4 July 1974; *Star*, 14 February 1976). From 1976 the army employed women both in administrative and clerical posts, and in such tasks as doghandling, topographical work and draughtsmanship. The commandos, where the biggest deployment of women takes place, employ women as adjutants, radio operators, pay clerks, stores managers, personnel officers, and a range of other administrative roles (*Star*, 24 June 1978). But even these new job categories for women perpetuate a distinction between male servicemen in active, decision-making roles and women in back-up services. Women members of the permanent force are barred from active service and similar restrictions apply to women in the commandos.

Women members of the SADF are virtually invisible in the higher ranks. By 1979 there were only two women brigadiers, five colonels, and 581 women holding rank, although the total number of women serving in the permanent force numbered around 1000. The most senior women officers have responsibility for welfare services, the training of women recruits and personnel management (*Star*, 12 July 1979; *Cape Times*, 30 November 1980). The areas of strategic planning and overall defence policy, to say nothing of active service, are closed to white women officers.

Although women in the services earn the same basic pay as men in the same job categories, it is difficult for them to qualify for all the benefits for which men are eligible. Until 1981 women serving with the permanent force had no access to housing subsidies, and the prohibition on women going on active service prevents them claiming the 'danger money' bonuses with which men supplement their pay. Although child-care is generally not a problem for white South African women because most white families employ a black servant, the low priority given by the SADF to the needs of the children of working mothers in the permanent force is illustrated by the tale of the nursery at Voortrekkerhoogte near Pretoria where large detachments of the permanent force are stationed. In 1976 the Women's Federation at Voortrekkerhoogte founded a nursery school, but the only accommodation they were provided with was a prefabricated hut opposite the detention barracks. There were sixty children enrolled, and a long waiting list. It took nine years before more suitable accommodation and adequate staff could be provided by the army command (*Paratus*, December 1985).

Despite these inequalities the SADF projects itself as an exemplar for the rest of the society. Major-General Neil Webster, at the time a member of the President's Council and an influential policy-maker in the SADF, stated:

If a conservative organisation like the army can accept the equality of women, why should the rest of the civil service and the private sector not do the same? Discrimination based on sex is morally wrong and economically indefensible. If more organisations could genuinely accept women as equals – instead of just paying lipservice to this ideal – a lot of the country's staff shortages would be alleviated. (*Sunday Times*, 22 November 1981)

Major-General Webster's portrayal of the army as an ideal version of the society masks the way in which the SADF continues to perpetuate discrimination against its own white members (to say nothing of its role in maintaining in power a regime which has created and perpetuated thousands of political, legal and economic constraints making for the oppression and inequality of all black women and men).

The reason why the SADF is portrayed as an equal-opportunity employer, and the creator of 'spiritual and material welfare', seems to lie in the new role it has taken on as the guiding hand navigating apartheid policies away from their hidebound past, condemned by the world, to a new dynamic future in which, it is believed, the rulers of South Africa will be able to sit down in comfort with other conservative world leaders. There have been attempts to portray the SADF as the epitome of the new South African society, where blacks serve side by side with whites and petty apartheid has disappeared. It is as part of this image-building by the SADF that statements about the equality of women within the armed services must be seen. White women are no more equal in the SADF than blacks are, but they, and the society of which they are a part, must believe they are in order to accept the SADF as a go-ahead institution and the engine of a new dynamic form of apartheid. This role for the SADF was made explicit in the farewell message of General C. L. Viljoen, who retired as head of the SADF at the height of the state of emergency in 1985 as troops patrolled the townships, assaulting and killing:

> We in the Defence Force serve South Africa to the benefit of all its people. If we continue to do our task as well as we have in the past we will gain enough time and maintain the peace long enough for peaceful solutions to be found to our problems. If we fail all the inhabitants of this country will face chaos, poverty, famine and civil strife. We must accept that this is a worthwhile task, protecting all our people against the disaster that is revolution. (*Paratus*, November 1985)

Military training for women

Although the SADF career structure makes it plain that women will be confined to administrative jobs and support roles, the training given to women at the George College stresses toughness and endurance. There is an emphasis on combat situations which is out of key with the fact that the women are unlikely to encounter these within their actual working lives.

The training at the George College for women going into the permanent and citizen forces involves nine weeks of basic training in the use of firearms, parade ground drill, military discipline and fieldcraft, including map-reading and long-distance marches in rugged country (*Star*, 24 May 1978). Subsequently women in the permanent force get training similar to male recruits, but with more emphasis on clerical tasks and somewhat less emphasis on physical activity (*Paratus*, December 1982). Young women doing the one-year training course, not necessarily for a career in the SADF, have the same basic instruction with special courses in telecommunications and administration and lectures on current events, the army and revolutionary war, and much stress on crafts and music (*Paratus*, October 1985).

It appears puzzling that women who are going to be office-bound are given so much costly, traditional, basic military training, and that women who know their work will never involve active service elect to undertake a training that is so very 'macho' in tone, and in the face of which they have to work so hard to maintain their 'feminity' (see below). But this contradiction dissolves if women's participation in the SADF is seen to be as much about maintaining an ideology as it is about fulfilling labour requirements. The training of women seems to stress the inculcation of *esprit de corps*. The feeling of 'belongingness', which the SADF promised its recruits, can well be cultivated under the stress of route marches or in parade ground drill. Training women in the use of firearms underlines the political role they will play in maintaining white supremacy, even though they will never use these skills. If women are being recruited more because they are white than because they are women, it is important that their training gives them a sense of their race being under threat and of their contribution to white unity. Hence, the heavy emphasis on tasks the women will never perform except in imagination by identifying with white men fighting in defence of the regime.

Minnie Dreyer, an award-winning student at the George College in 1980, said of her training:

> It has really been worthwhile because you get to know yourself. A woman should know how to shoot, to do first-aid and to be prepared for whatever may happen in life. It's not necessarily preparation for war. (*Cape Times*, 14 April 1980)

Despite the disclaimer, according to Minnie Dreyer, all the skills the training had inculcated are skills associated with maintaining a society under threat. This seems to be the essence of the ideas the women acquire at the George College and which may be much more important than any work-experience as clerks, typists or personnel officers. In the words of the College song their training brings the young women together:

> In endeavour heart and mind
> To protect our citizens
> We shall be strong and conquer.
> (Own Trans. from *Paratus*, November 1985)

At the passing-out parade in 1978 Desirée De Swardt, who joined the Air Force as a member of the Permanent Force, gave her reasons for taking this course:

> I could do something for the country, study through the Air Force, be treated as a lady, and get almost the same salary as a man. (*Rand Daily Mail*, 21 April 1978)

I suggest that the country for which she wanted to do something is the territory of white power. The rigorous training which the SADF recruits undergo ensures that the women will define their country in these terms, and forge links of fellowship with other recruits in a way that a typing course or ordinary nursing training could not.

Soldiers and 'femininity'

In counterpoint to the strenuous military training the women receive is the heavy emphasis placed by the George College officers, the SADF apparatus, and the women recruits themselves on maintaining their 'femininity'.

Paratus, the SADF magazine, commented: 'These women soldiers are brave and capable, and yet we are assured they are ever-feminine' (quoted in *Resister*, 25 April–May 1983). At the passing-out parade in December 1982 Brigadier P. M. Lombard said to the women recruits: 'You must never lose your femininity. Never stop being a woman' (*Uniform*, December 1982). In promoting the George College, *Paratus* stressed in 1985 that it was out-and-out a military college with discipline, but that at the same time women should be as feminine as possible. In addition to the marching and the gun practices, young students are taught special courses on feminity, how to dress, diet, and manage a household (*Paratus*, October 1985). Daleen Scholtz, who attended the George College in 1981 held the view that:

> Our training helps us to become prepared, but still remain women. (*Citizen*, 14 April 1981)

The emphasis on preserving an element of gender identity suggests that the 'feminine' seems much more than merely a recognition of actual sexual *difference*. It appears to me that amongst officers and recruits the maintenance of 'femininity' is an appeal to perceived *traditional values* of gender difference which need to be preserved in times of stress and change. It is notable that although Afrikaner nationalist hagiography is rich in images of pioneering women who fought in the battles of the nineteenth century in the conquest of South Africa from its African rulers, no appeal is made to these symbols of fighting women by the modern defenders of white rule. It is possibly because the images of the *voortrekker* (pioneer) women are the ideological property of the far right, from which the SADF wishes to detach white women, that they are given no prominence.

Interestingly, women in the services are not portrayed as (or indeed given the role of) caring for male soldiers. The 'feminine' qualities of caring for children and visiting the sick are not publicly and ideologically ascribed to women soldiers. The Southern Cross Fund, a charity run by white middle-class women with some participation by wives of members of the permanent force, collects money for comforts for troops serving in the operational area, conducts Christmas-time visits to soldiers in hospital, and organises a ride-safe scheme for national servicemen hitchhiking home on leave. The women members of this fund make *koeksisters* (dough-nuts) and other home-made foods, publicly portraying themselves as super-mothers, while at home so much of their cooking is done by servants. The activities of the Southern Cross Fund underline the ambiguous identity of white women recruits, whose ideological role is neither that of carer nor comforter, despite their strenuous efforts to preserve other aspects of femininity.

White South Africa's view of women soldiers

The sanctified and esteemed role the SADF confers on women soldiers within white South African society, by word if not in deed, does not reflect all views of women soldiers, which in certain circles or at particular times range from the patronising to the openly hostile or dismissive.

The press, for example, has a condescending tone when referring to white women in the services. They are often depicted by diminutives, for example 'Botha's Babes' (a reference to P. W. Botha who introduced women's recruitment when Minister of Defence), 'trooplets' and '*soldoedies*' (an Afrikaans diminutive of the word for soldier). In other characterisations they are identified with rather useless, specifically feminine accessories, for example as the 'powder-puff squadron' and the 'petticoat privates'. In all of this the press mirrors the marked sexism of white South African society as a whole, which has been virtually untouched by the moves towards sexual equality which have been an important element in the post-war history of so many countries.

Another view of women in the services is held by women who identify politically with the far right – The Kappie Kommando (formed in 1982). The name honours the *kappies* (bonnets) worn by the Voortrekker women and the kommandos that carried out the defence of Afrikaner nationalism against British imperial policy during the Anglo-Boer War. The Voortrekkers were pioneers who travelled north from the Cape in the early nineteenth century in search of land and in protest at the liberalism (particularly with regard to race), as they saw it, of British imperial administration at the Cape; they engaged in the wars of dispossession against the African people. The women of the Kappie Kommando dress in Voortrekker costumes, often in black, as an indication that they uphold 'traditional' political values. The main focus of their protest has been the moves made by President Botha to allow some blacks to sit in Parliament and engage in an exercise of power-sharing. For the Kappie Kommando, women in military service are prostitutes. In 1982, at the time when there was widespread speculation that national service would be introduced for white women, a leading Cape member of the Kappie Kommando stated:

> Under no circumstances will we allow our daughters to be taken up into an integrated army for the purposes of prostitution. This is what happened in the last war. Only women from the lower classes joined the army and they were for prostitution. (*Argus*, 20 March 1982)

These views were supported by the national vice-president of the movement:

Women in the army during the last war were used for prostitution. If they were recruited to the army now the same thing
would happen. They would definitely not come out of the army as
virgins. War and the army destroy women's moral standards.
(*Argus*, 23 March 1982)

Whatever traditional values the SADF wishes to maintain in its
constant stress on women soldiers preserving their femininity, such
values are clearly not preserved sufficiently for the women of the
Kappie Kommando who consider any women in military uniform as
women sacrificed to vice. It is plain that within conservative white
political circles there are differing views on which traditional values
are to be maintained and what are the best ways of doing so. In
terms of the 'total strategy' of Botha and others, the enlistment of
white women bolsters the view of a society under threat and of all its
white citizens staving off disaster. From the point of view of the
Kappie Kommando, the presence of white women soldiers under-
mines the very values the regime should be preserving, symbolically
identified with their women's virginity. Interestingly enough, the
Kappie Kommando itself does not lay claim to the tradition of the
fighting Voortrekker woman, but to those aspects of the Voortrekker past that stress religion, rectitude and the preservation of white
dominance.

Conclusion

I have shown how the use of women in the SADF was born not so
much out of the need for women's labour as the need for women's
identification with white supremacy in a context where the majority
of the population is black. The expansion and modernisation of the
SADF has led to some use of skilled women workers, but their role
in the services has been portrayed not for what it is, a continuation
of white women's subordination to white men in terms of pay and
job opportunities, but as an advertisement for the modernity of the
SADF and as an instrument to create white political unity. Women
in the military have helped to maintain white identity in South
Africa. Their training, which stresses white unity and aspires to the
'feminine', attempts to preserve certain 'traditional' white values.

In my judgement, recruitment into the armed services on these terms is no liberation for white women, it is merely an advance into backwardness.

Note

1. I would like to acknowledge the help of several people who assisted me in the writing of this study. The Committee of South African War Registers helped me find some of the research materials used in this paper, Gavin Cawthra allowed me to see the then unpublished manuscript of his book on the South African military and he, together with Sharon Macdonald, made very useful comments on early drafts of the paper.

References

Cawthra, G. (1986) *Brutal force: The apartheid war machine* (London: IDAF).

Davies, R., O'Meara, D. and Dlamini, S. (1984) *The struggle for South Africa: A reference guide to movements, organisations and institutions* (London: Zed Press).

Grundy, K. (1983) *Soldiers without politics* (Berkeley: University of California Press).

Argus (Cape Town).

Cape Times (Cape Town).

Citizen (Johannesburg).

Paratus (Pretoria).

Rand Daily Mail (Johannesburg).

Resister (London).

South African Digest (Pretoria).

Star (Johannesburg).

Sunday Times (Johannesburg).

Uniform (Pretoria).

7

Living with images of a fighting elite: women and the Foreign Legion

ROSEMARY McKECHNIE[1]

Although the imagery associated with war and warriors is primarily focused on fighting men, the women attached to these men are also drawn into its classificatory vision. This study explores how the rigid ideals of womanhood and femininity that arise as a function of the 'maleness' of the military context affect the lives of one group of women attached to a regiment of the French Foreign Legion: the wives and concubines[2] of non-commissioned officers and those women attached to unranked men. The ethnographic material comes from eighteen months spent in Calvi in Corsica, base of the *Deuxième Régiment Etranger de Parachutistes*.

Few armies are so wrapped in exotic military imagery as this mercenary force that has fought through colonial wars from the desert of North Africa to the jungle of Indo-China. The Legionnaire[3] has come to epitomise the figure of the professional soldier, a construction of exaggerated masculinity that appears to preclude female participation. Traditionally, one of the main tenets of Legion mystique is the absence of the female. But if women have been excluded from this most masculine of armies[4] (and not only from the battle-field: in the past the Legion demanded total dedication from its soldiers, only officers could marry), they have never disappeared; in folk-belief and literary representations the Legion is defined as the army men join because of women:

a number of men are in the Legion on account of women; a good deal because they could not marry the woman whom they loved; a good many because they did marry her . . . most *légionnaires*, celibates of circumstance, talked and thought a very great deal about women. (Wren, 1931, p. 241)

If women were seen to be the reason men went to their death they also provided a reason to live; the symbolic role of the female as the 'other' was magnified and crystallised by her absence. In the asymmetric male world of warfare men may do the fighting but images of the female (both negative and positive) have assumed a particular potency. The theoretical implications of this complex imagery about war and death, atonement and sacrifice are to a great extent outside the scope of this study – here I am principally concerned with the problems faced by women today, who live with the ideas that have evolved around this imagery both inside and outside the institution.

The historical background and traditions that have made the Legion what it is have created an institution somewhat ill at ease in its present context of modern France. After almost 150 years at war, it is having to come to grips with the changes brought about by two decades of peace. One of the 'problems' that has accompanied this relative stability is the appearance of women within the 'family' of the Legion. Women's traditional roles in the old order of things were necessarily limited: the 'camp-follower' or prostitute was liminally attached to fighting units while the wives of officers waited for their men to visit. Nowadays women are not so easily categorised or contained. The dichotomy prostitute/wife is no longer apt (if it ever was[5]) to describe the women who are connected to the Legion in different ways, and the exclusion of women from the domain of total control exerted by the Legion over its men is increasingly difficult to maintain.

Just as enlisting is a matter of choice, so is marrying 'into' the Legion, but as most women have little knowledge of the institution beforehand they are often unprepared to cope with the rules that order life within the Legion 'family' and the stigma attached to their position (see Hutter, 1981, p. 25). They have to learn how other people see them, and this can be a painful experience. It is in defence against this view of themselves, in an effort to maintain a reasonable self-image, that women turn to the alternative roles offered as antithetical to that of camp-follower, with an exaggerated portrayal of the 'decent' wife and mother.

Historical background: the formation of a fighting elite

The formation of the French Foreign Legion in 1831 marked the beginning of a force that was to participate in 150 years of constant warfare. From the colonial wars of the nineteenth century, through two World Wars and, more recently, the conflicts in Indo-China and Algeria, the Legion has been in the front line of the French forces. The loss of Algeria marked the end of an era.[6] The Legion's regiments are now based in France, though they do provide a constant military presence in several Third World countries friendly to France.[7] From its beginning as an ill-trained battalion of mercenaries the French Foreign Legion has fought its way to worldwide recognition as a courageous and efficient fighting force. This reputation holds, despite the fact that there have been no wars to fight in over twenty years.

The *Deuxième REP* has a special reputation within the Legion itself.[8] Legionnaires classify themselves into two categories, *seigneurs* and *corbeaux* – the parachutists of the *REP* being the 'lords' while the rest are 'crows'. There is fierce competition to serve with the regiment, amongst officers as well as non-commissioned men. Most commissioned men are from St Cyr, the most prestigious military school in France, and although they are likely to stay only two years with the regiment, they will proudly wear its insignia for the rest of their career. This elitism is recognised economically, too, in that men who serve in the REP are paid about 3000 francs (c. £280) a month more than other regiments.

Views of Legion women

Ideas about the women attached in any way to the Legion are woven around those held about Legionnaires, and I think it is necessary to consider these here, albeit superficially. The men who join the Legion come from all over the world and whatever are their reasons for enlisting – be they criminal, political or personal – new recruits leave their identity, possessions, nationality and family behind.

They are given a military identity card bearing a new name, date of birth and nationality. In the past, the *légionnaire*'s lot was a hard one; the pay was low, fighting was constant, and death was a distinct possibility. Today the conditions are less arduous and the soldier has every chance of surviving, but the stereotype of the Legionnaire has not modified; if anything it has been embellished since the force returned to France.

The imagery associated with the Legionnaire – that of the professional soldier who is disciplined, dispassionate, even brutal – is seldom contradicted in literary or popular portrayals. Over the years the French public have been treated to a stereotype-reinforcing parade of ex-members of the REP who have made headline news by doing just what one expects Legionnaires to do.[9] The pictures that spring to the minds of English speakers, flavoured by the novels of P. C. Wren (or more recently the account of Murray[10]) and memories of Gary Cooper striding over the desert as Beau Geste, are perhaps a refinement of the more ambiguous glamour exercised by the Legion in Francophone countries.

The attraction and repulsion exercised by the institution are fundamentally rooted in the vision of war and death that has evolved within the historical perspectives of Western society. In the face of military threat the breaking of fundamental laws against killing are justified in terms of patriotism, of protecting one's people, or of safeguarding the heritage of future generations. It is difficult to use this reasoning to explain the actions of the Legionnaire. He is a soldier by inclination and has already deserted his country and past. While the soldier 'gives his life' for his country, the Legionnaire kills for another. The 'human' side of the soldier who goes off to war but then comes back, who can be seen as a fellow-countryman, father, husband, or son, is missing. In his case there is no softening of military characteristics, no integration back into another role in society, no sympathy for the hardships he has suffered. The idea of reintegration by atonement, French if not by blood then by blood spilled (*par le sang versé*) loses meaning in times of peace.

France is a nation that seems to be preoccupied with military power. Its own somewhat shameful record of defeat this century no doubt plays some part in this, but it should also be remembered that the Fifth Republic itself was born of a military coup; force has played an important role in shaping the French constitution. The figure of the paratrooper has assumed a particular significance in this light, and not only because he is associated in the popular mind with the heroism of Indo-China. Aron describes how the ambiguity of this French obsession was exacerbated by the actions of the military during the Algerian crisis (Aron, 1984, p.165).[11] The 'paras' of the Foreign Legion are seen as a dangerous weapon to keep in reserve, their presence on French soil is viewed with suspicion. The very qualities that excite awe in the context of war can be viewed with mistrust and disdain in times of peace; the brutality that is acceptable when society is under threat seems reprehensible in retrospect, and we distance ourselves from those who were directly involved, leaving the stigma of responsibility with them.

This stigma is also carried by the women who associate with Legionnaires. The qualities attributed to the professional soldier define him as unnatural and dangerous, and women who are seen to be attracted by these are strongly censured. The stereotype of the Legionnaire is clear about his attitude to the female; virile but cold, his needs are sexual not emotional, a combination that should repel all respectable women. War is clearly a male domain as is interest in war; only men may admire it, or admit being drawn to martial imagery. If the women attached to armies are often categorised as camp-followers, and seen as prostitutes, that is doubly true of those who have relationships with Legionnaires. They lose the respect accorded to 'decent' women.

There is a certain symmetry in the imagery attributed to the professional soldier and the prostitute that is worth noting here: both are 'mercenary', and the negative evaluations inherent in this term speak for themselves. Since their stereotypical appearance exaggerates masculine and feminine characteristics to the extreme, the imagery presents caricatures that exclude individuality or personality. The process of categorisation marginalises them so that they are regarded as dangerous, abnormal, and 'deviant' by the society that makes use of their services.

La grande famille: the basis of the mystique

The ambiguous glamour generated by the Legion is rooted in more than simple machismo. It is a complex institution that not only bounds its adherents from the outside world, it binds them with something that cannot simply de described as loyalty. In surviving 150 years of fighting it has knit together a constant turnover of new recruits of many nationalities, and it continues to attract men despite the discipline and hard treatment it is known to dispense (some seven out of ten applicants can be turned away). Whether the recruit enlists for pragmatic reasons or in search of an ideal there is no partial commitment. Five years is the minimum term of contract and during this time his entire life is subsumed within the military persona he has assumed. Young describes this in terms other than escapism:

> The French Foreign Legion is far more than a simple sanctuary for men who have abandoned their past and seek to escape to a new life. It is a family.

He goes on to quote a colonel he talked to:

> These men are for us another family and not just soldiers we have to form and train. (Young, 1984, p. 142).

The Legion is in fact referred to as *la grande famille* in everyday conversation. The motto painted over the barracks' headquarters is *Legio Patria Nostra* (the Legion is our country). Men will say that their loyalty is to the Legion first with France coming a poor second. The attitudes of officers, the songs that are sung every meal-time,[12] the ritualisation of everyday actions, all combine to keep alive this ideology. In the past, joining the Legion was a renunciation in the grand style: of the past, of one's name and nationality, of a normal role in society – and, quite possibly, of life itself. The imagery found in poetry and prose written by men[13] is of the misfit who has been rejected or has rejected society, who has given body and soul to the Legion. '*La Légion*', the Legion, is feminine; it is mother, family and country to its men. Those who belong do not say that someone is a good Legionnaire, they say '*Il croit au fond*' (he believes absolutely), the reverse being '*Il ne croit plus*'.

As Williams has pointed out, against our background of Western secularised and individualistic thinking it is difficult to understand a group whose reference point is not the individual but the whole (Williams, 1975, p. 106). The aim of the Legion is to create a disciplined and dependable armed force from the disparate elements who join, most of whom do not even speak French. It can function only if the cultural and individual heterogeneity is mini-mised. Everything that differentiates one individual from the next is reduced to the lowest common denominator, a label for the military persona that comes to take precedence over the person. This nominalisation results in a schematic social configuration of stereotypes – a world of Kiwis, Paddies and Fritzes – where the everyday confrontation of cultures produces all sorts of linguistic and non-verbal misinterpretation (see Chapman, 1982, for a description of how cultural stereotypes arise and are reified in such circumstances). These strengthen rather than contradict generalisa-tions, making judgements on a more personal level difficult. The forcible imposition of a rigid code of behaviour means that, on the surface at least, relations are maintained on this level: one must be seen to act the part. This is undoubtedly relevant in considering the male/female relationship; if the relations described appear to be unrealistically formalised then it must be remembered that indi-vidual responses are habitually hidden in such a repressive situa-tion.

If armies are mainly men's worlds, then the Legion is more self-consciously so than most. '*La Légion*' may be feminine and all-encompassing, but it encloses a purely male world of war and death. Young quotes Antisthenes: 'When brothers agree there is no fortress so strong as their common life' (Young, 1984, p. 161). Nowadays women are causing problems within the Legion fortress. Women provide a context for the non-military person to exist: in their life-giving capacity, women are able to create a family that rivals the 'family' of the legion for the devotion of its men. The conflict between that part of men's lives enclosed in the Legion sphere and that which is outside often leads to disillusionment; this results in men leaving to find a career that is less restricting to their private life. Many men have girlfriends, are married and have families; a Legionnaire may be a husband and a father too. The conflicting claims of *la grande famille* and the family are played out in each relationship.

Keeping women in their place: rules and regulations

Marriage

The Legion has retained one prerogative that most European armies renounced in the nineteenth century (Macmillan, 1984,

p. 91) – unranked men are not allowed to marry, and even if a man was married before enlisting his new identity is single. Although men are now permitted to live outside the camp, this is not encouraged, and the demands made on their time are such[14] that it is virtually impossible for them to sustain any kind of external relationship. The directives of the force are relayed to the men through the company commanding officer, and I have heard many stories of how these officers have tried to keep 'their' men away from women. One woman related how when she met the man she is now married to, they had to wait two years before spending any time together; each time he asked for leave it was refused, and when his *capitaine* learnt that she had come to visit, he spent three weeks confined to barracks, much of it on guard duty outside the camp brothel. Officers often lead the censure levelled at the legionnaires who spend time away from camp to be with a woman: they are labelled '*cas sociaux*', 'social cases'. This insult implies that those concerned are not capable of fulfilling their role within the regiment, that their allegiance is elsewhere.

The control exercised over the lives of unranked men has serious consequences for those women who attempt to sustain a relationship with them; their position is one of constant insecurity. A woman can make no legal financial claim on her partner, nor can her children be recognised by him. If he is injured, or sent away without notice, as often happens, she will not be told. Information is released only to wives. As the men are not allowed to drive, rent property, even open a bank account, women have to take complete responsibility for all of these things, but at the same time they are usually at least partially dependent on the men's salary (there is little work to be found in the area outside the tourist season and many women are eligible for only limited state benefits, or none at all). This creates terrible problems, as when men are away, they are either unable to send money back or are not paid until they return.

The discipline that is imposed on unranked men controls their sexuality until they are considered able to control it themselves. Although this discipline has led to the Legion being likened to medieval orders of celibate knights (Young, 1984, p. 161), it has never required celibacy of its adherents. In fact until a few years ago there was a brothel within the camp.[15] Far from denying men sexual access to women, the Legion provides it on the 'premises', and so is able to limit the contact to an impersonal transaction. This is institutionalised in the *rite de passage* that marks the promotion of an *élève*,[16] which often includes a ritual visit to the brothel with the commanding officer footing the bill. Women in other more threatening capacities are firmly excluded from the male preserve of the camp.[17] Prostitutes are talked of in terms of 'sexual hygiene', they fulfil an anonymous function as the outlet for the sexual drive that might otherwise interfere with the men's performance or turn towards other men. In the Legion's reductive 'world-structure' sexuality is amputated from all other aspects of womanhood, and personified in the despised image of the whore. It is interesting that in the context where homosexuality is strongly condemned the frequenting of transvestites, whose appearance portrays to exaggeration the stereotypes of the sexually available woman, is relatively acceptable.

The administration is sensitive to outsiders' perception of the regiment, aware that their position in France (and especially in Corsica) is barely tolerated. The control exercised over men's sexuality during *formation* fulfils two functions; it makes clear that women should not interfere with their primary obligation to the Legion and clarifies the distinction between the kind of women suitable for marriage (and integration of the Legion family into French society), and the kind of women who can be used for the satisfaction of sexual needs. This polar 'division of labour' results in the familiar schematic categorisation of the female sex into those fit to be whores and those fit to be mothers, and those attached to the Legion's sphere in any other capacity than the latter are automatically defined as the first.

Christmas: virgins and godmothers

Before going on to look at the implications of this for the women concerned I would like to pause and look at what is probably the most solid symbolic statement of the exclusion of women and the dangers they represent: Christmas. The other *fêtes* on the Legion calendar are marked by balls to which the consorts of ranked men are invited. Christmas is different, however, precisely because it has come to symbolise the unity of the family: *la grande famille* makes no bones about imposing its precedence over the family. It is a week of unrelenting activity, in which work often spills over into free time as preparations for the celebrations and various contests between companies get under way. One of these contests is for the best *crèche* scene, and the somewhat bizarre themes of these should perhaps be illustrated by a few examples. For instance: the Virgin kneels humbly before a standing paratrooper who holds the baby Jesus in his arms; a traditional scenario, somewhat marred by the fact that it is constructed inside a rocket-shell with paratroopers suspended in the background amongst the angels; a crib artfully placed on the deck of an amphibious tank with the traditional farm animals replaced by sundry marine fauna. There is obviously much material worthy of analysis in this Legion version of peace and goodwill to all men, but here I will restrict my enquiry to focus on the fact that there is but one female figure in the exclusively male 'family' grouping at Christmas – the men joke about the only virgin who has ever been seen the inside of the camp. J. R. Young describes a Christmas Eve celebration he attended:

> Celebrating Christmas is something very special for Legion-naires. Few of them have homes to go to, unless they are married. The Legion is their 'home' and the bonds of its own family are tight. So much so that, traditionally during Christmas, all officers and *sous-officiers* remain with their men until after the *réveillon*. Wives and sweethearts accept this custom as a normal part of sharing their lives with a Legionnaire. (Young, 1984, p. 157)

What Young doesn't seem to have noticed are the extra guards posted around the camp to make sure that nobody decides to break with tradition. The Legion seems to suspect that the bonds that hold its family together may need a little support, or perhaps the wives and sweethearts are less passive than they appear. Nevertheless, festivities continue into the night with a long circular bar-crawl. The men are allowed to go home in the morning, if they are in a fit state to do so.

The First Regiment at Orange is singular within the Legion in that it invites a woman to participate in the first part of its Christmas celebrations. She is the Comtesse Ladislas du Luart, who was made an honorary *brigadier-chef* of the regiment in 1944 for her patron-age. She has also been decorated with the *Croix de Guerre* and is an Officer of the Order of Merit, as well as Commander of the Legion of Honour. This extraordinary woman is known as the *marraine*, the godmother of the regiment. Young says of her:

> She is a handsome woman . . . You cannot mistake the distinct
> military bearing, and yet she radiates a simple motherly quality as
> she moves round the room. Every man present receives a light
> kiss on each cheek. These are her 'boys', her Legionnaires.
> (Young, 1984, p. 157)

I won't go into the role that Catholic religion plays in sustaining the
ideology of the Legion here, but I would like to note what Hastrup
has said about the anomaly of the virgin mother being a potent
symbol of the relationship between the natural and supernatural
world (Hastrup, 1978, p. 60). This anomaly must increase in such a
context, where the virgin is seen to be so out of place. She also
points out that women beyond the age of having children are
anomalous in a world where child-bearing is very much the central
role of women. In this light the presence of the Comtesse at the
Christmas *réveillon* of the First Regiment is not at all contradictory.
She is the godmother, the spiritual mother, quite different from
those who are waiting alone for their men to come home.
Completely removed from the sexual and procreative role of wives
that threaten the central core of Legion ideology, the essence of her
spiritual role is enhanced by her aristocratic background and
military honours, dignifying the Legion's creed of purity and
elitism. Despite the fact that it would be difficult to imagine a
personage less like the stereotype of 'legionnaire's woman' – or
rather because of this – she plays the symbolic role of mother within
la grande famille perfectly.

Women and wives

Once a man moves up in the hierarchy and become responsible for
others, the controls exercised over the private sector of his life are
relaxed. His mature position indicates that he is considered capable
of organising his life so that it does not interfere with his own work
or harm the reputation of the regiment. He may, at last, ask
permission to marry, but before this is granted, the background of
each woman is investigated by the military police. Supposedly this is
to check her political background. In fact the main aim of research is
to find out if a woman is 'morally suitable' and if it is discovered that
she has been a prostitute or has worked in a bar, the prospective

husband will be then advised that the marriage would endanger his career. Ethnic background is also a significant factor, and apart from North African women, few ranked men choose a partner who is coloured.[18]

The files amassed during this process of screening are supposedly confidential but information is often disclosed. One woman, for example, was understandably upset when her husband was informed that she had once been a prostitute in Paris for many years and advised not to marry her. Conjecture about the past of women is common, and details are freely bandied about. The administrative officers complain about the quality of the women *sous-officiers* live with and discuss ways in which they could be excluded to save the regiment's reputation.

Women are constrained to accept this vetting because of the control exercised over their husbands (a man would certainly lose his position if he were to marry without permission), and because of the difficulties experienced by non-recognised consorts. In addition the material benefits of marriage are substantial; as a family man her husband will be given extra money and a subsidised flat in the military apartment blocks in Calvi. In order to become part of *la grande famille* a woman has to accept that no domain in her life will be private – that is, unknown to her husband and to the regiment. She also has to accept the Legion's evaluation of her life, and the fact that her husband's career may well depend on her classification and performance.

The categorisation of women as 'fit' to be wives comes from a classifactory model that orders all the women that orbit around the regiment and I think it is important in the context of this study to describe not only those women who have married 'into' the Legion but also those who are more loosely attached. To begin with I should make clear that apart from the tourist season there are relatively very few women, considering the size of the garrison (about 1200 men), and local Corsican women are not included in the model I am about to present. With very few exceptions Corsican women from Calvi do not mix with Legionnaires – just to be seen talking to one or in a bar that caters for the regiment damages a girl's reputation almost irretrievably. At the same time, the evaluations of Legionnaires and those of their women that are present in the Corsican context (at once particular to the area and a reflection of a wider French set of ideas) are the basis of the ideas that women enounter in their immediate contact with the outside world.

Just as the *Deuxième REP* attracts men from all over the world and from diverse backgrounds, so too does it attract a number of women. They come to Calvi for a variety of reasons. Young has this to say:

> The tourist office will remind the visitor . . . that the small town of Calvi in its NW corner was destroyed by Nelson in 1794. In recent years Calvi has become famous for something else as many a pretty girl will tell you . . . Broadly speaking, most well-brought up Frenchwomen have mixed feelings about Legionnaires – that is, apart from those that have married into the Legion . . . However there can be no doubt that, for some women, there is a touch of magic about the white kepi and those who wear it. As any member of the *2ème REP* will tell you, during the summer months the beaches of Calvi are awash with the most attractive girls . . . searching for a Legionnaire to share their annual holiday. (Young, 1984, p. 88)

The picture he presents of the *Deuxième REP* as a magnet drawing women from all over Europe is something of an exaggeration. The beaches of Calvi are indeed awash with tourists in summer, but it is unlikely that the regiment's presence was the deciding factor in their choice of holiday venue. However, there are some who come because of the garrison, a number of whom could be described as 'well-brought up' (I did meet one banker's wife who spent a month in Calvi every year and swore it did her marriage the world of good). Perhaps the most amusing example of the ambivalent pull of the Legion I came across was that of a party of social workers who worked to rehabilitate girls with backgrounds of petty crime and prostitution. The Legion appeared so often in their files that they came to Calvi, curious to meet with Legionnaires 'in the flesh' as it were. The somewhat surprising outcome of their foray was the marriage of four of their number to men of the *REP*.

What is certain is that many lasting relationships are formed at this time of the year. The men regard the tourist season as their main chance to meet 'decent' women. Young perhaps exaggerates the numbers of young female tourists who visit Calvi because of the *REP*, but he omits to mention the other women who come in the wake of the Legion. Many prostitutes are regular winter visitors in

Calvi – arriving as the tourists leave. The 'professionals' work to an agreed tariff system from certain bar counters while others turn to prostitution only in times of need. In addition, a new privately owned 'closed' brothel situated some 20 yards from the camp[19] has taken the place of the military one.

More numerous than prostitutes, however, is the floating population of women who live off the Legionnaires in a casual way. Many work in bars, or simply spend most of their day in them. They will sometimes sleep with men for free, sometimes ask for 'presents', and often they depend on admirers to pay for clothes, and apartments. In general (though not always) they are young when they arrive, often from an economically disadvantaged background, having had little or no education; many are of North African origin and their families may be in an irregular position within France. As a rule these women do manage to attach themselves to an unranked man, or one who has recently been promoted to sergeant, fairly quickly on a permanent or semipermanent basis.

A few women organise their financial dependence on the men of the *REP* in a more systematic way. They do this by setting up a series of what are known as '*pigeons*', in other words, they elicit a fixed sum of money every month from several men by spinning them a hard-luck story about some problem – paying the rent, debts, caring for children – that could be overcome by a little steady financial help. This strategy does not include sexual inducement, in fact its success depends on the men being convinced that the woman concerned is 'decent' (*une fille bien*). An intelligent choice of victim and careful management of personal life are essential if the ploy is not to fail. The system is very profitable if practised assiduously. One woman (who did in fact have a genuine problem) worked in a bar undeclared while claiming state benefit and collecting a regular contribution from six or seven *pigeons* – the monthly total reputedly exceeded 20 000 francs (c. £1800).

The status of these women is vague; they do not consider themselves as prostitutes, and their own view of their position may or may not take into cognisance their economic dependence. Young women talk in terms of being free to go with whoever appeals to them, and of soldiers falling in love with them. They are preoccupied for the most part by the glamour of their own appearances and the power their sexual attractiveness gives them. Older women who remain unattached, or who are 'between relationships' tend to discuss their position in much more prosaic terms that makes little usage of romantic terminology.

Whatever their own view, women are stigmatised both by society and by the Legion world. Those who have gone from man to man accumulating children (often in order to claim the benefits available to single mothers) present problems that the small social work department at Calvi cannot, or will not, deal with. The fact that they have been categorised as Legionnaires' women certainly affects the view taken of their case, as one woman put it: 'I am an Arab, I have worked in a bar and I have a child so people assume that I am with a Legionnaire'. Its a 'Catch 22' situation, as women in difficulty end up desperately looking for a Legionnaire as the only economic option open to them.

In general the women who frequent the Legionnaires' social circuit are thought by the men to be economically active; they are there to make money. Just to talk to a woman is expensive (a drink in these bars can cost up to 60 francs) and if the relationship should go further there is a meal and a hotel room to pay for; perhaps a 'present' to take into consideration. Men say that at least prostitutes offer a 'clean' (*net*) transaction that is more 'honest' than paying for silly conversation, and false smiles. The other women are seen to be dangerous, they may trap a man into settling with them or even marrying. There is even a gesture to symbolise this: that of claws hooking inwards; she is said to be 'well stuck on' ('*elle est bien accrochée*').

This brief description of the women who gravitate around the *REP* makes no pretension of being holistic or well detailed; of course, many women fall outside the definitions offered above. What I hope it will do is provide a background into which the following analysis can be set with more clarity. Many men meet their wives and girlfriends elsewhere – at home, abroad or on mainland France – and bring them back to Calvi. The *REP* extends its boundaries around an extremely heterogenous set of men and women, representatives of many races, religions and classes: it would seem likely that such a random selection of people would generate a flexible model of male and female roles. However, just the opposite is true; they are bound together by a rigid system of values based on ideas about Legionnaires and Legionnaires' women, that come from both outside and inside the group.

If wives are looked on with respect by the men it is only to the extent that they fulfil the specifications of a respectable woman. Since this excludes women already present in the Legion world, ideally a wife should come from outside the context, of whom nothing is known, who is seldom seen and who is therefore not discussed: 'the best woman is she of whom men speak the least' (de Beauvoir, 1972, p. 122). Older women are noticeably more acceptable as wives than in outside society; associated more easily with the role of housewife and mother they are thought to control their sexuality while interfering less with the men's lives. It is considered important that a man is '*bien casé*' that he is comfortably housed and that his wife is capable of taking care of domestic problems by herself. The men's (apparent) acceptance of this formalised model is more readily understandable in terms of the role they have undertaken and the context they find themselves in. I would like to look more closely at how women perceive the situation.

Living with the Legion: *la cité des cocus*

'*Tu vois, ici il y a de tout, la moitié des femmes sont des putes l'autre moitié sont des bourgeoises*' (You see, here there is a bit of everything, half the women are whores, the other half are middle class). Whether female stereotypes are from inside or outside the Legion world they have in common a generalisation that masks the heterogeneity of the women they describe. As the woman I have quoted above remarked, the women who find themselves as wives living together in the *cité de cadre*, more usually known as the *cité des cocus* (literally 'The cuckold's estate'), have come from every walk of life. Their arrival within the Legion world often comes as a shock. Experiencing the regulations that intrude into their private life while realising that so much of the men's time and energy is bound up in the Legion is the first thing they have to come to grips with. The next is the image of themselves that they encounter both in society at large and in the Legion context.

The censure of the outside world is often first encountered by women on breaking the news of the relationship to their family: even if a parent has little against the Foreign Legion, the prospect of a Legionnaire marrying one's daughter is seldom welcome. For some brides there is an element of rebellion in their choice, and they are aware of breaking with the constrictions of their family background. Few can say that their families were not opposed to their relationship to some degree. One well-educated woman described with relish the reactions of her father on learning that she (an only daughter) had decided to marry a man ten years her senior, a Jew of rather miserable Turkish origins, and a Legionnaire to boot.

The full weight of the stigma attached to being a Legion woman only becomes clear on settling into life in Calvi. Knowing people have ideas about a group is quite different from being a member of it and experiencing the translation of prejudice into the reality of everyday life. Hostility is seldom openly articulated by local people, although this does happen; women simply find that after years of living in Calvi they know no-one outside the Legion world. The only society open to a Legion woman is that of other Legion women and its fulcrum is the *cité*, even those women who live outside the *cité* (often to escape the 'claustrophobia' of its confines) find that their social life revolves around it.

First impressions of the *cité* are cheerful; large white buildings are set around grassy courtyards, lines of washing and pots of flowers colourfully festooning each apartment's balcony. Contact with neighbours is soon established, and the newcomer finds that she is almost immediately in possession of information concerning the lives of those around her (she too will be pumped for details about her background and her relations with her husband – as everyone will tell her, gossip is the drawback of living in the *cité*). She soon learns that there is a strict notion of hierarchy, that her husband's position affects very much her own; she learns the importance of housework, that the washing on each balcony is not as innocent as it first appears, that if her appartment's floor is not washed by ten o'clock in the morning people will discuss it; finally she learns that some of the 'things that go on' are indeed shocking. The judgements passed on the scandalous behaviour of others will soon make clear just how her own life must be managed to escape being categorised in the same way as those held to have transgressed morally.

Even women who have been loosely attached to the Legion before may not understand the behaviour expected of a wife or the negative moral evaluation held of their marginal involvement in the Legion world. For example, one girl who had several Legionnaire boyfriends on a casual basis settled with a sergeant. At first life continued pretty much as before: during the day she did the housework and visited friends; in the evening she prepared herself to go out and then went to a bar where she drank coffee and gossiped. First her husband objected to the make-up she wore, he said it was 'tarty' (*ça fait pute*). In camp men began to tease him because she was seen out alone, and occasionally talking to other men, with the result that he forbade her to go out in the evening, even when he was away. Further, he required her to stop talking to most of her friends, including her sister who was having an affair with a friend of his while her husband was overseas and so had a 'reputation'.

By completely reorganising her life this woman became acceptable to the Legion men as a wife – after a few months his friends admitted that she seemed to be 'behaving'. However, she did not automatically become acceptable to other wives. While not disagreeing with the primary definition of Legionnaire's women (of which they are surrounded by so many concrete examples) wives can only claim that it is not true of themselves. The women 'police' themselves. Rigidly adopting the rules that define wifely conduct, they accept to stay in their homes and take on an exaggerated housewife/mother role; they also dissociate themselves from women who do not, and lead the censure levelled at them. This results in fragmentation of the group. One cannot take the risk of being friendly with a woman who breaks the rules or seems as if she might; one might be 'tarred with the same brush'. There is little organisation of group-activities, as one might expect in such a situation,[20] or mobilisation of the group as a whole against the many regulations that often make their lives miserable (Christmas being a good example). It is simply a matter of maintaining a positive self-image in a situation where each woman feels she can deny the moral slur only at an individual level.

Hilary Callan has pointed out that the military context offers an example of direct replication of hierarchy, each wife taking a position that accords with her husband's chain of command (Callan, 1984, pp. 11–12). The Legion world is no exception in this respect: as in other contexts it is often said that women are even keener than their husbands to observe the military hierarchy, '*elles portent les galons de leurs maris*'. I often heard wives say that the women most anxious to assert their status are those from the worst backgrounds; that they seize on their husband's rank to pull them from their own lowly position in the world. Others blamed middle class women for trying to assert their superiority. The situation is perhaps singular because of the variety of backgrounds present and the fact that there is no correlation between the education or class of married partners. Stripped of all the superficial signs of their prior identity the men are inserted into a hierarchy that is based on military criteria only, while the women find themselves lumped together with others whom the 'ground-rules' of society would normally divide them from. In conversation, women almost always maintained that hierarchy didn't matter to them, but many obviously found it difficult to accept a hierarchy that attempted to rank them as equal or inferior to women whom they considered morally and socially beneath them.

The female hierarchy fits closely with the male military one, distributing characteristics along its continuum from prostitute to respectable housewife. The women who have relationships with unranked men are stereotyped as mercenary, insincere, uneducated and vulgar – all in all hardly flattering. When a man is promoted, his partner's position is at least recognised and stable, and as his rank improves her claim to wifely status is increasingly difficult to challenge. The struggle for recognition of rank is one for moral status and if it is conducted with some bitterness that is perhaps understandable in a situation where women find themselves having to fight just to retain (or attain) the barest respect due to a married woman. The weighting of her husband's status is clearly more important than her own. However, if a woman's past position and achievements mean less, they are not meaningless: the Legion is a total institution and as the female appendage of a male member, the prior standing of a woman indicates how well the man has placed himself in French society.

Her behaviour continues to reflect back on his position, particularly when he goes up in rank and her fulfilment of the moral ideal becomes more important. Gossip can be seen to play an important role in this context, it is the primary means by which the code of values particular to the context is transmitted and imposed, and it enables the evaluation and isolation of those who are dangerous to associate with. Through gossip woman are in possession of knowledge of that part of the men's lives normally outside the jurisdiction of the camp – the only access the camp has is through the medium of 'des histoires de bonne femme'. In fact the system is very effective, these 'simple-minded women's tales' may be ridiculed by the men

but they carry them back to the camp, and they are often acte
with uncanny speed. The Legion does not hesitate to interfere in
'private' sphere of its men's lives and men may lose promotion o
even be sent from the regiment if their conduct (or that of their
wives) falls beneath the standard expected of them. On one level
wives seem to be 'informing' on each other, but on another, gossip
can be seen to give them some control over their situation. The
camp discipline is directed at those whose actions damage the
reputation of the group, and it can also affect the standing within the
camp of men who rival their own husband's interest. Apart from the
'pecking order' aspects, gossip is used in a positive way to force the
camp to deal with men who mistreat their wives, for although
violence is considered as a valid means of control, should it reach
the point of scandal, perhaps visible beyond the Legion boundaries,
then the perpetrator will be punished.

Reality and imagery: women's views

The fact that the reaction against the set of ideas ordering their lives
tends to be contained at an individual level does not mean that the
wives see themselves (or their marriage) in terms of the models
offered by society or the Legion itself. As Edwin Ardener has
pointed out, women may accept men's definitional models when
they share the same definitional problems, but the models set up by
women bounding themselves are not included in the dominant
models (Ardener, 1975, p. 6). Legion wives may actually redefine
their moral status positively, by challenging certain basic premises
of the man's model. The articulation of these ideas is 'muted'
however, limited to 'women's talk'; they do not penetrate beyond
the boundaries of a purely female context. Again the contradictions
that arise between experience and the imagery are often restricted
to a personal level. For instance, women can gossip about the sexual
exploits of one soldier or another, mythifying the exploits of those
who fulfil the libidinous expectations of the stereotype, immediately after discussing the difficulties of coping with a largely celibate
life. For the men are not only absent much of the time, often they
are so exhausted by the day's physical activity that they have to
make an effort to stay awake long enough to eat before going to
bed. This is a subject that by its nature is discussed only with

...ever, and elements of self-doubt and loyalty
...eralisation of the view that Legionnaires,
...ale potency, are often 'under-sexed'.
...out the ideas they had of Legionnaires
...ey have 'mixed feelings' with regards to their
...is not, in general, because he is tough and military.
...onnaires may be seen to fulfil the expectations raised by
...ereotype, to be brutal and cold, but unlike them he is quite
...uman, perhaps even sensitive and affectionate. The characteristics
that fit the stereotypes crumble away from reality under any but the
most superficial scrutiny. Women know that their men are not like
that (just as each husband knows that his wife is different from the
women he discusses every day), and it is rather amusing that the rest
of the world should think that they are.

This contrast between reality and imagery is articulated not just
by rejecting the ideas concerned but by turning them on their head.
Men are often referred to as children who 'play' with guns and
weapons, the war-like training they participate in is seen as a series
of games. This image is reinforced by the fact that almost all non-
military tasks are carried out either by the Legion or by wives,
leaving men unable to cope with even the most simple of practical
matters. There is also their variable mastery of the French language
– men often go through several years of child-like inarticulacy.
Another contributing factor may be that many men have not
experienced 'normal' family lives, and coming from a variety of
cultural backgrounds they are often inexperienced at displaying
affection, unfamiliar with the norms that pattern the expression of
emotion. Some women regard military discipline and values as
admirable, but many wives claim to be '*anti-militaire*' and further
maintain that their contact with the military world through the
Legion has strengthened this opinion. Often they excuse the fact
that their husbands are mercenary soldiers in terms of their past: the
men are described as '*paumé*' or '*traumatisé*' (lost, traumatised).
The amoral tendency is still present, but the child-like irresponsi-
bility of the men in their model is easier to live with.

This recategorisation of dangerous Legionnaires as '*gros gosses*'
('big kids') enables women to maintain a more positive self-image.
Rather than being attracted by an aura of brutality or cold sexuality,
they see themselves as motherly and responsible, able to take care
of this immature male figure. The mother role can be seen to be of

central importance to the lives of *sous-officiers'* wives – it is never sacrificed to that of wife as in the case of officers' wives (Macmillan, 1984, p. 97). The Legion does not call on the services of the first in any capacity beyond their domestic functions. As they accustom themselves to the frequent absence of their husbands, caring for children become the major occupation in a context that offers little else.

The fact that the men are absent so often enables the ideal roles of all concerned to take on more solid aspect. While the men are away in warm, exotic places, in an all-male military situation, the women have to cope with household and family problems by themselves, so the role of the mother is strengthened. At the same time, the stereotype of the 'scarlet woman' increases in significance since the wives are no longer under direct control (hence the most 'macho' of men are also cuckolds). As one would expect, 'policing' activity among the women increases noticeably in the absence of men; gossip, anonymous letters, accusations and counter-accusations publicise the slightest straying from the straight and narrow. The duality of female imagery is intensified at this time, and the 'sheep' are separated from the 'lambs'.

The dualism of the imagery is powerful and its influence at an ideological level is clearly very strong; the control it exerts over women keeps them in their place much more effectively than the regulations that are the Legion's obvious tools. By using the stereotypes already available in the larger society the Legion has marginalised and isolated the women who have come to be included in its world. These women are there for various reasons – they may have been attracted by the glamour, by commitment to their partner, or by the possibility of financial security – and their reactions to the evaluations and strictures placed on their existence vary enormously with past experience and expectations held of married life (for example, many men marry North African women who are familiar with a model that restricts the wife's role to the home).

For some women, the glamour continues to be attractive as they live out their fantasies within the marriage, and elements of the imagery can provide the sugar that coats the bitter pill of reality (this is undoubtedly easier with the frequent absence of the men). These women prefer a husband to maintain his military persona even within the privacy of their home: this may be marked by their use of his Legion surname rather than his 'real' name; or they may like him to come home in his uniform, to have his hair cut even shorter than necessary; or they may observe the unwritten and often broken rule that one never asks a Legionnaire about his past.

Ultimately the women feel no loyalty to the Legion itself; on the contrary they frequently voice hostility towards the institution which dominates their lives. Many women do leave, others stay (accepting that there is little possibility that their situation will change). One woman relating her experience of twelve years at Calvi tried to express the hopelessness and humiliation she felt after struggling to maintain some kind of family life during this time: she said '*finalement la Légion ça prend tout*', 'in the end the Legion takes everything'.

Notes

1. The material for this paper was collected while carrying out research on Corsica which was financed by the ESRC. I would like to thank Sharon Macdonald, Pat Holden, Shirley Ardener and Lucy Rushton for their help in preparing the paper, and J. M. D. Smith for much useful advice and criticism.
2. Since many men are unable to procure the necessary papers from their country to marry under French law, the Legion extends recognition to the legal institution of *concubinage* (the nearest English equivalent would be common-law marriage). Hereafter in the paper 'wives' refers to recognised consorts of both sorts.
3. Throughout this paper 'Legionnaire' denotes any member of the force while '*légionnaire*' refers to the rank of private soldier.
4. Several women it seems have succeeded in enlisting in the Legion: Wren's account of 'The Memoirs of "Mary Abree" The English Woman Legionary' (*Sowing Glory*, 1931) is prefaced by an article from the *Daily Telegraph* of 19 June, 1931 reporting the rumour that a women in the Legion's ranks had escaped detection. A previous infiltrator in 1908 had been discovered during a shower bath parade . . . 'Similar precautions are to be taken now, so that the regiment in which identities are cloaked in mystery, shall, at least be sure its members are all males' (Wren, 1931). Helene Deutsch also notes the case of a young Polish woman who was discovered only after being wounded during the First World War (de Beauvoir, 1972, p. 425; Deutsch, 1946, p. 327).
5. Although I have so far found little textual evidence, it seems that until the end of the last century 'canteen women' followed soldiers to colonial fronts, some of whom did marry non-commissioned officers. From biographical accounts of Indo-China it seems that at least some

of the 'prostitutes' attached to fighting units were attached to one man (several married afterwards), and others acted as nurses to sick men. During the conflict in Indo-China some of these women were awarded medals in recognition of their courage.

6. The Legion fought in the Crimea, in Italy, in Mexico, in Tonkin, in Madagascar, Algeria and Morocco. There was no break in the cadence of fighting until after the First World War in which the Legion suffered appalling losses. It quickly regained its numerical strength however, and by 1940 there were some 45 000 men of over 100 nationalities in its ranks. The Legion was already present in Indo-China by 1945, where it constituted 40 per cent of the European force and lost over 12 000 men. Those who did survive were sent directly to Algeria. There the losses were only one-fifth of those sustained in Indo-China, but the loss of Algeria was significant in another way, as Bergot has pointed out: the town of Sidi-Bel-Abbés was the Legion's base and in a way they were defending their homeland (Young, 1984, p. 43; see also Morin, 1974). The mutiny that broke out amongst the officers of the Legion, the so-called '*Putsch des Genereaux*', resulted in the disbanding of the *Première REP*.

7. Djibouti, Central Africa, Tahiti, French Guyana and now Chad.

8. The *REP* consolidated its reputation as a fighting force in 1978 when its quick intervention saved hundreds of hostages taken by Angolan guerillas in Kolwezi, Zaire.

9. In the last year (1985) alone news items have drawn attention to figures such as Sulac the Yugoslav 'Robin Hood' whose escape from prison ended in death; the author of 'Oro' who wrote a best-seller relating his experiences as a gold-miner in Puerto Rico; the member of the right-wing SAC (*Société Anti-Communiste*) organisation who carried out politically motivated murder of a family in Oriol; the three recruits who murdered a North African worker on the train taking them to training camp.

10. In *Legionnaire* (1978) Simon Murray relates his experience as a Legionnaire during the Algerian war; several British men in the *REP* said they had enlisted after reading his enthusiastic account.

11. *Cela fait quinze ans que le mythologie des paras hante l'imagination populaire, quinze ans qu'on les redoute et qu'on les aime, toujours en première ligne dans les circonstances douloureuses, parfois appelés, surtout engagés, affectés a la Légion où a des unites specialisés, tous freres dans la fierté. De quoi exalter un peuple nourris d'élitisme au point de reconnaître a la noblesse, au XIX siècle, par la fiction, le monopole d'honneur qu'elle a perdu: voyez le succeś des trois Mousquetaires.* (Aron, 1984, p. 165).

12. The work of the young American poet Alan Seeger is interesting in this context (see particularly 'I Have a Rendez-Vous With Death'). Here I include a short extract from the poetry of Capitaine Bourgin:
    J'ai engager ma vie, seigneur, sur votre parole
    Les autres peuvent être sages, vous m'avez dit qu'il fallait être fou
    D'autres croient a l'ordre, vous m'avez dit de croire a l'amour.

D'autres pensent qu'il faut conserver, vous m'avez dit de donner.
(*Le 2ème Régiment Etranger de Parachutistes* 1984, p. 50).

13. An example:
    '*Le soleil brille, preparez-vous,*
    Déjà les moteurs tourne, vite, equipez-vous,
    la porte est ouverte, serrez les dents et va-t-on.
    De a bataille, de la bataille, légionnaire tu ne reviendra pas,
    La bas, les ennemis t'attendre maintenant nous allons au combat.'

14. Men in combat companies can expect to be away from Calvi nine or ten months every year; on top of this they often have to stay in the camp on guard duties during their time in Calvi. The day of unranked men begins at 6 a.m. and they may not ask permission to leave the camp until 6 p.m. (the request is granted or refused at the discretion of the commanding officer).

15. The practice of having brothels situated within military bases seems to have been dropped due to public opinion. However, overseas Legion camps do still have brothels included on the site.

16. Men who are taking the course in order to move up in rank from first-class soldiers to corporals are called *élèves*.

17. Apart from well-specified times when they may use the medical on sport facilities, wives are not allowed to enter, and, since the Legion takes pride in having men who can perform every task necessary to the smooth running of the regiment, virtually no women work there (there are in fact only three women, from the regular army, who mend parachutes).

18. I don't have space here to go into the *rationale* of a force composed to a great extent of the colonial nationalities it used to fight against. There is however a very rigid hierarchy of race implicit in the regiments' organisation (there is only one black *sous-officier* in the regiment) and this is extended to apply to the women. The attitude that is current amongst the men is perhaps illustrated by this intercepted personal communication: '*Je ne peut pas me payer que des négresses en ce moment – la vie est triste en noire et blanc*'.

19. In a closed brothel the women have to live and work on the premises. There are four to six prostitutes there at any one time and they are replaced every four weeks or so. Relations with these women are strictly limited to the economic transaction that exchanges money for sex; this seldom takes longer than the time to buy a drink plus fifteen minutes. It is possible that the women are penalised if this time is exceeded; the men certainly have to pay double.

20. The organisation of activities for the wives is limited to keep-fit classes twice a week and a few artistic activities attended by only a very small group of women.

References

Ardener, E. (1975) 'Belief and the Problem of Women', in S. Ardener (ed.) *Perceiving Women* (London: J. M. Dent).

Aron, Jean-Paul (1984) *Les Modernes* (Paris: Gallimard).

de Beauvoir, S. (1972) *The Second Sex* (Harmondsworth: Penguin Books).

Bergot, E. (1984) 'The history of the Legion', in Young (1984).

Callan, H. (1984) 'Introduction', in H. Callan and S. Ardener (eds), *The Incorporated Wife* (London: Croom Helm).

Chapman, M. (1982) '"Semantics" and the "Celt"', in D. Parkin (ed.), *Semantic Anthropology* (London: Academic Press).

Deutsch, H. (1984) *The Psychology of Women: A Psychoanalytic Interpretation* (London: Tavistock).

Hastrup, K. (1978) 'The Semantics of Biology: Virginity', in S. Ardener (ed.), *Defining Females* (London: Croom Helm).

Hutter, B. (1981) 'Introduction', in B. Hutter and G. Williams (eds), *Controlling Women* (London: Croom Helm).

Le 2ème Régiment Estranger de Parachutistes (1984) (Aubagne: Kepi Blanc).

Macmillan, M. (1984) 'Camp followers: A Note on Wives of the Armed Services', in H. Callan and S. Ardener (eds) (1984).

Morin, J. (1984) 'Les Légionnaires Parachutistes', in *L'Histoire Mondiale des Parachutistes* (Paris: SPL).

Murray, Simon (1978) *Legionnaire* (London: Routledge & Kegan Paul).

Williams, D. (1975) 'The Brides of Christ', in S. Ardener (ed.), *Perceiving Women* (London: J. M. Dent).

Wren, P. C. (1924) *Beau Geste* (London: John Murray).

Wren, P. C. (1931) *Sowing Glory* (London: John Murray).

Young, J. R. (1984) *The French Foreign Legion* with an introduction by Len Deighton and a 'History of the Legion' by Erwan Bergot (London: Thames and Hudson).

8

Women and the pacification of men in New Guinea

JESSICA MAYER

In the mid-1960s the Australian colonial government suppressed inter-tribal warfare in New Guinea. In many parts of the Eastern New Guinea Highlands, warfare had been a persistent and visible feature of village life; and among the Ommura, who are my focus here, warfare was the exclusive preserve of men. Perceptions of gender and of appropriate male and female roles, rights and privileges, were an integral part of ideas related to the practice of warfare, and to the significance that warfare was seen to have in the society. The potential implications of the Australian government's action for gender relations were, therefore, far-reaching. The basis for gender relations was exposed in the peace process. Adjustments to old values, and new justifications for supporting traditional prestige systems, were required; and women became a new focus of activity for men deprived of their war pursuits.

Ommura society before and during pacification

The people who call themselves Ommura occupy three *mata* or villages, each of which is associated with a distinct territory.[1] I lived in Yonura village for a year, in 1975–6,[2] about ten years after the advent of colonial government. My information about warfare and gender before colonial times was gained mainly from the reminiscences of Yonura women and men, from answers to my questions, and from current stories and rituals, viewed against the background of my knowledge of contemporary Ommura culture and society.

Warfare in Ommura took the form of bow and arrow fighting between Ommura villages, or between a village and a neighbouring non-Ommura group. An invasion would be launched, usually resulting in damage to crops and property, injuries and a few deaths before the invaders returned to their home village. All activities relating to war such as making the weapons and training in their use, mobilising and planning, as well as the fighting itself, were the responsibility of the men of the village. Women were not even allowed to be present at military deliberations, let alone take part.

Fighting was seen as an extremely tough and arduous duty. Within the village, the war objective was always represented as being defensive, deterrent or retaliatory – a counter-stroke when harm had been done or threatened to be done to people or resources in the village. Men were thus perceived as strong people who had a special responsibility to protect the village community against life-threatening forces from outside. As I shall show, this notion underlay a whole complex of other assumptions regarding proper work-roles, rights and privileges of men and women.

In the mid-1960s, about ten years after their first patrol into Ommura, the Australian colonial government took control of the area and ordered the people to stop fighting. A government patrol post was set up in Yonura, staffed by officers with guns and riot control equipment. The Ommura were warned that they could be shot or imprisoned if they so much as drew their bow strings.

The suppression of war remained for some years the only really conspicuous 'modernising' change in Ommura. In contrast to the more direct administrative intervention in many other parts of the highlands, Ommura did not, for example, have a taxation system or a local government council until 1973. A number of Ommura men were recruited for wage labour on coastal plantations during the 1960s, but this was discouraged later in favour of a 'local development' policy. Access to significant amounts of cash for the majority of people began only in 1976, when coffee (recently introduced as a cash crop) started fetching higher market prices. Even then the people were still living basically from subsistence cultivation, producing the old crops by slash and burn techniques and using cash mainly for small luxuries. The only Christian mission in Ommura at that time (founded in 1964) had so far attracted few converts or school pupils.

It therefore seems legitimate to characterise this first decade of colonialism as specifically 'post-war' – a transition time in between the 'traditional' past and a future time of probably many more far-reaching economic, social and political changes – and to consider gender developments during this period specifically in relation to the process of pacification.

The view that men were uniquely endowed with the strength necessary to protect the village community provided them with a charter for a wide range of prerogatives and privileges in both public and domestic contexts. Men monopolised the conduct of public village affairs. At home they left the greater share of labour to their wives, but claimed ultimate rights of disposal over valuable commodities the wives had worked together. As I shall show, women accepted these arrangements, despite occasional resentments, because they accepted the definition of themselves as less powerful beings whose lives depended ultimately on masculine protection. They understood that in labouring at production they left their husbands free for war, the vitally important 'men's work' which determined their own and the community's survival. Both sexes held to these assumptions. Although women had some separate perceptions of their own, these were subsidary rather than genuinely alternative, conforming to the same basic notions of what was properly 'masculine' or 'feminine', and only valuing some of the 'feminine' items higher.

Men as protectors

Pacification was at first, so to speak, a gender shock which produced some unsettling effects on these traditional notions, and particularly on women's acceptance of the domestic imbalance, as I shall describe. However, it was not long before the old assumptions seemed firmly re-established with both sexes. Men were again being viewed as protectors of the community and women as dependent for their lives on masculine strength.

A new threat, however, began to be apparent. Instead of the former military threat Yonura people now began to feel threatened by increasingly severe illnesses, which they attributed to dangerous new sorcery performed by their enemies outside. A new healing cult, *assochia*, now appeared in the village, operated exclusively by the men. *Assochia* constituted an unprecedented degree of intervention into village health, in directions which dramatically re-affirmed the principle of superior male control over life-threatening forces. Even illnesses which patients would formerly have managed on their own had now to be publicly 'chased away' under the men's guidance at frequent and impressive new ceremonies involving the whole village. I shall describe how men created the need for (and used) the opportunity to 'resocialise' those women or men who had been losing their old regard for masculine strength.

As I shall show, the vivid reaffirmation of the masculine protector image in this arena had much to do with the fact that Yonura women did not achieve any substantial change in their own self-definition, or in the domestic balance of power, at least at this stage. At first it had seemed right to them that their husbands, being relieved of military duties, should be pressed to take on a greater share of productive work, but the moral basis for such challenges largely fell away now that men were seen to be doing real 'men's work' for the community again.

As will be noted, Yonura men speaking from within the dominant ideology themselves acknowledged a certain element of institu-tionalised male conspiracy, saying that great care had always been taken to exclude women from male initiations and war deliberations because women could not be allowed to become powerful like men. After pacification some men imputed something like female conspiracy to women who were demanding more help from husbands, and openly discussed the need for male backlash.

Fighting and drudging

It has been suggested that 'internal war' – that is, fighting between neighbouring villages – directly favours a 'male supremacist com-plex' in the home community (Harris, 1977, pp. 31–43, 57–66).[3] For Harris, the elements of the complex include male control of economic resources and political and religious institutions; the acceptance by women of male supremacy, chartered by an ideo-logical belief in superior male ability, and the assignment of women to time-consuming 'drudge work', such as routine tending, proces-sing and cooking of subsistence crops, fetching firewood and water, and caring for infants and household possessions (Harris, 1977, pp. 57ff; see also O'Kelly, 1980, pp. 119ff and 137ff).

In Harris's interpretation, these arrangements serve as a system of rewards which motivate men to undertake the dangerous work of fighting; and the most viable way of motivating men to undergo the hardship of battle is to reward them with privileges at the expense of women. If such a system is to work smoothly an appropriate gender ideology is required, ensuring that women no less than men will be 'reared to accept male supremacy'. In the interests of this ideological underpinning, not even those stronger and swifter women who would make better warriors than the weaker men can be candidates for the fighting force: 'No woman could be permitted to get the idea that she is as worthy and as powerful as any man' (Harris, 1977, p. 43).

It is not necessary to accept the whole of Harris's interpretation in detail to see that traditional Ommura was an instance of the much wider social phenomenon he identifies: namely, the association in band and village societies between internal war, exclusively male fighting forces, and the elements of the 'male supremacist complex'. Two aspects of the Ommura complex may now be illustrated in more detail namely the asymmetrical content of ascribed gender roles, with the emphasis on men fighting and women drudging, and the associated gender ideology which made such arrangements appear proper or 'natural'. Except where otherwise specified the description applies equally to the time of my stay and the time before pacification.

Women's responsibilities and rights

Cultivation among the Ommura was practised by slash and burn techniques. It produced the main subsistence crops – sweet potatoes, yams, corn and various edible greens – and also sugar cane and bananas, prestige crops cultivated primarily for exchange and ceremonial purposes. The most valued exchange commodities were pigs. The household – typically consisting of husband, wife and their unmarried children – was the basic unit for both crop and pig production, with neither sex usually working in groups. But the husband normally spent much time in the communal men's house, while a wife's subsistence activities occupied the greater part of her day. All the planting, day-to-day tending, harvesting and transporting of staple crops was defined as 'wife's work', the husband being expected to assist with these tasks only in emergencies or when supplies ran low. His principal subsistence tasks – far less regularly time-consuming than hers – were to clear land for new gardens and construct and maintain garden fences.

Except when menstruating, a woman was also expected to prepare daily meals for her husband and children. Pre-adolescent children assisted their mothers with routine gardening and childcare but were not expected to do so on a regular basis. Babies and infants were cared for by their mothers, elder siblings and other village children. Only after they were able to walk did their fathers generally take a significant amount of responsibility for their care.

As to prestige and exchange valuables, the daily care of the household pig herd was defined as 'wife's work', while husbands did the more occasional tasks – built pig shelters, fetched in new litters from the bush and hunted for animals that went astray. Bananas and sugar cane were generally planted by men and tended by both men and women. Arrows were manufactured by men and string bags and grass skirts by women.

The fact that the wife contributed more labour than her husband to day-by-day subsistence did not entitle her to greater control over the allocation of subsistence crops within the household. Both spouses had the right to harvest vegetables from the household gardens for their own consumption or to feed their personal friends or kin. Similarly, rights over household pigs did not reflect the fact that wives devoted more time to breeding them. It is true that spouses were often represented in the abstract as being the joint owners of the pig herd, and that a man was obliged to consult his wife before disposing of any animal. However, where the couple could not reach an agreement the husband had the ultimate right of disposal. Moreover most ceremonial payments required pork rather than live animals, and the capacity to slaughter pigs was defined as a skill exclusive to males. It was imparted to them during initiation ceremonies from which females were strictly excluded.

Married women were recognised as owning the string bags and grass skirts they produced, and they often donated them to their favourite male kinsmen for use in ceremonial payments. Even so, it was generally agreed that a wife was obliged to 'help' her husband on occasion by allowing him to use these items for his own exchange purposes. He had no corresponding obligation to allow her access to exchange valuables of his own.

While wives thus had some small say regarding the allocation of exchange valuables produced in the household they did not ordinarily initiate exchange themselves or participate in ceremonial presentations in their own names.[4] Extra-domestic exchange was defined as a male activity. As elsewhere in the New Guinea Highlands there were no formal political offices, and participation in exchange networks served men as a means of forming politically significant alliances and gaining prestige and influence.[5]

These details take on extra significance when we consider that Ommura people, like certain others in New Guinea, laid a marked cultural emphasis on the principle of balanced reciprocity (*hini* in Ommura language). Their marriage ideology itself represented the ideal marital relationship as one characterised by *hini*. During the marriage ceremony the couple were exhorted to make sure that the value of goods and services with which they provided each other would be generally balanced so that neither party would feel aggrieved.

Female dissent

Both sexes were aware of a potential contradiction between the reciprocity principle and the accepted allocation of tasks and resources between spouses. It was well understood that wives often felt grievances, over the disposal of pigs in particular. For example, a wife was often eager that the best pigs should be reserved for gifts and ceremonial presentations to her own natal kin. Moreover women sometimes formed strong sentimental attachments to particular pigs that they had reared and made strenuous attempts to prevent them from being killed or exchanged. They felt it manifestly unfair if their wishes were not granted, considering that they had to do the main work of pig-rearing themselves. In the attempt to pressurise husbands into complying they would sometimes spend less time on gardening, refuse to cook for the husband or threaten to 'pollute' him with menstrual blood. The husband, backed perhaps by his fathers and brothers, might retaliate with verbal insult, shaming or beating. However, he was rather limited by the fear that the wife might indeed 'pollute' him and make him ill, or might even run away. Loss of a wife was regarded as one of the worst disasters that could befall a man. A crucial source of labour had been lost, and it was rarely possible to recoup the marriage payments.

Such frictions might be common, but all they questioned was the husband's use of privilege in specific cases and not the privilege itself. That was rendered both morally justified and practically necessary in the eyes of both sexes by the fact that the men of the community played such a crucial role in protecting the lives and livelihood of its members. This was the true reciprocity in Ommura eyes – that although 'husband's work' did not balance 'wife's work', 'men's work' more than balanced women's.

Men's work and the ideology of masculine strength

Warfare

In traditional Ommura, before pacification, world views were strongly shaped by a sense that the village community was under perpetual danger of attack by enemies from neighbouring villages. Younger men engaged in active combat and raiding while the older ones made weapons, advised on strategy and kept guard for enemy raids. As elsewhere in the Eastern Highlands of New Guinea (see, for example, Mandeville, 1979) warfare, raiding and peace-making were traditionally the main forms of political interaction between villages.[6] There was not the emphasis on peaceful exchange relationships between political groups found in certain other parts of Papua New Guinea (Strathern, 1971; Feil, 1984). The image of men as warriors was highly elaborated: most public gatherings involved episodes in which men engaged in flamboyant displays of military prowess and in boasting about recent victories over other villages, while women praised the strength of the men.

Protection and healing

Less tangible external forces were also seen as constituting a threat to people's lives, although up till pacification they were accorded less significance than the military threat. The most important of these were mystical forces that caused humans or pigs to fall seriously ill and the crops to fail. Protection of the community against these less tangible external forces was likewise categorically defined as 'men's work' and performed collectively by the initiated males of the village. The most important public rituals other than those associated with war were crop and pig fertility ceremonies, at which the men officiated while the women and children cheered them on. These rites were seen less as procedures for positively encouraging growth than as processes of 'attacking', 'killing' or 'chasing away' the harmful influences that it was taken for granted external enemies had applied to the pigs and crops.

Traditional public healing ceremonies for dealing with sickness regarded as life-threatening had also to be performed collectively by the men of the village. (Only the treatment of women's fertility problems, and other ailments defined as gynaecological, was the prerogative of senior women.) Again, the main emphasis was on symbolically killing, shooting or chasing away the afflicting agent (always an external force), or persuading or tricking it into releasing its hold over its victim, rather than on strengthening the patient's body or providing symptom relief. However, before the suppression of war men devoted relatively little time to such public healing activities, because disorders not regarded as serious were usually diagnosed and treated by the patient herself or himself.

Only men were capable of performing these various activities on which the survival of the community depended, because they alone were seen as sufficiently well endowed with *kyapukya*, a quality which I shall gloss as 'strength'. Being 'strong' in this sense involved having the ability to control or influence people or non-human forces, whether through physical prowess, magic, persuasion, reasoned argument or trickery. While all men and women were seen as having some degree of *kyapukya* only men were considered 'strong' enough to be able to vanquish external life-threatening forces and, by extension, to publicly participate in intra-village political affairs such as the settlement of disputes.

Sickness and weakness

This view of the different strength of women and men was also reflected traditionally in the diagnosis of sickness (Mayer, 1982).[7] For example, Ommura illness categories were distinguished less by their symptoms than by the agencies believed to cause them. Hence each had specific connotations regarding the sufferer's degree of control over harmful forces. Having a kind of disorder 'caused' by what was regarded as a relatively weak illness-causing agent – such as a centipede or a very large yam – must imply that one cannot have very much influence over life-threatening forces. By contrast, a sickness attributed to a stronger agent – such as sorcery – did not generally imply this lack. This obvious logic was that people who lack strength are incapable of resisting even the weakest of harmful forces, while it takes a very potent force to reduce a strong person to sickness. My research indicated that before the suppression of war men regularly perceived their own sicknesses under the categories associated with 'strong' illness-causing agents, while women would refer theirs to 'weaker' agents, thus conforming to the paradigm of women as being relatively lacking in *kyapukya*.

Some men were regarded as being weaker – having less *kyapukya* – than others. Yet it was held that every male acquired sufficient strength to be capable of vanquishing at least some life-threatening forces as he passed through various stages of male initiation. Indeed, most attributes or capabilities defined as essentially masculine or feminine were seen as being acquired through the processes of male or female initiation rather than as innate or inherent. In keeping with this, women were strictly prohibited from witnessing male initiations, and men took great care likewise that women must not overhear their discussions regarding political affairs or rituals, lest they learn how to perform these masculine activities and become as strong as men.

Women's world-views

It was not disputed that women's productive and reproductive activities were important for survival. However, in terms of Ommura social ideology it was men rather than women who were *ultimately* responsible for the perpetuation of life, because the children, pigs and crops that women produced would perish without men's protection. Women as much as men were socialised into this perception, hence into accepting their own responsibility for routine production. In girls' initiation ceremonies senior women told the initiands: 'If your [future] husbands stayed in the gardens and grew vegetables you and your children would be killed and all your pigs and food would be dead. If men stayed in the gardens who would protect us from the enemy? Have you ever seen a woman who could shoot men with arrows?' Girls were brought up to see themselves as naturally and irresistibly attracted by male strength, and this fact appears also to have played a role in disposing wives to concede their husbands' privileged claims.

The arduous nature of the men's work in protecting the community was seen as maintaining balanced reciprocity in the marital relationship in spite of the husband's lesser productive effort and greater control over resources. It was fundamental to the dominant world-view and value system that a person's social worth depended primarily on what she or he was considered capable of contributing to community survival, and hence on the extent of his or her strength. Different skills or types of work were evaluated according to this measure. In this light, women and women's activities necessarily appeared as less important than and inferior to men and men's activities. Moreover, notions of masculinity were far more elaborated than images of feminity. Beliefs about fundamental distinctions between the sexes were not, as in many cultures, elaborated in terms of symmetrical dualisms. Rather, women and men were located at different points on a single scale, so that women tended to be defined as people relatively lacking in the masculine attribute 'strength' rather than in positive terms relating to, say, their reproductive capacities.

Alternative models

While women often spoke of themselves in terms of this dominant paradigm they also drew on alternative, less systematically articulated, models which accorded physical strength and the vanquishing of harmful forces a less central position. From this other perspective there was greater emphasis on the value of certain attributes and capabilities regarded as particularly feminine, such as the capacity to work steadily for long periods or to tell jokes successfully and amuse people. Women could rate 'wife's work' as important and valuable for reasons not to do with social survival, for example the way in which women beautified the environment by laying out vegetable gardens in intricate and aesthetically pleasing patterns.

Pacification: impotence

With the establishment of the patrol post and the cessation of large-scale military activities in the area, Yonura men were left with a great deal more spare time, most of which they filled by sitting in the men's houses reminiscing about past military exploits. Some husbands began to devote a little more time to gardening. As noted above, not many men went away to work outside the area, and not much time was so far being givien to coffee production either.

It was a confusing time for perception of gender as a whole and of marital reciprocities in particular, given the fact that men could no longer fight or impress women with flamboyant displays of their military prowess. The traditional perceptions had been so closely interrelated with beliefs about the constant threat of military attack that its suspension was bound to introduce a new element of doubt, starting with the men's image as strong people and protectors of life.

Several women told me that they had taken to complaining more outspokenly when they first realised that they and their children were no longer threatened by enemy attacks. They had argued that nowadays men were 'just sitting around in the men's houses rather than doing real work', and that it was therefore no longer necessary or consistent with *hini* (balanced reciprocity) for them, the wives, to keep doing so much of the daily work on their own. Men were accused of staying in the men's houses 'just talking and playing cards'. Some women recalled that when their husbands had stopped carrying bows and arrows and periodically attiring themselves in war regalia, they had ceased to find them so attractive and felt less disposed to please them by striving hard to fulfil their wifely obligations. They did not go so far as to question their exclusion from direct participation in extra-domestic exchanges and other affairs.

There was much debate in the Yonura men's houses. On one side some husbands began to respond more readily to their wives' requests for assistance with gardening work and/or their wishes regarding the allocation of pigs. They apparently felt this to be necessary in order to maintain an appropriate degree of balanced reciprocity in their relationship with their wives, now that they had been deprived of their military role. Moreover they feared that because women no longer felt so dependent on men, a thwarted wife was now more likely to run away from her husband or make him ill by deliberately polluting him with her menstrual blood. (Since the imposition of Australian control over the area a runaway wife ran far less risk of being attacked by men of enemy villages.) On the other side, there was a growing sense of alarm among the more conservative men. As one man put it:

> Because our wives no longer saw us painting our faces for war and
> decorating our fighting shields they began to think that we [men]
> were weak like women, and that wives could now sit around all
> day making their husbands grow the food while they [wives] just
> ate up this food and tried to make us sick [through pollution] if we
> didn't send the pigs out to their own kin.

The suppression of war was also the beginning of changes,
disturbing from the traditional viewpoint, in perceived patterns of
illness. Whereas it had been exceptional for a man to attribute his
illness to a 'weak' agent or a woman hers to a 'strong' one (p. 157
above), this now became much commoner, suggesting that women
were beginning to regard themselves as men's equals and men to
lose confidence in their own powers. During a male initiation
ceremony the initiands were warned that they must keep a constant
eye on their future wives because women were increasingly coming
to see themselves as '*kyapukya* people who contracted illness from
wera [a 'strong' force connected with experience in the wider world]
and had the right to tell their husbands what to do'.

Assochia: potency regained

However, within a decade of the patrol post being established,
Yonura men had introduced another innovation of their own,
through which the image of men as the protectors of life was being
powerfully refurbished in a new idiom. This was *assochia*, a novel
form of public healing.

At this time, despite the pacification, Yonura people were again
coming to think of themselves as under perpetual threat from their
enemies outside. Now the danger was seen as illness-causing forces
rather than military attack. As they saw it, illness was becoming
more and more severe, due to external enemies who could no
longer resort to armed warfare and who were making them ill
instead through new and increasingly powerful forms of sorcery.[8]

Assochia is the name of a tree bark chewed by practitioners to
enable them to 'see' the cause of illness so that it can be 'chased
away'. Pharmacologically speaking it probably has mild halluci-
nogenic effects. The *assochia* public healing ceremony had been
introduced into Yonura two years before my arrival by a local man
to whom it was said to have revealed itself during a visit outside the

Ommura area. Since his return he had taught the skills to two other village men.

When I was in Yonura, *assochia* seemed to have put all other healing techniques into the shade. A majority of all cases of illness were being defined as serious and brought to it for public healing. This was a significant reversal of the traditional pattern, in which the majority had been defined as light enough to leave to patients and only a few as requiring the traditional public rituals. Hence *assochia* was being performed on average several times a month – far more frequently than any other public healing ceremony had ever been. It was also far more elaborate.

Although the three skilled practitioners were sometimes referred to as 'the *assochia* men' it was a key point that all the adult males of the village had to perform the ceremony collectively. All men, it was emphasised, were in the process of learning to chew the bark, and even those who had not yet mastered the technique played an important part in helping those who had. Thus *assochia* had been firmly typed as 'men's work' on the exact lines of warfare and the life-protecting rituals in the past: a class of work which required strength, and of which all men had to be capable for the community's sake, although some might be more experienced and skilled than others. Women did not dispute that they were not strong enough to perform *assochia*. It was said that any women who attempted it would go mad.

The assochia ceremony

Both sexes had come to see *assochia* as necessary for their health and as much the most powerful (*kyapukya*) form of treatment available. The ceremony was performed in an unusually solemn atmosphere, after dark, in a specially enlarged hut, with men and women sitting on opposite sides. The women kept up a slow hushed singing of special *assochia* songs, while the men, turning their backs, helped the three practitioners to interpret the image they were seeing after chewing the bark. Only after lengthy discussion would the men turn around and explain their insights to the women, who then joined in 'chasing' the illness away.

Assochia ceremonies were thick with the imagery of power. Many of the symbols were associated with the new 'foreign' political and economic power structures: with government officials, magistrates, expatriates, missionaries, or urban living. The practitioners kept breaking into praise of the unique power of the insight they had acquired through *assochia*. They would then liken it to a Colman lamp (the most powerful kind of kerosene lamp seen in the area), an electric light, a photograph, a camera or a movie film: 'When we eat *assochia* we see inside everything. The stones break apart, the trees break apart, the ground breaks apart, the mountains break apart. . . . Before, we could only see as by the light of a bamboo torch. Now *assochia* shows us everything, like a Colman lamp'. In some episodes they would mime pilots taking off and liken *assochia* to an aircraft 'flying us to the place where the [cause of sickness] has been hidden'.

The ideology of diagnosis

A patient would come to *assochia* complaining of an illness in the terms of what he or she had perceived to be its cause. Quite often the practitioners would forcefully reject the self-diagnosis and establish a different one, even if it seemed less to the patient's satisfaction. I discovered that the underlying strategy was ideological rather than therapeutic. Men's illnesses were being consistently rediagnosed into 'stronger' categories, and women's into 'weaker' ones, whenever the notion of superior masculine strength seemed at risk.

The practitioners made no secret of what they were doing in this respect. For example, a man who claimed to be ill from menstrual pollution or from food that his wife had handled would to be told he had no right 'to put shame on all the men and women here' by suggesting that men were so weak that their wives could make them ill. After one such occasion the practitioner explained to me:

> *Assochia* tells us that we [men] must show everybody that men are strong, that women cannot make them ill. If we did not do so people would [disbelieve] that we [men] [have the strength] to 'see' the sickness with *assochia* . . . Then men wouldn't be strong enough to perform [*assochia*] properly and everyone would get sick or die of *irama* [poison brought by sorcerers]. Also women would become so lazy that they never did any work in their husbands' gardens.

It was a village woman who told me:

> Now women think that they are *kyapukya* like men and that only
> *wera* and *irama* can make them sick. But if all the men and women
> in *assochia* see a woman [as being] sick from *wera* or *irama* they
> will say that women are as strong as men and needn't listen when
> men tell them to work hard in their gardens. If that happened we
> wouldn't have any food. Also men wouldn't be able to see clearly
> in *assochia* and kill the *irama* our enemies leave for us.

Towards the end of my time in Yonura some men were asserting
that *assochia* could even cure women of infertility, a disorder
traditionally treated by senior women. This was the first time to
anyone's knowledge that men had claimed such direct control over
women's childbearing capacity. It was the point on which women
remained most dubious so far.

In *assochia*, then, on one level Yonura men were responding to a
generally felt need for means of coping with a perceived increase of
severe illness. On another level, and no less explicitly, they were
reacting to the perceived effects of the suppression of warfare on the
sexual balance of power, particularly in marriage.

I never heard them mention a third possible motivation which
may well have been present also: a need to affirm their own strength
in face of frustration and impotence after a stronger 'foreign' power
had forced them to lay down arms, and when a wealthier 'foreign'
economy and lifestyle were confronting theirs.

Conclusion

I have shown how closely traditional Ommura conceptions of the
capabilities, rights and proper work roles of women and men were
bound up with the practice of internal warfare, and that in the main
women concurred in viewing male life-protecting strength or
kyapukya as the most admirable of all human qualities, though
among themselves they could also draw on less systematically
articulated models which gave it a less central position.

The suppression of war initially shook Yonura women's faith in
some of the traditional gender perceptions and social arrangements, but did not radically transform their notion of themselves as

the weaker sex, who properly accepted the labour of production, without expecting to control the product, in the conviction that they depended on men for their survival. The men, deprived of their conspicuous male role as warlike guardians, were quickly able to construct a kind of alternative, and the women quickly gave it their assent.

In part no doubt this reflects the fact that economic and social change had not yet gone far enough in Yonura for the women to have been extensively exposed to new experiences or models. They still had no basis for converting their rather tentative challenges into systematic attempts to redefine marital roles and obligations, or into active demands for a share in public affairs. So, whatever the men might feel they had lost during the first decade without warfare, so far the women had not been substantially the gainers.

Notes

1. In contrast to many other parts of the New Guinea Highlands, the men of the local group do not use an agnatic idiom to conceptualise their unity and solidarity. They represent the village as constituted by 'people of the same ground' rather than by, say, 'fathers and brothers'.
2. Fieldwork was financed by the Social Science Research Council of Great Britain (SSRC), to whom I am most grateful.
3. 'Internal war' is contrasted with 'external war' by Harris. The latter, conducted by large raiding parties against distant enemies may result in an improvement of women's position insofar as they are left in charge of economic and public affairs previously managed by men. Sanday (1974) makes a similar argument.
4. In certain other parts of the New Guinea Highlands women play a much more active role in extradomestic exchanges and can initiate exchanges themselves (Feil, 1984).
5. The large-scale ceremonial exchanges found in certain parts of the New Guinea Highlands (e.g., Strathern, 1971) have never been practised in Yonura and male status depended more on military prowess than on control of material resources.
6. In this area of the New Guinea Highlands the village is the effective political unit.
7. By 'sickness' I am referring here and elsewhere in this study to the class of disorder which Ommura people classify as *nriqa viro*. *Nriqa viro* sufferers feel generally unwell and withdraw at least to some extent from their everyday activities. This class of disorder is contrasted with *ati nriqa* or 'minor ailments' which are always represented as being localised rather than affecting the whole person and are often considered not to require treatment.

8. Medical data for Yonura before the establishment of the patrol post are so scanty that it is not possible to determine whether the incidence of disease, biomedically defined, actually had increased since that time. Epidemics of yaws, gonorrhoea and influenza – diseases probably introduced or exacerbated by European 'contact' – had long been known in parts of the Highlands and had apparently reached Ommura as long ago as the early 1950s. A government inspection in the early 1970s found no active cases of yaws in Yonura.

References

Feil, D. (1984) 'Beyond Patriliny in the New Guinea Highlands', *Man*, 19:1, March 1984, pp. 50–76.

Harris, M. (1977) *Cannibals and Kings* (New York: Random House).

Mandeville, E. (1979) 'Agnation, Affinity and Migration among the Kamano of the New Guinea Highlands', *Man*, 14:1, March 1979, pp. 104–23.

Mayer, J. R. (1982) 'Body Psyche and Society: Conceptions of illness in Ommura Eastern Highlands New Guinea', *Oceania*, 52, pp. 240–60.

O'Kelly, G. (1980) *Women and Men in Society* (New York: Van Nostrand).

Sanday, P. (1974) 'Female Status in the Public Domain' in Rosaldo, M. and Lamphere, L. (eds), *Women in Culture and Society* (Stanford: Stanford University Press) pp. 189–206.

Strathern, A. (1971) *The Rope of Moka* (Cambridge: Cambridge University Press).

9

Passive in war?
Women internees in the Far East
1942–5

MARGARET BROOKS

During the Second World War thousands of women were interned in the Far East.[1] These female 'enemy aliens' were missionaries, nurses, teachers, or wives of military personnel, businessmen and government officials. On the face of it, interned women are completely victims of war – confined, subjugated, compelled – about as passive a position as possible. Nevertheless, these internees' own descriptions of life in the camps show how, despite the apparent helplessness of the women, they developed a sense of group consciousness and cohesion, and through ritual and symbolism drew the strength to survive.

In the late 1970s and early 1980s the Imperial War Museum recorded for its Sound Archives personal reminiscences of women who had been interned by the Japanese during the Second World War, and it is these women's own expressions of their experience that I discuss here. As only first-hand testimonies were recorded, we are dealing necessarily with women who were under about forty years old during internment, and who survived the experience. These women are all British of European extraction, primarily middle class,[2] and in some way part of the colonial system.

Women were interned not for personal misdemeanours, but for reasons of nationality. Some were taken *en masse* from evacuation ships, others were notified to report to a specified place and taken to internment from there, while some were arrested individually.

Often they had time to pack suitcases hastily to take with them, though the things they chose to take were not on the whole practical (as would have been knives or malaria tablets) but more often of sentimental value (photographs, prayer books, clothes and so forth). One recent bride took six new handbags from her trousseau; and most women took cosmetics and jewellery. Some women took sanitary towels which were a great waste of space as only a limited supply could possibly be carried.[3]

As most women had not held positions of authority they were not usually interrogated by their captors, though a woman who had been in such a position might be questioned and bullied. A hospital matron, for example, who had been interrogated about thirty times before she was interned, described the procedure:

> We went to the Commandant's office. 'Sit down', said my guide, pointing to one of the chairs. This seemed queerly polite treatment but I sat down and waited. What next? Not two minutes later a clout on my head and several blows in my face from behind completely took me by surprise, as it was meant to do. 'Get up, you bitch, how dare you go and sit in a chair'. I got up and turned. Two Japanese were standing behind me. 'I was told by the guide who brought me here, sir.' I had to kneel, stretch my feet out straight behind and sit on my heels. Try that for even five minutes and see what it feels like. 'Get up and bow. Sit down'.[4]

Her treatment, however, was not harsh by the standards men were subjected to, which was perhaps one of the few benefits for women to be derived from the low opinion held by the Japanese of female capabilities.

The internment camps

There were about fifteen main internment camps for women of 'enemy' nationalities in the Japanese-occupied Far East, with most British women being interned in the major islands of South East Asia.[5] The camps were sometimes purpose-built, but more often consisted of an isolated set of buildings or a village that could be fenced in and put under constant guard. The accommodation itself varied but was usually cramped. For example, in the relatively comfortable, formerly Dutch, houses in Java and Sumatra women lived about eight to a room with one earth closet lavatory in the house.

It was up to the women themselves to organise their lives within the camp. We should remember that these women probably did not even all share a common language: they were of various nationalities and from a range of occupations and social backgrounds. Initially the organisational structures the women employed in the camps were based on nationality (British, Dutch, and so forth), occupation (for example, nurses or missionaries) or status (for example, officers' wives).

Some form of centralised organisation was necessary for liaison with the Japanese, who usually requested that there be a spokeswoman. The arrangements made by the women were generally democratic; a representative from each house (or similar unit) being elected by consensus, and an overall leader emerging by consensus from this committee of 'house captains'. The committee took and disseminated orders from the Japanese commandant at the camp gate, and dealt with such matters as food distribution, room allocation and camp hygiene. In some camps democracy was taken as far as holding elections, and the women went to great effort to find scraps of paper for the secret ballots. Despite the fact that military terms were often used by the women (for example, 'commandant', 'officer' and 'captain'), the structure itself was flexible:

> If anything happened that the house captain wanted to step down for some reason or they were ill then automatically somebody else would step in. It wasn't anything very serious. Every household got to know each other because we lived in such close proximity that everybody knew everybody so intimately that it was obvious who would just step in.[6]

Sometimes, particularly in the later period when inmates were increasingly debilitated by illness, the arduous role of house captain was rotated. The military nomenclature was simply a reflection of the familiarity most of the women had with the military in their colonial lives. I have only come across one case in which the internees were said to have deliberately avoided military terminology and used instead the term 'house mother'.

Although a hierarchy based on status within the colonial system soon broke down in the camps, it was usual for the leaders to be educated, of mature years, and with some experience of organising and leading others. Such women were specifically spoken of as being 'the leader type'; and in different camps they were, to take some examples, a doctor, a senior colonial official's wife, a mother superior and a ship's stewardess.

Life in the camps

Life in the camps was very different from the white colonial woman's previous experience of life in the Far East, where, especially as a wife, she represented and upheld the colonial system.[7] In the camps there were no husbands and no servants, though children of both sexes were interned with their mothers. Everybody in the camps, unless too ill, had to participate in the daily tasks of cooking, carrying food and supplies, collecting refuse, looking after the sick, and dealing with sanitation; and all these had to be done in a hot and humid climate and on a poor diet. The following description by an internee describes graphically the problems of organising the food supply:

> They sent in food. The idea was – they told us – they would send in food every day, which wasn't true. We never knew when it was coming and how much was coming. And when it came – although we asked – they didn't tell us or they told us wrongly how many days it was for. So sometimes when very much more than usual came in, which we realised was more than usual, we would say, 'But how long has this to last?' And sometimes they would say, 'Oh, more tomorrow'. And sometimes it didn't come in again for two or three days.
>
> On the other hand they would sometimes send in sacks and sacks of rice with no idea how long that had to last us which was extremely serious because for the women – who were pretty hungry by then – to be confronted with sacks of rice their immediate idea was to eat it. But we didn't know how long it was supposed to last. It was very difficult to ration it out ourselves. We did want to ration it properly ourselves.
>
> You couldn't have hundreds of people rushing at these rations

or else it would have been chaotic. So one of the committee was always there. And one was sort of ration officer and to oversee the distribution and division. And the difficult part was that all these houses were not occupied by the same number of people. So that sometimes there were say, fifteen of us, sixteen next door, twenty-four opposite, eleven . . . and so on, different numbers. And then by the wisdom of Solomon this amount of rations had to be divided up as fairly as possible to give each house, each lot of people, an amount which was worked out fairly per person. It was very difficult especially when they dumped meat, just threw a chunk of meat on the ground. It was terribly tough old meat just on the bone. And people would be hacking at it with penknives and table knives to try and cut up this chunk of meat lying in the roadside and try and give pieces to all these different numbers of people.

And eggs would come in sometimes. By this time there were over four hundred of us. And supposing thirty eggs came in what do you do with thirty eggs among four hundred people? And all this had to be decided. And it was a very good thing that we were sensible enough to elect a committee and somebody who had the final say-so to what happened to these things.[8]

The women were also given work by the Japanese: sewing, gardening and water-carrying for instance. The jobs were allocated by the camp committee and women were paid by the Japanese in cash or kind.

Civilisation inside the fence

The women also organised educational and leisure activities. Despite the lack of books, children's schools were set up; classes were arranged for learning the languages of the different national-ities in the camp; and lectures were held on such subjects as travel. Some internees even managed to create a camp newspaper for a while. At Palembang in Sumatra the women initially held country dancing meetings, but as their health deteriorated they replaced this with a thirty-piece 'orchestra' with the sounds of the instruments being represented by humming. Verbal exchanges of recipes were popular in most camps. The women were creative in their uses of any foodstuffs available (such as chopped and boiled banana skins), but on the whole the recipes were not for immediate use, but were recollections of old favourites from their pre-internment days. One woman told me how she still uses a Yorkshire pudding recipe that she was taught in Los Baños camp in the Philippines.

Many of the activities organised by the women did not serve any practical function, but they brought the women together and gave some sense of cohesion and self-identity. Brownfoot (1984) has argued that European women (*memsahibs*) in colonial Malaya had an important symbolic and practical role as a civilising influence through which the white community's prestige was represented. In the camps, though unable to fully elaborate their traditional female conventions, such as attention to dress, home, appearance and meals, the women retained as far as possible their symbols of civilisation. Although there was usually only enough food for one daily meal (if that), the women maintained a three-meal routine plus elevenses and afternoon tea. These latter consisted of hot water, which was an effort in itself to make as both fuel and water supplies were variable and fires were difficult to maintain in a damp climate. The women even managed to create 'special' occasions.

> We used to run little concerts for our birthdays and Christmas and that sort of thing. We would acknowledge people's birthdays and try to find something to give them. We'd go through our own possessions and try and find something to give. Or people who'd still got some needles and cottons would make something. Or if you could pick any wild flowers you'd make them a little pot of flowers in a coconut shell or anything that you happened to be able to get. And we tried to excuse them from all duties. We always said 'No, you're not to do anything today, no work, it's your birthday'. And if they'd got any decent clothes left they'd put on these birthday clothes, and sit around like ladies for a day. It was rather fun and made something of the day.[9]

Sometimes celebrations were expressly forbidden, as happened one Christmas at Bandoeng, Java; but despite the possibility of punishment the women went ahead with the rituals:

> Nothing daunted, the women held a little service of their own in a room right at the back of the compound which was usually used as

a clinic. The singing was heard however, by a guard who promptly reported it. In the middle of the sermon, held by myself, in walked the Japs for inspections. We stopped and, rummaging in the medicine chest, started handing out pills and bandaging perfectly good elbows and legs. The Japs drifted off and we took back the pills and continued, although I didn't find it easy to recover the thread of the sermon which had to be delivered by heart and without a Bible.[10]

In the evenings some women continued to 'dress for dinner' as was their peacetime custom, though in the camp this meant only changing or rearranging rather dilapidated clothes, and perhaps putting on make-up:

Even in 1944 it was still pleasant to see that towards evening, when the work was done, the women who had looked like drudges during the day somehow or other managed to dress as well as possible, did something with their hair, their face, their hands and strolled about looking almost as usual. It kept their spirits and their morale up. The last things a woman would part with were her cosmetics, especially her lipstick. Here the old adage was apparent that women not only dress to please men but just as much for their own pleasure and self-satisfaction and from a sense of rivalry towards other women and there was no doubt about it that this was a sort of triumph to look, feel and be well dressed and well groomed in spite of the disgusting surroundings one had to live in.[11]

During the 1940s there was far less emphasis on eyes than at present, the most important cosmetics being red lipstick, pale pink face powder carried in a compact and sometimes rouge cheek colour. Most well-bred British women in circumstances of their choosing would not be seen without lipstick. For interned women, the lipstick in no way hid the ingrained dirt, the bruises or the tropical sores and ulcers, but it was a matter of individual and group self-respect. Indeed, some women who had brought a good supply with them wore cosmetics during the day as well, even at the risk of punishment by Japanese guards. Punishment for this and other misdemeanours could include teasing (for example, giving contradictory orders), repeated roll calls, face-slaps and beating, extra labour, and being made to stand for hours in the vicious sun.

It is perhaps difficult for us, forty years on, to understand why the women risked so much for what seems essentially an unnecessary adornment, and even one which can be seen as part of a system of exploitation of women. For the internees, however, lipstick was a statement of positive personal attitude, and the wearing of it was perhaps a small personal victory[12] against the Japanese. The symbolic value of good grooming is not of course confined to defeated displaced women. Patients in hospital are permed and made-up, or shaved as appropriate, to aid in recovery and rehabilitation.

Fastidiousness about cosmetics would have been the more important because internees were obliged to manage without the hygiene and modesty which were previously important. When they were not available in houses, toilets were normally latrine ditches in full view of anyone who cared to look, and bathing was generally done with the aid of a bucket or can in a public area.

Protection through symbolism

The women were obviously vulnerable to sexual harassment by the guards, though there seems to be little evidence of women being sexually abused.[13] Perhaps this was due in part to the group cohesion of the women and their own sensitivity to the power of symbolism. The following anecdote, recalling an event while the women were bathing, illustrates this well.

> And then one morning we suddenly heard this guard. And of course we were all a bit scared. And I said 'Well girls, just turn round and bottoms up, because if we just do exercises and he just sees bare bottoms he'll never be able to identify you'. And so it happened and it was never reported because he knew he'd lose face.[14]

This recourse to nudity to shame a man has many cross-cultural parallels as Shirley Ardener discusses (1975, pp. 29ff; 1987).

In another incident, the Japanese guards requested that some women be sent to the club for junior ranking officers:

Well of course we had a very good idea why they wanted them to go because they'd only chosen a few and they were all the very shortest and youngest of the nurses. So we were very worried about that. We wouldn't let the few go. Six I think were selected. We wouldn't let them go alone: all the sisters went. And they put on nurse's uniforms. They all donned their nurse's uniforms and marched stolidly to this place they'd been told to go. Of course the Japs had a great surprise. They'd only asked for the six but the whole column of thirty-two marched down in uniform. The doctor [spokeswoman] made a very strong protest about it and it never happened again.[15]

Survival and death

About one-third of the women and over half the men did not survive the Japanese internment camps. Basic conditions do not seem to have been significantly worse for men, though men do seem to have been more likely than women to attempt escape or otherwise risk torture. On the whole, women seemed to be better able to accept that submission was appropriate, and to build a structured life within the oppressive boundaries. In that symbolic niceties, such as lipstick and tea parties, represented law and order and control in the internees' lives, they were of psychological value to survival.

When women did die, mainly from conditions resulting from malnutrition – as happened increasingly as time went on – some attempt was made to see that the dead departed in a traditional and 'civilised' way. The body was wrapped in a blanket and until the burial, friends stayed to keep away rats. An internee burial party went under escort outside the camp, and the graveside was decorated with wild flowers or even a home-made wooden cross inscribed with a charred stick. The perilous position of the living, however, had to take precedence over the dead: the blanket in which the body had been wrapped was brought back to the camp, for blankets were in short supply. The personal belongings of the deceased would be apportioned between her friends and neighbours. Some women wrote wills to try to prevent the squabbling which might break out on such occasions.

In order to acquire food, or other necessities, some women would sell anything they had, or could obtain, to corruptible guards or the indigenous population. Other women chose to die with their wedding rings, which tended to annoy and distress the doctors and nurses who felt the money might have helped to save them. The rings were usually all the women had as mementos of their husbands, whose fate they did not know. The best survivors seemed to be those women who could put thoughts of anything troubling, including missing relatives, to one side and concentrate instead on the exigencies of living.

> We developed into an art the attitude of trying not to worry about things that we could not remedy. If it was possible to help, even ever so little, no trouble or risk was too great. But if it was quite, wholly, absolutely impossible one had to try not to let things penetrate too much or you might easily go quite crazy and that didn't do anybody any good. That is also why on the whole one doesn't worry overmuch about the people one has been separated from. They were not a part of the actual scheme of things and one couldn't do anything about them anyway. Sometimes I began to wonder what the outside world was like. This thought is the beginning of all unrest, I put it out of my mind; no good striving after the unattainable.[16]

Their symbols replaced the unthinkable losses and fears which then, indeed, did not bear thinking about.

In the latter part of the war, as the women grew weaker, social life was sometimes adapted to suit the disabilities. In some camps large-scale communal activities were discontinued, and the women formed small family-sized units to deal with specific tasks instead. The principles of consensus and sharing, and voluntary rather than enforced participation, continued. The supposed characteristics of women together – bitchiness and hysteria – seemed by and large absent, though there were, of course, occasional disputes, particularly about food or space allocation.

Victories

Though the Japanese left the women to their own devices in many ways, they also made sure their presence wasn't forgotten. Sentries and patrols were constantly present, and the women were subjected to twice-daily roll calls and seemingly arbitrary punishments. The women were required to bow deeply in the Japanese custom to their captors. They did not, however, regard their position with shame or humiliation, but rather with wryness.

Very rarely the women took the offensive, as on the following occasion in Sumatra:

> When some of our volunteers, our noble volunteers, who used to empty the cesspits for us – had to do it every day – they had to also fertilise the Japanese gardens with this stuff. They [the Japanese] had just little Dutch bungalows outside the camp and they had their gardens for food. So these girls got up early, about half a dozen of them I think and they told these girls to take the manure and put it on their gardens. So they dashed and got as much of this stuff as they could and they rushed and put it all under the windows of these bungalows. Well there wasn't any glass; as a rule there were just shutters, open shutters that you closed if it rained. And they kept on, they were working as hard as they could, rushing before the Japs realised what they were doing, running with these great cans of stuff and tipping it madly all under these windows. And when they'd finished the Jap who was in charge of them was so pleased that they had worked so hard that he gave them each a little piece of soap. Now, soap was like gold, I mean that was like giving them two or three pounds because they had worked so well. And they came in absolutely triumphant. We all gathered by the slits in the camp fence with our noses, to see what happened. Of course by afternoon when the sun was well up this stuff under their windows began to exude this terrible odour. And there they were, all the Japanese, coming out of their houses wondering what was all this smell. Oh dear, it was absolutely lovely.[17]

Usually the internees only won small psychological victories, by pretending the guards were not there, or by delaying and dawdling when engaged in tasks for the Japanese. This response was probably similar to that the women once received from their own former servants.[18]

For some of the surviving women amongst the supposedly passive victims, it seems that ultimately there was a form of personal victory:

It seems strange but I think for the first time in my life I had become an independent person in my own right. I'd been the youngest in the family. I was always told what to do more or less. And I married quite young. And in the Army one isn't exactly independent, you do what the Army tells you. And I automatically took it for granted that my husband made the decisions. I was quite content to go along like that. But of course it was all different: interned I had to be myself. And I did find that I perhaps was a bit of a different person from what I'd thought I was. I found my independence. I found that in a tight spot I had enough there to depend on myself, something that I would have doubted if anyone had told me that I'd got to do this and face this. I'd never survive. But you see I found I did have the strength and the will. And I also came away with an extremely high regard for members of my own sex which I didn't have before. I used rather to shy away from women's company. I wasn't awfully fond of women's company. I found I was much more at home in men's company and found women boring and vapid. The women I knew thought nothing about anything except their children and their servants and playing mah-jong and gossip. But when I came out of camp I had a healthy respect and regard for women which I have retained for the rest of my life. I know that women are dependable and women are strong, extremely strong in a crisis. I do admire women very much.[19]

Notes

(Accession numbers in the notes are for oral history records in the Imperial War Museum Sound Archives.)

1. Civilian evacuation in the Far East was late in beginning and about 20 000 British civilians, male and female were interned, primarily following the fall of Singapore and the Dutch East Indies.
2. Lower ranking clerks or soldiers would not have been so likely to have wives or daughters resident in the East.
3. The problem of periods was solved after a few months, when with only a poor diet women's periods stopped.
4. Oral history recording in the Imperial War Museum Sound Archive: DJ 6210/7.66.
5. Women were nearly always interned separately from men, and were unlikely even to receive news of their husbands or events outside the

camp. In a few camps women and men were permitted to meet under guard for such events as religious services and to do the laundry.

6. Imperial War Museum Sound Archive: MC 6229/11.4.
7. See Brownfoot (1984).
8. Imperial War Museum Sound Archive: MC 6229/11.47, 49, 50.
9. Imperial War Museum Sound Archive: MC 6229/11.101
10. Imperial War Museum Sound Archive: DJ 6210/7.11.
11. Imperial War Museum Sound Archive: DJ 6210/7.86.
12. See, for example, Okely (1978, p. 123); in a girl's boarding school taking the lift from the beach instead of the steps constituted a 'triumph'. See, too, final section of this study, pp. 175–7.
13. There was probably a racial element in this. I have only heard of one British woman being raped and she was Eurasian.
14. Imperial War Museum Sound Archive: HG 6476/6.31.
15. Imperial War Museum Sound Archive: MC 6229/11.58.
16. Imperial War Museum Sound Archive: DJ 6210/7.76, 83.
17. Imperial War Museum Sound Archive: MC 6229/11.105.
18. Shirley Ardener discusses how 'minor deviations and rebellions can nurture the confined soul. Simple acts . . . can become charged with emotive force . . . and can have greater expressive effect than some grosser confrontations . . . Such small gestures are the vivid language and satisfaction of some muted groups' (Ardener (ed.), 1978, p. 29; for 'muted groups' see Ardener, 1975). See also Okely (1978).
19. Imperial War Museum Sound Archive: MC 6229/11.11.

References

Ardener, S. (1975) 'Introductory Essay', pp. vii–xxiii, and 'Sexual Insult and Female Militancy', pp. 29–53, in S. Ardener (ed.), *Perceiving Women* (London: J. M. Dent).

Ardener, S. (ed.) (1978) *Defining Females: The nature of women in society* (London: Croom Helm).

Ardener, S. (1987) 'Gender Iconography: the Vagina', in P. Caplan (ed.), *The Cultural Construction of Sexuality* (London: Tavistock).

Brownfoot, J. N. (1984) 'Memsahibs in Colonial Malaya: A Study of European Wives in a British Colony and Protectorate 1900–1940', in H. Callan and S. Ardener (eds.), *The Incorporated Wife*, pp. 186–210 (London: Croom Helm).

Okely, J. (1978) 'Privileged, Schooled and Finished: Boarding Education for Girls', in S. Ardener (ed.) (1978) pp. 109–39.

10

Perceptions of 'Peace Women' at Greenham Common 1981–85: A participant's View

LYNNE JONES

Any woman from anywhere in the world can come, go, return; and be welcomed. No questions are asked. There is no hierarchy, no structure. There is no distinction of race, creed, colour, money, age, class or nationality. These unpretentious women in their beat-up warm clothes, have become a world-wide symbol and model for countless ordinary people who also say NO. (Martha Gellhorn, *Observer* 12 February 1984)

Sue Hanson, a sprig of a girl from Mid America's Heartlands, believes she is more liberated than any of the Greenham Common women on the other side of the missile fence – both literally and ideologically. Lieutenant Hanson, a bespectacled blonde, is the only woman in the Cruise programme in Britain capable of obliterating Leningrad at the touch of a button . . . 'My face will never be as lacking in makeup as theirs, . . . I'm a liberationist not a feminist'.

It is also predictable they will be deeply upset to discover that the operator in control of Cruise is a mature life loving young woman who cherishes peace just as much as most of us. (Brian Vine, *Daily Mail*, June 1984)

Think of the image: 'a young woman cherishing peace'. What comes to mind? When I reflect, try as I will, I cannot avoid images of domesticity. She sits with a child on her lap or playing at her feet.

179

She sews, she knits, she cooks, she plants and harvests, she makes music. Utterly reasonable of course, for all these activities are incompatible with war: peace requires some kind of home and stability. Domesticity is equated with peace, woman with domesticity and therefore with peace. If I try to shake free of this image and see 'peace woman' in another light, the image that comes to my mind immediately is of a woman being like a man. She springs out: Pallas Athena in shining armour, Joan of Arc, an Amazon, a Nicaraguan woman in battle fatigues.

The strangest thing is that I do not come up with an image of myself in spite of the fact that I have spent the last three years as what the media call a 'peace woman', and although along with my sisters I seem perpetually to be involved in one long 'struggle' (I prefer that word to war). So pervasive is the influence of the media, and the effect of art and literature passed on through formal education, that it is easier to exclude myself, because I don't 'fit', than to readjust the images. This chapter, therefore, is an exercise in perception; an attempt to deal with images and to understand how they are created. I want to see myself more clearly.

In April 1982 my own involvement in the Peace Movement, and in particular with the camp at Greenham Common, had grown so much that I resigned my job as a casualty officer in a Liverpool hospital. Over the next two years I lived for varying periods at the camp, moving there completely in the summer of 1983 and remaining until September 1984. This chapter comes out of my personal experience of living there and my continuous involvement with the camp and the process it has begun. It is a personal statement: other women may have different perceptions. We can each tell our own story.

Media images

I began by writing down all the words I could think of which are used to describe Greenham Women (see Table 10.1) and found, not surprisingly, that they fell into two columns, positive and negative. At first sight it might appear that there are two types of women. This idea is supported by the 'myth' that originally there were the 'good' women, who made sacrifices and started the camp, but who were later supplanted by the 'lazy' women who cared little about the issue

Table 10.1   *Media stereotypes*

Positive	Negative
Sacrificed comfort of home	Abandoned children
Living in horrid conditions	Living in squalor
Brave/committed	Bloody minded, stubborn, aggressive
Standing up for beliefs	Won't admit defeat
'Suitably dressed'	Doesn't care about appearance
Not materialistic	Doesn't care about other people's property/scrounger
Idealistic	Naive
Feminist, lesbian	Women's libber, man-hater, lesbian
Vanguard of peace movement	Holding back peace movement
Symbol of resistance	Lost cause
Spiritual	Spiritual
Imaginative	Crazy
Creative	Kinky
Non-violent	Passive
Egalitarian	No leadership
Communal	Disorganised
No hierarchy	Chaotic, no structure
Having no leaders	Being manipulated by a few
Small valiant group	Tiny minority

and just wanted to scrounge off the dole. But then I noticed that some words appeared in both columns, and all I had to do was change my tone of voice. 'Image' is created by those doing the looking – not by those being seen. The media of course do more than just look – they present and create, and after a time almost everyone's view is filtered through the media image. This is why I want to look at media presentation in some detail.

A chronological account of media descriptions shows how various perceptions of Greenham women developed and altered with the contingencies of the moment. At first very little was said ('As few stereotypes as in the average bus queue' (*Standard*, 2 December 1981)) and only the element of sacrifice was mentioned. Jane who gave up her job as a teacher was quoted: 'I could no longer stand in front of the children and talk about their future when I didn't believe [in] my own'. Over the following year there was an increasing note of admiration:

Warm hands join to defend the Peace. (*The Times*, 22 March 1983, describing the first blockade)

Ring of resolve to stop Cruise. (*Guardian*, 20 December 1982)

This built to a crescendo around 12 December 1982 when the 'Embrace the base' action received very favourable world-wide coverage. However, in February 1982 Michael Heseltine, the Minister for Defence, visited Newbury. Women did a 'Die in', lying down outside the building where he was speaking. The large numbers of police who had organised themselves literally to smash through the barrier of prostrate bodies tripped up as they carried Mr Heseltine across. The headlines the next day read:

Mobbed! Heseltine is floored. (*Daily Star*, 8 February 1982)

Angry Peacegirls rough up Heseltine. (*Sun*, 8 February 1982)

Jeering peace protestors punch Minister. (*The Times*, 8 February 1982)

Was this change in tone because we were becoming too popular? Opinion polls at this time showed for the first time a majority against Cruise Missiles and, moreover, that the presence of the women had been a factor in publicising the issue.

In September 1982 the camp, after a second eviction, had been deprived of caravans, and enormous boulders had been dumped on the site. But by November 1982 no one had yet commented on the wet bales of straw used as seats, bins for food, the mud everywhere and plastic sheets draped across a washing line for shelter. However, in the Spring of 1983 the press descriptions of the camp began to change:

The sad truth that shattered a dream . . . The desolate filthy camp site was bad enough, the few women squatting round the fire was a total shock. (*Daily Mirror*, 11 July 1983)

In July 1983 with sunlight, dry ground and our first 'benders' (structures of wood, bent and set in the ground with plastic stretched over) we were described as living in a 'mixture of filthy disease ridden shacks' (*Sun*, 26 August 1983). 'It's time to go home', we were told. 'What is being achieved by depriving children of proper family life and decent secure homes?' they asked in a column placed on the same page as a large cartoon dealing with paedophiles. This showed a large and evil-looking spider (the paedophile) crouched in the corner of a web reaching over two small children. Below this a leading article dealt with the 'EVIL MYRA [Hindley]'. The juxtaposition of these two unpopular stories of child abuse with reports on Greenham women seemed to me to be clearly intended to bracket them by association.[1]

In October 1983 the American Army occupied Grenada and the press suddenly took a new interest in our views. As the missile deployment date neared, the eyes of the world (their perception directed through the lenses of the media) were fixed on us to see how we would react. Cameras and recorders were thrust in our faces, and we felt like gladiators in a ring.

Yet the virulence remained. We were accused of manipulating the media and deliberately scheming for publicity by all manner of means:

Sharp tactics behind those woolly hats. (*Mail on Sunday*, 26 November 1983)

Dirty tricks that hit the thin blue line. (*Daily Mail*, 14 November 1983)

There have been times when these 'ladies' pinned their used sanitary towels to their clothing or hung them on the fence for us to remove. They like to make a point of squatting to relieve themselves on the path we patrol and if we're watching . . . better still, and their other little joke is to stand in front of us rubbing themselves or touching each other up. (P. C. Carpenter to reporter, *Daily Mail*, 14 November 1983)

The Greenham Common action is one of the most sophisticated 'agitprop' operations ever before seen in Britain . . . Television programmes always desperate for news pictures have been manipulated. (*Mail on Sunday*, 20 November 1983)

What I did learn in those two years was that the media image has little to do with what one presents and more to do with the political space one occupies. Therefore, there is little point in 'modifying' one's image for publicity's sake.

This was never more apparent than after what the media referred to as 'The Eviction' of 5 April 1984. In fact, the four camps on the north side of the base had, over the previous three weeks, been 'evicted' daily. Bailiffs would come and tear down structures and remove the belongings that women couldn't claim or carry off quickly enough. The bailiffs would then leave and the women would settle down again. '*The* eviction' of 15 April consisted of some 300 police and 50 bailiffs moving in again to clear and fence off two sites, each 300 yards square, at the main gate. It was little different from what had been going on every day during the previous three weeks. The camp continued that particular day on the other side of the road, as did the other ten camps. The media, however, used the occasion to write our obituaries:

They were not sluts or harridans as the *Daily Express* for one viciously described them. What brought them together was a passionate belief that the world was racing towards nuclear catastrophe. It was to avert that fate that some of the women left their homes and families, and were called lesbians for it by those who never felt such passions for peace. (*Daily Mirror*, 5 April 1984)

The ladies of Greenham have neither damaged the credibility of the nuclear deterrent nor been allowed to transform themselves into martyrs. These viragos of protest are fortunate to live in Britain. (*Mail*, 5 April 1984)

The women of Greenham Common will not be remembered as people who in the manner of the suffragettes helped to change the nature of things. But they have established themselves . . . almost as a kind of national institution. It seems that these eccentric and single-minded ladies have always been with us. Perhaps the government should give serious thought to setting up a permanent national home for the Greenham Common women, far from all human habitation but not so far that it could not be visited by curious students of human nature. (*Daily Telegraph*, 5 April 1984)

Nothing has done more to turn the British public against their case than the antics of this bunch of sceptical nuisances. (*Sun*, 5 April 1984)

Only the *Guardian* actually described what happened – 'Peace women remain after evictions' (*Guardian*, 5 April 1984). The media for the last two years (1985–6) have been silent, apart from fairly short news pieces in the *Guardian* or *The Times*. Perhaps the hope is that if we are not discussed we do not exist.

Public opinion

I said earlier that the way we are seen – and perforce see ourselves – is inevitably biased by media coverage. In September 1983 CND commissioned independent research into, amongst other things, attitudes to Greenham among 'the ordinary public' – that is, non-sympathisers. This revealed an acknowledgement that the Greenham women had succeeded in getting the issue discussed: 'I'm saying they haven't achieved anything, but here we are discussing it' (Male 23–35). There was also, however, a feeling that the picketing had gone on too long – 'It's boring – and that public interest had been lost – 'Those Greenham women have turned everyone off it' (Male 25–35). Much of the criticism was personal and hostile. The report stated, 'The personal attacks seemed to be fuelled by the unconventional appearance and behaviour of the Greenham women which most respondents found distasteful if not threatening' (*Report of Research*, 1983, unpub, pp. 15–6). Remember that most respondents had not actually visited the Greenham Common site but relied on the media for their view. The report went on to interpret and conclude:

Some of the personal attacks on the women may be seen as a defence mechanism. Greenham Common provides people with reasons which they can use to excuse themselves for not taking the nuclear issue more to heart. The Greenham women enable people to generate reasons why they have not taken CND or the nuclear debate more seriously . . . The protest has succeeded in awakening the public to the broad issue of the nuclear weapons but comments (as above) indicate that the continued media coverage of Greenham as the main source of publicity about CND is having a counterproductive effect. The Greenham women are burying a potentially popular cause in a tide of criticism levelled against them on personal grounds. They are discrediting the cause to which they profess allegiance. (*Report of Research*, 1983, unpub, pp. 20–3)

This report came out at a time when CND, nervous before the impending deployment of missiles and its own 'failure' in the light of that, could have been said to be looking for someone to blame. It might be noted, interestingly, that the critics of the peace women in this conclusion themselves pointed out that hostility is a mode of defence – before they proceeded to castigate the camp.

Others have also drawn attention to the psychological mechanism of denial in dealing with the threat of nuclear weapons. Dr James Thompson, a psychologist at the Middlesex Hospital, explains how, when people are presented with frightening or disturbing information, one way of coping is to denigrate the informant. Thus a patient who is told by his doctor to stop smoking or he will get cancer discovers he 'never thought much of his doctor anyway', so he changes to another. Similarly, a Greenham woman who talks about children burning and radiation damage, isn't listened to because her hair is considered to be too short (though it may be easier to manage) and because she's in dirty clothes (from camping in the mud). People may find it easier to talk about *her* than about the weapons. Her appearance gives them an excuse *not* to talk about the weapons. The CND report assumed that if you removed the dirty women the public would immediately focus on the issue again. It failed to recognise that such diversion of attention *is* a response *to the issue*, and that it will operate even against a clean old lady in a smart Persian lamb coat if the idea she presents is threatening enough.

An understanding of these defence mechanisms seems to me to be critical to an understanding of the way we are perceived. One cannot separate these perceptions from the fact that we have deliberately chosen to associate ourselves intimately with some of the most terrifying aspects of human existence. This same process of denial amongst the media was well evident. It was notable how much time they spent filming 'the camp' and various domestic rituals, such as cleaning our teeth, and how little attention they gave to the nuclear silos themselves. Moreover the public is not just threatened by the idea of nuclear weapons. The fact that Greenham women make deliberate connections between the weapons issue and other problems, such as violence against women, poverty, ecological destruction and fear of homosexuals means that in listening to any of the women a Pandora's box is opened. Even more threatening perhaps, is that the women believe that we ourselves can do something about those problems. The idea that an individual may have some personal responsibility, and may be required to act on it, is extremely discomforting.

Most threatening of all, to some men and women, is the fact that we are women who are challenging in our action and lifestyle the accepted female sexual stereotype. Witness Sheila Sheddon, a retired nurse, *who had not even visited the camp*, speaking on a 'Greenham Women Out' march that she organised in 1983:

> Speaking as a retired nurse, the place is ankle deep in human excrement, infested with rats . . . their behaviour is a threat to womanhood. They think they're martyrs. *Never* in 100 years. I'll tell you who the martyrs are: the children left behind. I saw a woman put a naked baby in a policeman's arms! If you or I left a child like that they'd be put in care. (Quotation from own notes, 1983)

And here is Alex Hutcheon of 'Ratepayers Against the Greenham Encampments' (RAGE):

> Self-indulgent women flouting the law of the land, who do in fact run lesbian encampments and create an immoral situation. (Own notes 1983)

Also John Learoyd (RAGE) who, when I asked him if he felt threatened by the base replied: 'I feel more threatened by nakedness'; and a member of 'the ordinary public':

> You see them coming out of prison and they go to one particular girl and give her a big hug. It's quite obvious they're lesbians. (Male, 18–24. *Report of Research*, 1983, unpub, p. 18)

Mary Douglas (1966) pointed out that 'dirt' is 'matter out of place', and that this then becomes taboo: that is, dangerous and threatening. It is interesting therefore to contrast the descriptions above of women and the camps with Caroline Blackwood's description in her book about Greenham:

> Pat was a very gentle and intelligent woman. She was sensibly dressed for the awful conditions in trousers, heavy boots and bulky jacket. The floor of the Blue Gate living room was mud. There was no water at the Blue Gate except for the water that was carried to the camp in white plastic containers. The containers certainly looked unaesthetic and added to the camp's cluttered appearance. The piles of wood for the fire also looked messy. So did the plastic cups and saucepans which were all on the ground because the camp had no kitchen. (Blackwood, 1984, p. 6)

How much has the perception of Greenham women as dangerous, threatening and dirty to do with the fact that in civilised Western life cups are not supposed to be on the ground, and women are supposed to wear nice dresses and be at home with husbands?

Self-perception

To pin down how we, the Greenham women, see ourselves, is much more difficult. One reason is that, unlike those who look at us, we don't spend much time talking about it. So even media descriptions from supportive journalists tend to run like those of Martha Gellhorn in the *Observer* (12 February 1984): 'A tall strong grandmother, a war widow with a wind- and sunburnt face, her hair pulled back in a rubber band', or 'A pretty brown-haired girl, a researcher'. One is still defined in terms of job, or looks, or one's relationship with another person.

What women give in their speeches in court or in their own writing is an account of why they are at Greenham, what they're doing, and what they believe. These beliefs, with some thousands of women passing through the camp, are impossible to stereotype. Some women come motivated entirely by fear and a sense of urgency, others are attracted by a women-only community. Moreover, any woman staying at the camp for any length of time finds her ideas and values changing:

They simply do not go back to becoming ordinary housewives and live in semi-detached houses and do nothing else – they become politically active. Every woman who comes here is touched by the idea of her own power. (Liz, 1984, own notes)

What can be drawn out are a certain number of key beliefs that all of us share. They are interconnected but there is no order of priority. They are commitments to a women-only space; to non-violence; to each individual's personal autonomy, and the need for a non-hierarchical, leaderless form of organisation; and to a belief that the Cruise Missiles are only a symptom of a much larger problem. Although these commitments are in themselves interconnected and given different emphases by different women, for clarity's sake I will try to deal with them separately.

'Women only'

How the decision to be a women-only camp was made is documented very clearly in Barbara Harford's and Sarah Hopkins' anthology *Women at the Wire* (1984). I won't report much of it but recommend it for an understanding of people's feelings at the time. Reasons for the decision differed. Some felt it was wise tactically since the police overreacted when men were present. However, now, five years and a great deal of police and army brutality later, it is clear to us that reactions can be just as hostile to the sex which is not generally supposed to be threatening.

Some women living at the camp when it was mixed were fed up with sliding into the conventional female role of tidying and nurturing. Others, myself included, felt very strongly that we needed the space 'to develop our own ways of working'. I wrote at the time:

We see more hope for the future in the process emphasised by the women's movement – shared decision making, non-hierarchical leaderless groups, co-operation and non-violence – than in the hierarchical and authoritarian systems that prevail in mixed groups. We want a chance to develop skills we are not normally expected to acquire – organisational and practical ones – and to express those characteristics normally devalued in society at large; caring, compassion, trust. Human characteristics which *all* of us need to reclaim if we are to survive. (Jones, 1983, *The Greenham Factor*)

This was explained by another woman:

Having women's actions has got nothing to do with excluding men. It's got to do for once with including women. It's so women who have been told they can only function in one small closed-in area to do with children can come out of those areas and take part in politics and action and begin to affect and change the world. That's WHY WOMEN. It's got nothing to do with excluding men. (Katrina, 1983, *The Greenham Factor*)

Others took it further. Io's commitment to 'women-only' was also a commitment to political lesbianism which she explained as follows:

Political lesbianism is about making men understand. I suppose it's a kind of blackmail by withdrawing emotional support – so that they can come to their senses and see what they're doing. I see withdrawal as a means to an end. To some women lesbianism makes sense because men no longer have the capacity to fill women's human needs – they've become detached. A lot of men don't understand. They're very hurt. The hatred that we are facing has to do with men's fear and their hatred because of it. (From own notes, 1983)

This is how the 'women-only' decision was received: All hell was let loose. The men went completely mad. Their worst elements came out. One, who had come specifically to give a workshop on self-control, couldn't take it, bashed into a cauldron of boiling water, almost spilling it over one of the women, and then he just stormed off. Someone else was going wild saying 'I built this structure', and picked up an axe, and started to chop down the tarpaulin. (Sarah G., in Harford and Hopkins, 1984, p. 32)

Political motivation

Thousands of women have been politically motivated by Greenham over the past four years (1982–6); both the issue and women have become visible. Indeed, the effect has gone far beyond the camp:

At a CND conference I went to a non-violence workshop run by Greenham women, and I came out overjoyed because I'd been able to talk about my feelings without people sniggering and I'd cried and no-one had minded. I came out feeling purposeful with friends and a sense of people caring. Then I went home and started organising to get coaches of women to Greenham for December 12. (Interview with woman visiting the camp, Summer 1983)

This awareness of the importance of feminist ideas to the disarmament movement had helped me and other women to insist on organising our local mixed groups so that it does not reflect the values and structures we are rejecting. We've tried to create the sort of atmosphere in which everyone can speak and help to make policy. We do simple things like welcoming newcomers and introducing ourselves, which we feel is more important than the minutes of the last meeting. (*Spare Rib*, February 1983)

Later, miners' wives who became involved in strike action acknowledged the educative effect of the Greenham women. (*Guardian*, 1985)

Interestingly, in spite of the anger at the exclusion of males expressed in letters, visits, and at CND conferences (an anger that is only now waning as Molesworth increases in importance as an alternative focus), no men actually moved in or tried to take over, yet our decision was (and still is) protected only by our own belief that it is right.

Creative structure

As far as I was concerned, the main factor vindicating the decision to exclude men was the type of organisation that actually emerged, the like of which I have not experienced in any other political grouping. First (and perhaps most importantly) it is genuinely leaderless. Traditionally, we are encouraged to believe that in any group leaders emerge (whether named or not) by a process of natural selection. Several factors are generally considered to encourage this. Those who are dominant, by virtue of intelligence, articulateness, personality, sheer pushiness, or other characteristics, it is argued, find others looking to them to make decisions and become accustomed to being listened to. Outsiders, particularly the media, seem to demand a representative – a spokesperson – preferably the same one each time – someone who fulfils their image of a leader.

Greenham women have no special immunity to these forces, except a strong commitment to egalitarianism. Most arrived having just rejected some form of authority: being 'told what to do' by school, husband, prison, or by other peace groups. Further, the physical structure of the camp has actually helped to reinforce leaderlessness. It is impossible to dominate a group whose membership changes every day, whose constituents are spread around nine miles of perimeter fence, and whose 'central' financial resources rotate on a weekly basis (a different 'money-woman' deals with donations each week). Any woman taken up by the media may be away so much, making speeches, that she finds herself resented and rejected on her return. To call it structureless, however, is a misnomer: there is a structure that prevents over-structuring.

The immense advantage of this kind of group is that women who arrive, and decide to stay, very rapidly discover they can and have to think and act for themselves. The result is the release of an extraordinary amount of creative energy and a willingness to experiment. No idea seems too far-fetched to be seriously considered or even acted upon, as the following three cases illustrate:

> There was a group of us sitting in a bender . . . when I piped up I want to paint a plane. The others thought it was a good idea, so off we went to the main gate and announced it. Another four women said they wouldn't mind doing it, so we got the boltcutters and some paint. (Tracey, in Harford and Hopkins, 1984, pp. 154–5)

The painting of the Blackbird Spy Plane cost the American military 2¼ million pounds.

A second example is the 12 December 1982 encirclement and blockade, which was planned in a series of meetings both at the camp and in London. Decisions emerging by consensus, were reversed at the next meeting and subsequently changed again. Eventually a leaflet was produced. This was followed by a chain letter asking each woman to send it to ten others. The result was that 30 000 women arrived at the camp:

> There was nobody giving orders and telling us what to do. We'd each had a message from the Greenham women to bring a 'hymn' to express why we were here and that was all. The rest was left to us and somehow, through an intuition or a mysterious unspoken understanding, there was no conflict, there was no breakdown in communications, there was no paralysis of action. (Chris Malvey, in Harford and Hopkins, 1984, p. 92)

Another example was provided on 29 October 1983 when a chain letter was again sent, this time asking women to come to the camp dressed as witches as if for a Halloween party, but carrying bolt cutters. When the women arrived, they were told to find an empty patch of fence and wait until four o'clock. At four o'clock, to the surprise of the police (and to some of us!), at least four miles of fence came down.

These two events demonstrated our ability to learn from experience. The night of 13 December had been spent in detailed briefings as we trained ourselves for non-violent action. A year later, however, women, many of whom had not been to Greenham before, arrived in self-organised autonomous groups that needed no training or teaching at all.

The other main advantage of our fluid, flexible type of organisation is that it is almost indestructible. When an injunction was brought against twenty named, better-known women, it failed to disrupt the camp at all. Further, the judicial process of establishing guilt was made extremely difficult. Here is Ceri at the trial which was held in February 1983 for the Silo action which took place on New Year's Eve 1982–3:

Prosecutor:	When did you first know the base was going to be entered?
Ceri:	We talked about it a bit for a week.
Prosecutor:	Just give me a bit of detail. I want to know whose idea was it? Who planned it?
Ceri:	It was nobody's idea because we all meet together, women from all over. A suggestion comes up and we discuss it.

Prosecutor:	Who suggested it?
Ceri:	No-one, I don't remember.
Prosecutor:	Who was involved in the discussion?
Ceri:	All of us.
Prosecutor:	All 44?
Ceri:	No, more.
Prosecutor:	Who planned it?
Ceri:	No-one, we don't plan things.
Prosecutor:	Who alerted the press?
Ceri:	I don't know.
Prosecutor:	You don't know or won't tell?
Ceri:	I genuinely don't know.
Prosecutor:	Will you go in the base again?
Ceri:	I went in this morning.
Prosecutor:	Will you go in tomorrow?
Ceri:	It depends if we wake up tomorrow. (*Report of Court Proceedings*, February 1982)

Political symbolism

Communication of ideas

My own experience is that almost all political action relies to some extent on symbolism for its effect in transforming reality, although we tend to take most symbols for granted without noticing them as such. The Arms Race itself is in fact a symbolic game: extremely costly, dangerous and increasingly nonsensical, but still a game. Cruise missiles symbolise America's commitment to Europe and represent 'our determination not to back down'. Deterrence theory largely rests not on the military effectiveness of these weapons (Cruise and Pershing were not completely tested and guaranteed at the time of deployment) but on their 'political symbolism'. Language, itself simply a series of symbols, has been distorted to encompass the horrors of our time, and so has become part of a mechanism of denial. The linguistic symbols are used to disguise what would be a quite unacceptable reality. So an MX missile is called a 'peacekeeper'. A small nuclear attack (say twenty or so Hiroshimas) is a 'Strategical Strike'. Forty million dead equals 'acceptable losses'.

Faced with this, some of us see two alternatives: either to remain silent, to be left literally speechless; or else to create our own language and means of communication. As a result, perhaps the most potent 'effect' of the actions of the women at Greenham has been their capacity, not simply to close the base or obstruct the missile convoy (as does happen), but to communicate *ideas* both to the personnel in the base and a wider public. As indicated, one way of doing this has been to challenge the language used itself. So women charged with a 'Breach of the Peace' for various acts of civil disobedience and asked if they will be bound over to 'keep the peace' have invariably replied that they are doing so already. As Catriona responded in court:

> I will not be bound over to keep your peace. I am already keeping my peace. I will not take punishment, or recant, or admit guilt. I am responsible for this – for seeing the war machine grinding on, building silos arming the arsenals of the world with death and using all the non-violent means I can to stop it. I am asking *you* to keep the peace. We are not on trial, you are. (*Report of Court Proceedings*, February 1982)

Symbolic action

The other mode of challenge has been the constant use of symbolic action. Dancing on missile silos, for example, does nothing in practical terms to stop the building programme, but the image conveyed of women dancing, hands linked, on top of the hard bulge of ground intended to house the weapons, is a powerful one. The *idea* conveyed is that our language is stronger than theirs, and that it continues in spite of them.

On 12 December 1982 the fence around the military base was both 'embraced' (a word that immediately conjures up love, warmth, safety), and transformed into a 'Women's collage for life'. Women brought clothes, photos, weaving, pictures and objects of various kinds, and pinned them onto the fence in order symbolically to block out the ugliness of the base. On 29 October 1983, women again arrived at the camp dressed as witches. This was not only intended to be a reclamation of a reviled image of women and a symbol of power, it was also effective in convincing the police that the gathering was just a 'Halloween Party'. The women actually removed miles of fencing. This action had the very real effect of undermining the security of the base and also represented women's desire to remove the fence itself, since it was seen as a symbol of division and of power. As our press statement put it: 'This fence is our Berlin Wall. Before we can tackle the concrete and barbed wire that divides our continent we must start with that on our doorstep'. Another symbolic technique was adopted on 12 December 1983 when women used mirrors to 'turn the base inside out' and to make those inside see themselves (see Plate 4). Io wrote the following meditation on mirror symbolism:

> 'Mirari' is a . . . word that means 'to wonder' there are three words that come from 'Mirari' – 'Mirror' which is a reflective surface – which reflects heat, sound and light/images. 'Mirage', an optical illusion. 'Miracle' – an act/happening, that changes material – reality.
>
> . . . What do mirrors do? They reflect . . . Think of your mirror as a tool; what is it that you want to see? Would you like to see the base? Reflect these things inside from outside. Be creative . . . Try it on a policeman! Do they truly see themselves, do soldiers who carry guns know themselves, love what they are?
>
> I was going to write about non-violence and started to think about the symbolism of the mirror – and I find it is the same thing – about our non-violence and other people's non-violence. How can we show people who they are and what they are doing? We cannot change people's values – they have to do it themselves. We cannot take on that responsibility. Most people get caught up in conflict by mirroring others. Aggressiveness is not the way to change or transform violence into peace. Mirrors are excellent tools for showing people themselves. Let's hope for a miracle. Let's make it happen! (Io, 1983, p. 11)

One of the uses of symbols in language is not to substitute words for action, but to convey a large number of ideas by a single image. Consider the symbolism of the web: for the women of Greenham it represents connections between women, or between ideas; it can be started at any point; it is fragile, yet strong, and very beautiful. Moreover, weaving is traditionally women's work, individual yet also essential, constructive and beautiful. No two women will

Plate 4 *Women at Greenham Common hold up mirrors for the police to see themselves, 12 December 1983*

Source: Paula Allen

necessarily give the same interpretation. The web may be valued by some women not for its messages, but just for its practical ability utterly to bewilder police, or construction workers.

In one of the earlier actions, women dressed themselves up in papier-mache snake costumes and entered the base. Since then the snake, or serpent, or dragon, has occurred again and again in various activities becoming, for the women, along with the spider's web, a symbol of resistance, to be worn on earrings and bracelets, painted on benders and used for decorating articles and leaflets (see, for example, Plate 5). It is a symbol we apparently share with North and South American Indians and Australian Aborigines, among others, as Chris Knight explains in a Greenham newsletter:

> Women, as the custodians of all life-blood, are the guardians of life itself and of our future. When women have solidarity and strength, their reproductive cycles tend to synchronise with the periodicities of the tides and of the moon, so that the rhythms of human sex and life harmonise with wider cyclicities to form a coherent whole. This is the world-encircling 'dragon' or 'serpent' which lies at the heart of all traditional mythologies. Instead of dying, it merely changes its skin, as the moon does monthly, or as women do in menstruating. The 'dragon' is slaughtered by some patriarchal hero who established the present world-order from which we are suffering still. But however many times you kill the dragon, it has a tendency to rise up, fire-breathing as ever, with a new crop of heads. True, it hasn't been seen around for some time, now. But she seems to be stirring from her thousand-year sleep at last, her patience finally at an end. The Australian Aborigines and the American Indians, together with traditional people and women everywhere, will have the last word. (Pamphlet produced for Dragon Action, 24 June 1983)

It is easy to become fanciful or over-analytical about these things. I do not remember these connections being consciously articulated or discussed at the time. Yet if it was chance – what prompted it? Did women draw without realising it on some undisclosed culture?[2]

Symbols have also been used directly to confront the imagery used by those stationed on the military base. At Christmas 1983, crosses of coloured lights were put up by the personnel inside to decorate the base. Taking a cue from this, at Easter 1984, six

Plate 5 *Illustration from leaflet produced for the Dragon Action, Greenham Common, 24 June 1983*

Source: Catriona Howse

women took a large wooden cross into the base, stood it in the barbed wire, and read the Passion to the soldiers 'to confront them with the real meaning of the Crucifixion'. On other occasions the aim is to ridicule; activities such as roller skating down the runway, bike-riding round inside the fence, or dressing up as rabbits, make it difficult for Greenham's perceived role as a high-security base to be taken seriously.

It's often assumed that if an action is symbolic it can't be 'real' or 'effective'. At Greenham, with its emphasis on snakes, webs, mirrors, some thought that imagery had drifted off into the realms of fantasy: 'Very pretty, but how does it stop the bomb?' For example, in September 1984 at one action around the military base I was standing linking arms at the fence with a miner's wife who had come down with a group from Nottingham. We were confronting some fairly hostile and aggressive police. She and her friends were yelling loudly, 'Maggie Thatcher's Boot Boys!' I commented that I thought it might be winding them up more – 'Well I'll tell you', said one turning to me, 'we're just fed up with webs, mysticism, menstruation and magic!' But in each situation even the most straightforward symbolism adds a dimension that transforms the action, and underlines the ironies and paradoxes of the situation, so making people think. One can understand that the use of such simple, sometimes childlike activities such as dressing-up, weaving or painting, can be interpreted as simplicity or naivety. Such an interpretation, however, misses the point of the complexity of ideas that can be conveyed in this way, and the potential for establishing connections between issues in people's minds.

Symbolic connections and actions

Power of symbolism

Personally, one of the most attractive aspects of Greenham for me is that through my involvement I can directly and physically challenge a terrifying weapons system, whilst at the same time making it clear that Cruise is only one symptom of a much more complex problem. That problem is our complete lack of control over our own lives. Action at Greenham becomes for some of us a metaphor for action in other areas where we lack control. The kind of action we take, and the symbols we use, illuminate the connections between those areas.

Some of us believe, for instance, that the thinking that produces this kind of weaponry and calls it 'security', is the same thinking that condones (I use the word deliberately) male violence against women.[3] Some make similar connections between the deliberate destruction of the environment (in particular the common) and the perception of 'saving' a country by reducing it to ashes.[4] One way to demonstrate these connections is by symbolic action.

On 9 August 1984 (Nagasaki Day) women stripped naked, covered themselves and the ground with ashes and blockaded the main gate. The base personnel were horrified, reluctant to touch or remove the women (they eventually donned protective clothing to do so), and were profoundly disturbed. Of course the immediate connection was with the naked, burnt survivors of the Nagasaki bomb, and one can imagine others' reluctance at that time to handle them. The women performing the action wanted to confront the military with that reality. But they were also presenting the men with a challenge to their own stereotypes of naked women and how men assume such women should look (beautiful), where they should be (at the men's disposal), and how much power they should have (none at all – unless you count the power of an attractive object). These ugly and terrifying, yet naked and therefore vulnerable, women were stopping the men getting to work – work that many of the women perceived as a form of rape – and were confronting the men with the possible results of their work. Although the 'naked women' action could be seen as merely a show of our extreme vulnerability, it was in fact a clear statement of women's right to be ourselves. The women were in control. This action is an example of the power of symbolism, and also, to me, one of the best examples of feminist non-violence.

Non-violence

'Non-violence' is another of those words that produces an immediate stereotype in the mind of the hearer. It means to many 'passivity' and 'lack of action', therefore '*no* resistance'. Images of Jews trudging unresisting to the trains that took them to the concentration camps, or various religious sects who have willingly accepted any punishment handed out, and such like, come to my mind. Gandhi broke that particular mould. The struggle against British rule in India and the Civil Rights movement in the US gave us images of *active* resistance: of unarmed men willingly and repeatedly defying the blows of civilian police; of freedom marches, sit-ins, bus boycotts, and so on. Gandhi stressed the importance of humility and the willingness to accept suffering and thus convert the opponent by appealing to his/her moral sense. He called this 'The conquest of the adversary by suffering in one's own person'. It is this idea that makes non-violence an anathema to some feminists:

> The nurturing, peace-making, all-healing image of woman-patching-up-the-mess is just what we want to escape – she is part of the problem. It is a contradiction on the one hand to ask women to assert themselves and fight for their rights and on the other to say 'passively accept suffering in order to convert your opponent'. Women have been martyrs to self-denial and suffering all their lives and where has it got them? Lying down – either to be beaten up by a paratrooper or kicked by the police is just going to reinforce the perception of them as strong and us as weak. Moreover, fatalistically sitting in the mud declaring the end of the world and saying 'my conscience is clear' has nothing to do with active struggle. (*Breaching the Peace* 1983)

This is a valid point of view, but it ignores the reality of what is actually happening at Greenham. There is a great deal of difference between a woman victim of violence in a domestic situation which she cannot escape and a woman *actively* choosing her own weapons and site of action (her own body in the case of Greenham). I have not met any women at Greenham who see any virtue in suffering. We see it as an evil to be avoided if at all possible, though not by espousing the violent tactics of the system we are questioning. Over the past five years (1981–6) the way we act has changed to make us feel increasingly powerful. There are very few of the mass blockades of the early days. No woman is prepared deliberately to break her neck or martyr herself lying in front of the convoy, especially as we have discovered that our simple presence in the base before an excursion is enough to cause hours of delay. Today our action is flexible and spontaneous, and often very effective.

What is happening at Greenham is the non-violent equivalent of guerrilla warfare, and as with guerrilla fighters our effectiveness is based on constant attrition. Those who have seen the women as just 'sitting in the mud' forget the results we have had. An unarmed group of women with no telephone is *effectively* confronting a fully armed nuclear state. The base and dispersal exercises are continually disrupted. Greenham also acts as a permanent training ground for radicalising and educating women in anti-authoritarian non-violent resistance, and it is the inspiration for a network of peace-camps all over the world.

Successful non-violent action will always encounter violent repression in response, and as theorists like Gene Sharp have pointed out, this is part of the dynamic non-violent struggle (Sharp, 1973). The repression is not a sign of our failure; it actually generates an increased non-violent response, as has happened at Greenham.[5]

There is a paradox here – a woman who sees herself as 'at war' yet who calls herself a 'peace woman'. 'Men can go off and leave the children to fight, so why can't we?', remarked one woman. But there is a difference here; for the women 'to fight' means active *non-violent* struggle.

Greenham has provided a new stereotype of a 'peace woman'. For some, 'Greenham woman' has become synonymous with any woman who takes non-violent action, and this at least is broad enough to encompass numerous different women:

You do not need to be wonderful to set up a peace camp or take any other form of creative action. You just need to be fed up with other people taking decisions for you all the time and to not want to be blown up in the next few years. (From own notes, 1983)

Prosecutor: Did you go into the base by accident or desire?
Diane: It was by desire – to celebrate life.
Prosecutor: How often do you intend to go to Greenham Common?
Diane: Until the Government takes us seriously.
Prosecutor: Do you expect it to take you seriously?
Diane: I do. I represent half the world's population. (Report of Court Proceedings, February 1983)

Notes

1. This is not to suggest that I support the *Sun*'s view of Myra Hindley. I do not want to consider her here.
2. For example, Ancient Minoans worshipped the snake goddess as protector of the house, the serpent which shed its skin representing eternal life. This image was taken up in later Aegean culture as a symbol of healing (see Wolf, 1984, Chapter 2). The serpent around a staff is still a medical symbol today.
3. Note for example the fact that in June 1981 Gordon Asher was given a *six-month suspended* sentence for strangling his unfaithful wife while in 1980 the Maw sisters were given *three years* for killing their extremely violent father in self-defence (in Feminism and Nonviolence Study Group, 1983).
4. For example, Greenham women see a clear connection between the lack of self-determination for Blacks in South Africa and their own lack of self-determination over nuclear weapons.
5. *Two examples of this:*

    (a) The imprisonment of women in November 1982 was one of the factors leading to 30 000 women coming to the action in December 1982.
    (b) Constant incursions into the base resulted in new bye-laws being introduced in April 1984. These made entry subject to fine and imprisonment. As a consequence, hundreds more women immediately entered the base and have continued to do so, so rendering the bye-law impractical.

References

Blackwood, C. (1984) *On the Perimeter* (London: Heinemann).
Breaching the Peace (1983) (London: Onlywomen Press).
Douglas, M. (1966) *Purity and Danger* (London: Routledge and Kegan Paul).
Feminism and Nonviolence Study Group (1983) *Piecing it Together* (Feminism and Nonviolence Study Group).
Harford, B. and Hopkins, S. (eds) (1984) *Women at the Wire* (London: Virago).
Io (1983) 'Mirari', in *Women Reclaim Greenham: Handbook for Day of Action*, (London: CND).
Jones, L. (ed.) (1983) *Keeping the Peace* (London: The Women's Press).
Report of Research (1983) Advisory Project Commissioned by CND (unpub.).
Sharp, G. (1973) *The Politics of Nonviolent Action* (Boston: Porter Sargent).
The Greenham Factor (1983) (Greenham Print Prop).
Wolf, C. (1984) *Cassandra* (London: Virago).

'Did your mother wear army boots?' Feminist theory and women's relation to war, peace and revolution

RUTH ROACH PIERSON

We live at a time of widespread fear that our world faces extinction, a fear that not this particular nation, or this particular race, or this particular class, but all humankind will disappear in nuclear holocaust. Sara Ruddick has put forward the argument that the mothering experience of women, above all the 'preservative love' of women as mothers, is what can save us from this fate (Ruddick, 1984). Such a universalising, philosophical claim cries out for empirical testing. Although in no way definitive or exhaustive, a look at the historical record provides one approach.

What does a survey of the last few hundred years of Western history have to tell us about women's relation to organised violence in ideology and experience? Have there been any constants over time in women's relation to war and revolution? Has there been a distinctive women's position on war? Has motherhood kept women from involvement in organised violence? Has it been a source of opposition to war? What has been the experience of women in revolutions and wars? These are vast questions and the period under review is vast, but even an overview more episodic than systematic will indicate limitations to transhistorical claims with respect to women and organised violence.

Early feminist views on women and war

From early on feminists have tended to make generalisations regarding women and armed conflict. One can discern two main bases from which feminists have advanced claims for a distinctive women's position on organised violence. One is women's general exclusion from the formal societal apparatuses of power and coercion. The other is the involvement of most women in motherhood.

Two early examples of feminist statements on women and war adopt the standpoint of women's exclusion from power. In the late seventeenth and early eighteenth centuries the 'woman question' was debated in terms of the superiority and inferiority of the two sexes, and women who sought to extend the scope of female activities found themselves in the position of having to counter claims regarding the alleged inferiority of their sex. One countermove was to scrutinise men's historical record on questions of war and peace. This Mary Astell did in 1700 when she made a list of the many accomplishments of men and asked, sardonically, if it did not compel admiration of 'the Worth and Excellency of the Superior Sex':

> Have not all the great Actions that have been perform'd in the World been done by Men? Have not they founded Empires and over-turned them? Do not they make Laws and continually repeal and amend them? Their vast Minds lay Kingdoms waste, no Bounds or Measures can be prescrib'd to their Desires. War and Peace depend on them; they form Cabals and have the Wisdom and Courage to get over all the Rubs, the petty Restraints which Honour and Conscience may lay in the way of their desired Grandeur. What is it they cannot do? (Astell, [1970], p. 60)

According to Astell, men's arrogation to themselves of the power to decide the great issues of war and peace was evidence only of their overweening dominance, not of their superiority.

Lady Mary Wortley Montague, writing a generation later in 1739 as 'Sophia, a Person of Quality,' also felt constrained to defend the proposition that '*Woman [is] not Inferior to Man*'. Addressing herself to the exclusion of women from military service, she argued that it was in no way owing to a deficiency, incapacity or inferiority on the part of women. She could, she maintained, see no reason, physical, moral, emotional or intellectual, why women could not perform military service, indeed could not command either troops of soldiers on land or fleets of ships at sea. But possession of that capacity was, in her mind, beside the point. 'The real truth', she insisted, was '[t]hat humanity and integrity, the characteristics of our sex, makes us abhor unjust slaughter, and prefer honourable peace to unjust war'. Lady Mary Wortley Montague, then, used women's dissociation from warfare to establish their superiority not inferiority, while men's willing pursuit of 'war-like employments' and indifference to bloodshed signalled an unjust and cruel nature (Montague, [1984], pp. 26–9).

In *A Vindication of the Rights of Woman* (1792), Mary Wollstonecraft carved out another position on women and war. She castigated the bourgeois men of revolutionary France for excluding half the human race from the exercise of political power and sought to elevate motherhood from the 'ontological basement' to the status of active citizenship. While clearly preferring peace to war, she nonetheless allowed that 'defensive' wars were necessary and, therefore, just. Opposed to standing armies on the grounds that their hierarchies of command and the blind obedience they required were destructive of the intellectual independence and moral fibre of soldiers, she proposed citizens' militias as the force to fight the justifiable war. This advocate of equal rights for women, however, did not invoke their equal right to bear arms. Beating a speedy retreat from seeming to endorse that position, she reassured her readers that 'I am not going to advise [women] to turn their distaff into a musket, though I sincerely wish to see the bayonet converted into a pruning hook' (Wollstonecraft, [1967], pp. 45, 219). Although she implicitly assumed that the vocation of motherhood exempted women from arms bearing, Wollstonecraft posited no link between maternality and oppositon to war. Instead, in the polity of her dreams, she held equality between the sexes in active citizenship to be compatible with a division of labour which assigned the duty of military service to men and service as mothers to women.

The revolutionary tradition

Although Wollstonecraft wrote *A Vindication* at the height of British Jacobin support of the French Revolution, she did not address herself to the question of women's participation in the internecine strife of revolutionary conflict. In France, however, among the minority of consciously feminist critics/supporters of the Revolution there were women who, unlike Wollstonecraft, included in their demand for political equality the right to bear arms. Pauline Léon, the future leader of the Society of Revolutionary Republican Women, for example, submitted a petition carrying 300 signatures to the National Assembly in 1791 requesting authorisation for a women's militia on the grounds that women have a right to self-defence and to defence of the Revolution equal to men's. 'We only wish to defend ourselves the same as you', Léon pleaded,

> you cannot refuse us, and society cannot deny the right nature gives us, unless you pretend the Declaration of Rights does not apply to women, and that they should let their throats be cut like lambs, without the right to defend themselves.

Women also wanted, she persisted, the honour of sharing the trials and glories of their brothers in arms and 'of making tyrants see that women also have blood to shed for the service of the fatherland in danger' (Levy *et al.*, 1979, pp. 72–4). A year later the feminist Théroigne de Méricourt, a political moderate with pretensions to gentility, 'gave a speech at the Société fraternelle des patriotes de l'un et de l'autre sexe asking for a women's battalion, a company of Amazons' (Levy *et al.*, 1979, p. 104). For Méricourt, the militarisation of women was not only a question of imprescriptible right but a necessary step toward redressing the power balance between the sexes and fighting the enslavement of women by men. It '"is time"', she urged, '"for women to break out of the shameful incompetence in which men's ignorance, pride, and injustice have so long held us captive"' (Abray, 1975, p. 51). These female advocates of the extension to women of the full rights and duties of citizenship were critical of the revolutionary government's intransigence on this score, but they did not dispute the Revolution's need to defend itself by force against both internal and external enemies.

The mothering role of the women of the French Revolution did not necessarily serve as a source of non-violence or opposition to war. Women of the *menu peuple* played an important role in those revolutionary uprisings which were in the nature of bread riots, like the March on Versailles of 5–6 October 1789 for, as Olwen Hufton has argued, 'the bread riot was female, or rather maternal, terrain'

(Hufton, 1971, p. 94). Working women's attitude toward the Revolution was related to their role in the family economy, a crucial one in keeping the family from crossing the line between poverty and destitution. Also, in the face of the greater ease with which fathers opted out, responsibility for preserving the lives of children fell more heavily on mothers. Their support for the Revolution depended on its ability to protect their right to survival and their capacity to put food in the mouths of their children rather than on whether or not it used organised violence.

When revolutionary France found itself at war with the reactionary powers of Europe, common women donated their wedding rings, household linen, and great quantities of knitting in support of the Revolution's war effort. Fear of émigrés and foreigners, concern for the plight of husbands at the front, and patriotism led dozens of women to don male attire and actually enrol in the Revolutionary armies (Levy *et al.*, 1979, pp. 225–7). A few succeeded in serving at the front, and some, even after the Convention had ruled against female soldiers in April 1793, 'managed to evade its decree' (Abray, 1975, p. 49). But when the war threatened to disrupt the provisioning of Paris, *femmes sans culottes* protested in 'the form of spontaneous food riots, marketplace disruptions, delegations to political assemblies, and participation in popular societies' (Johnson, 1980, p. 122). The most militant and vocal group, the Society of Revolutionary Republican Women, pressured for economic legislation in the form of price controls and regulation of supply as well as for an internal revolutionary army to arrest and punish hoarders and speculators. While Hufton's picture of the 'doubly vindictive' women of 1793 seems misogynistically exaggerated, it does not appear that the *femmes sans culottes* flinched any more than their husbands, fathers, and brothers at the application of the Terror to those 'suspected of internal conspiracy' (Hufton, 1971, p. 101). What finally turned the women of the people against the Revolution was not its use of the guillotine or the bayonet but rather its turning of the Terror against the humble people, together with its failure to replace with any means of public assistance the charitable institutions of the *ancien régime*, or to create new sources of income for those thousands of women who, before the Revolution, had been employed in the luxury industries of lacemaking and the like. The final disenchantment came with the Revolution's failure to provide sufficient bread during the famine years of 1794 and 1795.

Most male revolutionaries disputed women's right to concern themselves with matters of state at all. In the view of the Jacobin Committee of Public Safety, the real crime of the royalist Marie-Antoinette, the feminist Olympe de Gouges, and the *Girondin* Madame Roland, was that they had trespassed on male terrain: they had intervened in politics. One opponent of the politicisation of women warned the Convention in the fall of 1793 that women started by meeting in clubs and wearing the red bonnet of the Revolution, but the next thing one knew, they were wearing gun belts and carrying guns. On 30 October 1793, the Convention voted, with only one member objecting, to suppress all women's clubs (Abray, 1975, pp. 56–7). The fear of women taking up arms may have contributed to the decisiveness of women's political suppression.

The tradition, however, of women involved combatively in uprisings of social protest and revolutionary civil war lived on. On the edge of Europe, in an economically backward Russia whose rulers welcomed western technology while seeking to keep out Western thought, the increasingly reactionary policies of the throne only served to fan a growing revolutionary fervour which drew young women as well as men to political terrorism. Women were prominent among the bomb makers and assassins of the anti-tsarist struggle of the 1870s and early 1880s. For one, Vera Zasulich, famous for shooting the tyrannical governor of St Petersburg in 1876, the struggle against social injustice included the struggle against the tyranny of gender. In her memoirs she remembered thinking as a schoolgirl:

It would have been easier, of course, had I been a boy: then I could have done almost anything . . .

And then, the distant specter of revolution appeared making me equal to a boy; I, too, could dream of 'acting', of 'exploits', and of the 'great struggle'. (Engel and Rosenthal (eds), 1975, p. 69)

In his *History of the Russian Revolution*, Trotsky credited women with taking the initiative in the Revolution's outbreak in St Petersburg in February 1917 (Rowbotham, 1972, p. 134). In the civil war which convulsed Russia after the October Revolution, the newly organised Red Army of the Bolsheviks utilised the skills of women in an extensive range of tasks including conventional combat. Women fought on every front of that far-flung land war,

> from Siberia to the Crimea, from the Baltic to Central Asia. They served as riflewomen, armoured train commanders, gunners, and demolition troops. (Griesse and Stites, 1982, p. 65)

Some women served in small all-female units, but most were integrated individually into predominantly male ones.

Separate spheres and the ideology of motherhood

When the chief officer of the Paris Commune was visited by a deputation of women protesting the dissolution of their clubs in October 1793, he reprimanded them for renouncing their sex and abandoning 'the pious duties of their households, their children's cradles' (Abray,1975, p. 57). While a *sans culotte* could spend his evenings drinking and talking politics in the *sociétés populaires*, his wife was to devote her entire being to hearth and home. Such an idealised picture of women's confinement to domesticity bore little resemblance to the real lives of working women in the 1790s. In the course of the next century's industrialisation, however, the sexual division of labour between male bread winner and dependent, home-bound wife became the ideological norm; domesticity for women took on the force of a cult; and motherhood, vocationalised, was also glorified. It became convenient for men caught up in the competitive hurly burly of the capitalist economy to assign the compassionate Christian virtues to women and the private sphere. While the archetype of the Angel in the House may have been imposed principally on the women of the propertied and professional classes, the doctrine of separate spheres came to pervade society from top to bottom (Taylor, 1983, p. 264). At the same time theories of sex differences emanating from exponents of the new discipline of sociology gave scientific validation to the equation of women with passivity and non-aggression, and motherhood with self-sacrifice and tender nurturance (Conway, 1972).

In the context of these ideological developments, the association of women with peace and the preservation of life gained credence, as did also its counterpart, the identification of war (indeed most killing) as a male enterprise. In 1911, with the waste and destruction of the Boer War in her mind's eye, the white South African feminist Olive Schreiner characterised a callousness toward life and death as 'instinctual' in men of certain cultures, as this passage makes clear: '"It is a fine day, let us go out and kill something!" cries the typical male of certain races, instinctively' (Schreiner, [1978], p. 176). In Schreiner's analysis one of the few irreducible differences between 'man and woman as such' was the 'somewhat differing angle' from which each sex looked at (and put a value on) the giving and taking of human life. The difference stemmed from 'their different sexual function with regard to reproduction':

> To the male, the giving of life . . . consists in a few moments of physical pleasure; . . . to the female, blood, anguish, and sometimes death. (Schreiner, [1978], p. 175)

For that reason, a woman 'always knows what life costs; and that it is more easy to destroy than to create it'. Schreiner denied that this gave women any 'general superior virtue', any greater mercy, or lesser cruelty – 'the woman will sacrifice as mercilessly, as cruelly, the life of a hated rival or an enemy, as any male; *but*', Schreiner stressed, '*she always knows what she is doing, and the value of the life she takes!*' (Schreiner, [1978], p. 176). It was '[o]n this one point, and on this point almost alone', Schreiner claimed, that 'the knowledge of woman' was 'superior to that of man: she knows the history of human flesh; she knows its cost; he does not'. It was, therefore, Schreiner's conviction that, when woman's 'voice is fully, finally and clearly heard in the governance of states', women would, because of their superior knowledge, because of their differing consciousness deriving from their different relation to human reproduction, eventually bring an end to war (Schreiner, [1978], p. 173).

Wherever the Victorian archetype of femininity held sway – as articulated in the cult of true womanhood and the idealisation of motherhood – the equation of female nature with the pacific virtues became a commonplace. This construction was used in women's struggle for entry into the public sphere, above all in the campaign for the female franchise. A firm plank of the woman suffrage platform was the claim that women's vote would weigh heavily on the side of peace. Mrs Emmeline Pankhurst, the leader of the militant British suffragettes, in defending the militancy of herself and her followers, stressed the careful distinction they drew between the violent destruction of property and the violent destruction of human life:

> Criticism from gentlemen who do not hesitate to order out armies to kill and slay their opponents, who do not hesitate to encourage party mobs to attack defenceless women in public meetings – criticism from them hardly rings true.

So Mrs Pankhurst declared on release from imprisonment for window-smashing in October 1912. In contrast to such men, she assured her audience:

> it has never been and never will be the policy of the Women's Social and Political Union recklessly to endanger human life. We leave that to the enemy. We leave that to the men in their warfare. It is not the method of women. (E. Pankhurst, [1979], pp. 264–65)

The impact of the First World War

After England's declaration of war, however, and once all suffragettes still in prison were released, the position of Mrs Pankhurst and her daughter Christabel shifted from opposition to the British government as enemy to support of its war effort against the foreign enemy Germany. According to Christabel, her mother justified the about-face with the question: 'What would be the good of a vote without a country to vote in?' (C. Pankhurst, 1959, p. 288). But, in fact, Mrs Pankhurst's *bouleversement* was less of a turnabout than it first appears, for while it had been politically expedient for her to argue the superiority of women's suffrage militancy over men's militarism in 1912 on the grounds of the former's greater respect for human life, her position had not been grounded in principled pacifism. Christabel, meanwhile, was promising already in September 1914 that, if the situation became so desperate that women were '"needed in the fighting line, we shall be there"' (Marwick, 1977, p. 30).

At the time of the disintegration of the Russian army under the pressures of war exhaustion and Bolshevik agitation for an immediate peace of 'no annexations, no indemnities', one woman combat soldier famous for her service with the Tsarist forces received permission from the Kerensky government 'to organize a women's shock battalion, [a] "Battalion of Death"' to shame deserting men to return to the front or, if that failed, to shoot them. Emmeline Pankhurst 'praised the unit and attended its farewell service' on her visit to Russia at the end of the summer of 1917 (Griesse and Stites, 1982, p. 64). Fighting on the battlefield remained, however, men's work in the British world, and the Pankhursts accepted this division of labour according to which men fight and women weep. The two-sided task of the suffragettes became: (i) to encourage women to enter the many areas of work opening up to them on the home front in support of the war, and (ii) to incite all British men to volunteer for the front. Although it was a man who first had the idea of handing out white feathers to any young men not in military uniform, many suffragettes joined with other women in performing these acts of humiliation (Marwick, 1977, pp. 35–6).

Other suffragists, however, preserved their anti-war stance (Vellacott, 1987). Sylvia Pankhurst, for one, 'to the deep chagrin of her mother', remained opposed to the war (Marwick, 1977, p. 45). Another, Mrs Emmeline Pethick-Lawrence of the Women's Freedom League, continued to preach internationalism and 'the need for concluding a negotiated peace as quickly as possible' (Marwick, 1977, p. 44). And Hannah Mitchell, a suffragette from the ranks of Labour, had all her life found 'the idea of men killing each other . . . so hideous' that she brought up her son, who was sixteen in August 1914, to resist war. 'As the time drew near for his call-up', she later recalled, 'I felt I couldn't bear to live if I knew he had killed another woman's son'. She was greatly relieved when he decided to become a Conscientious Objector (Mitchell, 1977, pp. 183, 186–7).

Despite the outbreak of the First World War, there were women suffragists in many Western nations who continued to hold on to the belief, as did Dr Aletta Jacobs, suffrage leader and first woman physician of Holland, that '[w]oman suffrage and permanent peace will go together', for women, she explained,

don't feel as men do about war. They are the mothers of the race. Men think of the economic results; women think of the grief and pain, and the damage to the race. (Eastman, 1978, p. 240)

In a United States still holding back from direct involvement in the war, several thousand women suffragists, representing a great variety of associations from the Women's Trade Union League and Woman's National Committee of the Socialist Party to the General Federation of Women's Clubs, converged on Washington, D.C., in January and founded the Woman's Peace Party (which later became the United States branch of the Women's International League for Peace and Freedom) (Costin, 1982, p. 307). A few months later over a thousand women representing twelve belligerent and neutral countries accepted Dr Aletta Jacobs's invitation to attend the International Congress of Women at the Hague in late April and early May 1915. Chaired by Jane Addams, the Congress protested 'against the madness and horror of war' and recommended immediate mediation by neutral nations in the current conflict, without waiting for an armistice to be negotiated. For the future the assembled women called for 'democratic control of foreign policy with equal representation of men and women', and a women's presence at the eventual peace conference ending the present war. Following the Congress, selected delegates travelled as envoys to both neutral and belligerent countries to place women's peace resolutions before their governments (Costin, 1982, pp. 311–12).

While the internationalism of the women's suffrage movement was severely shaken by the First World War, its outbreak dealt a death blow to the internationalism of the socialist movement in the industrial capitalist countries. Many socialist women of pre-war continental Europe had believed that involvement in their movement was advancing peace because the working people of the world who were committed to socialism would never take up arms against one another. The Marxist theoretician Rosa Luxemburg held that faith. When on 4 August 1914, the Reichstag delegation of the Social Democratic Party of Germany casts its 110 votes in support of the government's request for war credits, Luxemburg was devastated: the party whose leader in 1892, Wilhelm Liebknecht, had referred to the socialist movement as '"a great international peace league"' had capitulated to nationalism (Kempf, 1973, p. 28). Duped by the myth that Russian aggression made it a war of national defence, the leaders of the strongest socialist party in Europe declared their willingness to abandon class struggle for the duration. Like her friend Clara Zetkin and her comrade Karl Liebknecht, Luxemburg spent the war years in and out of prison for denouncing the war as imperialist and exposing the brutal hypocrisy of Germany's militarist, capitalist leaders for whom lives were 'the cheapest and most expendable commodity of all, especially proletarian lives' (Nettl, 1966, II, p. 631). The opposition to war of Luxemburg and Zetkin, like that of Liebknecht, stemmed from their unwavering commitment to the international proletarian revolution, not from feminism or a gender-essentialist pacifism.

As the Marxist Rosa Luxemburg held on to her faith that the working masses could be educated to an awareness that fighting for a German victory served only the interests of big business and the military, so the Swedish maternalist Ellen Key preserved throughout the war her faith in 'the motherliness of woman' as the only 'source' from which 'we may expect salvation' (Key, 1916, p. 100). That faith was challenged by the evidence, well-known to Key, of 'millions of women who have greeted a war in which their sons and husbands have been killed with enthusiasm' (Key, 1916, p. 201), of 'German women who are proud of the sinking of the Lusitania' (Key, 1916, p. 104), and of Russian and Polish and Balkan women 'who have dressed as men and entered the ranks' (Key, 1916, p. 199–200). Undeniably women had succumbed during the war to '*passionate nationalism*', 'just as much as men' (Key, 1916, p. 246). Equally undeniable were the examples of female combatants. By asserting that the women in both cases had contradicted their true nature, Key could maintain her belief in 'mother love and mother labours' as the only hope of future peace as well as the only justification for women's participation in public politics. 'To every body with any depth of insight', Key intoned,

the warring woman must seem a painful contradiction in terms. To be a woman implies the giving and protecting of life, and the whole future significance of woman's increased rights is dependent on her reverence for this mission and her abhorrence of all destruction of life, especially of the mass destruction of war. (Key, 1916, p. 199)

For Key there was a distinctive woman's position on war and she located it in motherhood. 'If women put themselves back in touch with the 'inmost strength of woman's nature' (Key, 1916, p. 100) – 'mother love' – and then gained a say in the politics of the public arena, military might would eventually be banished from the world.

Until that future state of international harmony was attained, however, Key granted that, for love of country – a justifiable sentiment distinct from self-aggrandising nationalism – defensive war would remain a necessity. As fighting and killing were tasks inimical to womanhood in Key's view, their burden would have to continue to be borne by men.

Key expressed the hope in 1916 that 'the motherliness of woman' would be 'so incensed by this war that it causes a mass-rising against the injustice of woman's position' (Key, 1916, p. 100). Certainly in the post-war Western world, promotion of peace and international-ism regained an important place in the women's movements of the 1920s and 1930s (Strong-Boag, 1987). Many a woman's pacifism dated from her experience of the death, physical maiming or psychological scarring by war of someone she loved. In post-war Germany artist Käthe Kollwitz took as her theme the opposition of mothers to war. In lithograph, woodcut and sculpture, she depicted the war-related suffering of innocent children, the grief of the parents and widows of the fallen, and the fierce determination of mothers to protect their young from the devouring evil of war. The images she thus created have survived as among the most powerful in the pacifist repertory (Klein and Klein, 1972, pp. 77, 81, 82, 85, 141, 150).

But the sacrifices of war left in other women a thirst for vengeance – just as, in contrast, actual experience at the front instilled in some men, such as Wilfred Owen, a pacifist abhorrence of war's senseless slaughter. Emmeline Pethick-Lawrence, who ran in the 'khaki election' of December 1918 on a platform of reconciliation with Germany, recalled in her autobiography how ironical it was for her, the pacifist proponent of women's suffrage, to find that her support came from the soldiers while the newly enfranchised mothers of children flocked to the 'Make Germany Pay' candidate (Pethick-Lawrence, [1984], pp. 322–3).

Virginia Woolf's *Three Guineas* (1938)

Virginia Woolf would have agreed with the British woman school teacher who, in a First World War poem, upbraided the female 'Dealer in white feathers' with the question:

Can't you see it isn't decent,
To flout and goad men into doing,
What is not asked of you? (Hamilton, [1981], p. 47)

In Woolf's analysis, those women who handed out white feathers
had helped to foster what she called 'the manhood emotion', men's
susceptibility to and fear of the taunt of cowardice. (Woolf, [1966],
p. 182). Written in the midst of the Spanish civil war, when Europe
stood poised on the brink of the bloodiest war the world has ever
known, Woolf's *Three Guineas* (1938) sounded a dire warning as to
the importance of seeing the connections between patriarchy and
militarism, patriarchy and fascism, patriarchy and war. With one
eye on the swaggering Italian Fascists and the other on the sinister,
jackbooted Nazis, Woolf was put in mind of threats and thunderings
closer to home. She recalled the battles of Westminster, of Oxford
and Cambridge and, most recently, of Whitehall and of York and
Canterbury – that is, the fierce resistance mounted by Britain's male
civil servants to opening the Civil Service to women after the
passage of the 1919 Sex Disqualification (Removal) Act, and by the
1936 Archbishops' Commission to the admission of women to the
Anglican priesthood. Woolf acknowledged that 'the monster' of
patriarchal tyranny had 'come more openly to the surface' and
'widened his scope' in Italy and Germany (Woolf, [1966], p. 102),
but she repeatedly pointed to the similarities between the dictates of
Englishmen as to what women should and should not do and those
of the Führer and the Duce. Both Hitler and Mussolini insisted on
the sexual division of labour, but so also, Woolf observed, did the
Anglican priests and the top-ranking civil servants as well as those
male heads of household who, claiming man's right to a family
wage, piously asserted their 'desire to support wife and children'.
The emphasis which men placed upon the necessity for separate
male and female spheres 'is enough', Woolf concluded, 'to prove
that it is essential to their domination' (Woolf, [1966], p. 180–1).

No matter how sharply separated spatially or normatively, the
male-defined public sphere and the female-defined private sphere
were nevertheless 'inseparably connected', Woolf argued; 'the
tyrannies and servilities of the one are the tyrannies and servilities
of the other' (Woolf, [1966], p. 142). Men's dominance in the
private sphere depended on women's exclusion from or restricted
access to the public sphere as much as men's dominance in the

public sphere rested on the relegation of women to domestic labour in the private sphere. It was this hierarchical division of labour by sex which fundamentally structured society in terms of dominance and sub-ordination and which fundamentally gendered dominance as masculine and subordination as feminine. And therein lay the germ of male dictatorship and female hero worship; of the fighting spirit of man and the war enthusiasm of woman.

Those unequal power relations institutionalised in the sexual division of labour were also internalised by men and women as 'sex characteristic' – if not instinctual. Man's conception of himself as 'manly' was tied up with his ability to dominate, his willingness to fight to establish or maintain dominion; woman's conception of herself as 'womanly' was tied up with her ability to serve men, to gain male approval. As the counterpart of male dominance was female subordination, so also were 'manliness' and 'womanliness' enmeshed in a reciprocal relationship. Woolf indeed perceived the men off 'in the immensity of their public abstractions' and the women immured 'in the intensity of their private emotions' to be locked in a pathological symbiosis (Woolf, [1966], p. 142).

If the patriarchal sex/gender system bred in woman submission, it bred in man a will to power and the belief 'that he has the right, whether given by God, Nature, sex or race is immaterial, to dictate to other human beings how they shall live; what they shall do' (Woolf, [1966], p. 53). In its extreme form, it was a disease, this compulsion to dominate, this need to feel superior, 'for whose gratification a subject race or sex is essential' (Woolf, [1966], p. 167). Woolf labelled it with the psychologists' term 'infantile fixation' (Woolf, [1966], p. 126–7). Its most alarming contemporary manifestation was the Fascist and National Socialist assertion of 'unmitigated masculinity' (Woolf, [1978], p. 98), the indentification of man with warrior. Both Hitler and Mussolini 'repeatedly' insisted that it was 'the essence of manhood to fight', 'the nature of womanhood to heal the wounds of the fighter' (Woolf, [1966], p. 186). If in the eyes of George Orwell the picture of future evil was of 'a boot stamping on the face – forever' (Orwell, [1952], p. 203), Woolf reminded her readers that the gender of the person wearing the boot would be masculine. For Woolf, 'the picture of evil' was the man in uniform claiming to be 'Man himself, the quintessence of virility' (Woolf [1966], pp. 142–3). That man posed the threat of war.

Prevention of war would require, then, the dismantling of the whole patriarchal sex/gender system: the desegregation of male and female spheres, and the depolarisation of masculinity and femininity. Men would have to emancipate themselves from the notion that war was a necessary proving ground of 'manly qualities' (Woolf, [1966], p. 8); women would have to cease 'concealing and excusing the disease of infantile fixation' in their men (Woolf, [1966], p. 134). And if, as Woolf wrote in *A Room of One's Own* (1929), 'mirrors are essential to all violent and heroic action' (Woolf, [1978], p. 36), then women would have to stop serving, as they had been for centuries, 'as looking glasses possessing the magic and delicious power of reflecting the figure of man at twice its natural size' (Woolf, [1978], p. 35).

In Woolf's view women were not by nature opposed to war, any more than men were by nature warlike. A woman combatant in the Spanish Civil War, a sergeant in the Republican army, proud of the fact that she had killed five, possibly six, enemy men, was an example of how quickly the 'fighting instinct' could be acquired by the female sex (Woolf, [1966], pp. 177–8). Wilfred Owen, the poet who through his experience in the trenches of the First World War came to abhor the 'inhumanity', the 'insupportability', the 'beastliness', the 'foolishness' of war, was an example how a man could acquire the pacifist impulse (Woolf, [1966], p. 8). Woolf seemed to believe that a simple look at the pictorial evidence of the results of war – a photograph of ruined buildings and mutilated bodies – should be enough to convince most rational people, male or female, of the brutality and horror of war. What subverted that perception were the structures of dominance and subordination. It was to break out of her stifling dependence that the educated man's daughter had rushed to serve in the First World War, in the Land Army, FANY, or the VAD. 'So profound', Woolf wrote, 'was her unconscious loathing for the education of the private house with its cruelty, its poverty, its hypocrisy, its immorality, its inanity that she would undertake any task however menial, exercise any fascination however fatal that enabled her to escape' (Woolf, [1966], p. 39).

Nonetheless, Woolf believed that, for social historical reasons, women had greater potential for opposition to war. She located this potential, however, not in motherhood, but in the historical exclusion of women from power and wealth. 'Through no merit of their own' (Woolf, [1966], p. 100), but rather because of their relegation to powerlessness and poverty, women had little or no investment in any one country's resources and institutions. It was from this position of outsider that Woolf could have her female pacifist say, ' "as a woman, I have no country. As a woman I want no country. As a woman my country is the whole world" ' (Woolf, [1966], p. 109). The women of Woolf's anarchical 'Outsiders' Society' would work to prevent war by earning their own livings but refusing to be co-opted by the 'system', by maintaining 'an attitude of complete indifference' (Woolf, [1966], p. 107) toward the allure of the uniform, by absenting themselves from patriotic displays, and by telling the truth about the nature of warfare.

The connection Woolf saw between war and men's identification of their masculinity with fighting might have led her to advocate combat for women as a way of breaking the male monopoly on the 'hard' virtues and thus divesting men of the need to prove their manliness through war. Woolf did note that because women were exempted by the state from the citizen's responsibility to bear arms, 'Pacifism is enforced upon women' while, in contrast, 'Men are still allowed freedom of choice' (Woolf, [1966], p. 177). Woolf's pacifist feminism, however, sought equality between the sexes not through admitting women to combat but rather through liberating men from militarism.

Contemporary feminisms

In contradistinction to Woolf, a contemporary US spokeswoman for female combatants entertains the possibility that the military could be degendered. 'The military in general, and combat in particular, is a masculine proving ground', Mady Wechsler Segal writes. 'If women are fully integrated into the military, then this arena loses this function. A young man cannot prove he is a man by doing something that young women can do' (Segal, 1982, p. 283). Segal is writing from a feminist position that emphasises equal rights and sees 'the issue of women in combat' as supplying 'a test of the logic of full equality' (Goldman (ed.), 1982, p. 17). A similar position was articulated, as we have seen, at the time of the French Revolution, but then pretty well disappeared from the dominant culture of Western and Central Europe with the sexual division of labour introduced by capitalist and male-dominant industrialisation. But under the impact of the second wave of feminism, the recent movement for equality between the sexes, attitudes have undergone tremendous change. In the US, for example, the subject of women in combat was rarely raised publicly during the Second World War, and whenever it was, it aroused in Congress 'protestations of deep aversion to the idea' (Quester, 1982, p. 219). Roughly forty years later, however, a Gallup poll of 560 Americans aged eighteen to twenty-four showed a majority of the young men and women in favour of including women in combat roles on a voluntary basis (Segal, 1982, pp. 284–5).

The male control of arms bearing is, some contemporary feminists argue, a bulwark of male domination and the male-dominated state. According to this view, while comparative studies indicate that women's exclusion from combat has been relaxed when societies have been undergoing social revolutionary struggle against repressive regimes, colonial or indigenous – as in wars of national liberation or 'people's wars', or when countries have mounted guerrilla resistance against invasion and conquest by a foreign enemy – the 'political and military decisions to put women into combat have almost always been made by men' (Goldman (ed.), 1982, p. 11). And once a stable state has emerged (or re-emerged), its domination by men is re-asserted and combat becomes male-exclusive again. In Israel, for example, women served as combatants in the defence of Jewish pioneer settlements before, during and after the First World War, in the anti-British struggle during and immediately after the Second World War, as well as in the war of independence of 1948–9. Once the state of Israel came into existence, however, and the Israeli Defence Forces were unified and regularised, women were excluded from 'All jobs involving combat, jobs that have to be filled under bad conditions, and jobs where physical demands are regarded as too great for females' (Bloom, 1982, p. 155). Feminist critic Aviva Cantor Zuckoff sees extending back into biblical times this link between patriarchy and the exclusion of women from combat except in dire emergencies. 'If we go through the Bible and legends carefully', she has written, 'we see that whenever Jewish survival is at stake, Jewish women are called upon to be strong and aggressive. When the crisis is over, it's back to patriarchy' (in Bloom, 1982, p. 157). Similarly, in the Soviet Union, the direct engagement in combat by more than half a million women during the Second World War was not 'a path leading to greater recognition and equality' for Soviet women in the public sphere, 'but rather a stopgap measure used by a desperate regime pushed to its ultimate resource, which it did not hesitate to exploit' (Griesse and Stites, 1982, p. 79). In the post-war years Soviet women were called upon to assume the triple duty of housewife, mother and worker, while the peacetime Soviet armed forces returned to being overwhelmingly male, with a small percentage of female personnel assigned mainly to administrative duties and technical support services. The implication of this analysis is that equality with men in military service and control over the military is a necessary precondition for women's full social equality.

Adamantly opposed to and appalled by the prospect of militarising women in a world threatened by global militarism and the nuclear arms race is another major stream of the second wave of feminism, a maternalist, pacifist feminism whose origins, we saw, lie in the modern intensification of the work of mothering and the ideology of idealised motherhood. Against the image of the 'Woman Warrior' these feminists invoke the powerful symbol of 'the Moral Mother – nurturant, compassionate, and politically correct – the sovereign, instinctive spokeswoman for all that is living and vulnerable' (Di Leonardo, 1985, p. 602). The mother/earth goddess/web-of-life-spinner/weaver imagery has inspired (and undoubtedly also empowered) women to mount and sustain women-only peace actions that have succeeded, however briefly, in capturing media attention and in exposing the deadly humourlessness of nuclear military installations (Reid, 1982, pp. 289–94).

No less concerned with the risk that nuclear arms build-up poses to all life on this planet is another contemporary pacifist feminist position, reminiscent of Woolf's. It does not locate a source of peace in women's innate or practised motherliness but rather a propensity for war in 'the domination of men over women', the sexual division of labour, 'and the subsequent polarisation of so-called male and female characteristics'. The Cambridge Women's Peace Collective concludes:

If the qualities of caring and nurturing are ascribed to those in society who have no political power, and the influence of those

qualities banned from international relations, the opposite attributes of forcefulness and competitiveness rule unhindered.
(Cambridge Women's Peace Collective, 1984, p. 7)

The feminist anti-militarist Cynthia Enloe, who cites *Three Guineas*
as one of her inspirations, shares with Woolf the conviction that
women as outsiders have a valuable perspective to bring to analyses
of war and peace. As Woolf exposed the threadbare nature of the
claims of patriotism on women, Enloe subjects the military's
definition of 'national security' to feminist scrutiny. Using its
privileged relationship to the state, the military, she argues,
interprets 'national security' in its own interests to mean 'not only
the protection of the state and its citizens from external foes' but
also, and 'perhaps even primarily', the preservation of the existing,
male-dominant social order (Enloe, 1983, p. 11). Following closely
in the footsteps of Woolf, Enloe investigates the structural and
ideological interconnections between patriarchy and militarism,
shedding new light on the complexities of their symbiotic relationship. The US military is dependent, she shows, on the ideological
construction of masculinity and femininity as complementary, the
former bound up with action and combat, the latter with need for
male protection and sexual accessibility to men. Probing the
contradictions in what military commanders want from women,
Enloe proposes, helps expose the cracks in an institution that seeks
to appear before the world as invulnerable.

Also surviving into the contemporary world is a revolutionary
feminism which asserts women's equal right with men to take up
arms against militarily enforced social, political, and economic
injustice. In the case of women's participation in the Nicaraguan
revolution, the two main sources of a distinct women's position on
war and peace – motherhood and powerlessness – have both led to
support for revolutionary violence. The primary motive Nicaraguan
women give for having enlisted in the Sandinista movement is
related to their socially assigned role as nurturant mothers: they
could no longer stand by and watch the violence visited by the
Somoza regime on their children. Secondly the women sought to
end their own defenceless vulnerability to the violent rape so widely
practiced by the Somoza National Guard (Randall, 1981). In the
aftermath of revolution, and despite the urgent need to defend the
new order against external aggression, the Nicaraguan women have

a continuing struggle against the powerfully entrenched culture of *machismo* which would limit and segregate their military contribution to national defence (Deighton, *et al.* 1983, pp. 50–62).

Conclusion

Are women by nature, or by socialisation, in ideology or experience, more pacific than men? The recent historical record would appear to be inconclusive. It has been possible to isolate two main sources of a distinctive women's position on organised violence: the experience of maternity on the part of the vast majority of women and women's historical exclusion from public power. But motherhood is an institution and neither it nor women's relation to public power is transhistorical and unchanging. Consequently, from these two perspectives, feminists have posited conflicting theories on women's relation to war and peace and women have, according to changing social historical circumstances, responded to warmongering and peace movements in a great variety of ways. The historic links between feminism and pacifism are counterbalanced by the instances when women have embraced revolution with hope and war with enthusiasm. There has not been a consistent women's response to war and revolution any more than there has been a uniform feminist position on women's relation to organised violence.

References

Abray, Jane (1975) 'Feminism in the French Revolution', *American Historical Review*, 80, pp. 43–62.

Astell, Mary (1970) *Some Reflections Upon Marriage* (New York: Source Book Press) reprint of the 4th London edn of 1730.

Bloom, Anne R. (1982) 'Israel: The Longest War', in Nancy Loring Goldman (ed.), *Female Soldiers – Combatants or Noncombatants? Historical and Contemporary Perspectives* (Westport, Conn.: Greenwood Press).

Cambridge Women's Peace Collective (1984) 'Introduction' to *My Country is the Whole World: An Anthology of Women's Work on Peace and War* (London: Pandora Press).

Conway, Jill (1972) 'Stereotypes of Femininity in a Theory of Sexual Evolution', in Martha Vicinus (ed.), *Suffer and Be Still: Women in the Victorian Age* (Bloomington: Indiana University Press).

Costin, Lela B. (1982) 'Feminism, Pacifism, Internationalism and the 1915 International Congress of Women', *Womens Studies International Forum*, 5, 34 p. 301–15.

Deighton, Jane, Rosanna Horsley, Sarah Stewart and Cathy Cain (1983) *Sweet Ramparts: Women in Revolutionary Nicaragua* (London: War on Want and the Nicaraguan Solidarity Campaign).

Eastman, Crystal (1978) ' "Now I Dare To Do It": An Interview with Dr Aletta Jacobs, Who Called the Woman's Peace Conference at the Hague', *The Survey*, 9 October 1915. Reprinted in Blanche Wiesen Cook (ed.), *Crystal Eastman on Women and Revolution* (Oxford: Oxford University Press).

Engel, Barbara Alpern and Rosenthal, Clifford N. (eds) (1975) *Five Sisters: Women Against the Tsar* (New York: Alfred A. Knopf).

Enloe, Cynthia (1983) *Does Khaki Become You? The Militarisation of Women's Lives* (London: Pluto Press).

Goldman, Nancy Loring (ed.) (1982) 'Introduction' to *Female Soldiers – Combatants or Noncombatants? Historical and Contemporary Perspectives* (Westport, Conn.: Greenwood Press).

Griesse, Anne Eliot and Richard Stites (1982) 'Russia: Revolution and War' in Nancy Loring Goldman (ed.), *Female Soldiers – Combatants or Noncombatants? Historical and Contemporary Perspectives* (Westport, Conn.: Greenwood Press).

Hamilton, Helen (1981) 'The Jingo-Woman' in Catherine W. Reilly (ed.), *Scars upon my heart: Women's Poetry and Verse of the First World War* (London: Virago).

Hufton, Olwen (1971) 'Women in the French Revolution 1789–1796' *Past and Present*, 53 pp. 90–108.

Johnson, Mary Durham (1980) 'Institutional Changes for Women of the People During the French Revolution' in Carol R. Berkin and Clara M. Lovett (eds), *Women, War and Revolution* (New York: Holmes and Meier).

Kempf, Beatrix (1973) *Woman for Peace: The Life of Bertha von Suttner*, trans. from the German by R. W. Last (Park Ridge, New Jersey: Noyes Press).

Key, Ellen (1916) *War, Peace, and the Future: A Consideration of Nationalism and Internationalism, and of the Relation of Women to War*, trans. Hildegard Norberg (New York: G. P. Putnam's Sons; London: The Knickerbocker Press).

Klein, Mina C. and Klein, H. Arthur (1972) *Käthe Kollwitz: Life in Art* (New York: Holt, Rinehart and Winston).

Di Leonardo, Micaela (1985) 'Morals, Mothers, and Militarism: Anti-militarism and Feminist Theory', *Feminist Studies*, 11, 3 pp. 599–617.

Levy, Darline Gay, Harriet Branson Applewhite and Mary Durham Johnson, (eds) (1979) *Women in Revolutionary Paris 1789–1795* (Urbana: Univeristy of Illinois Press).

Marwick, Arthur (1977) *Women at War 1914–1918* (Fontana).

Mitchell, Hannah (1977) *The Hard Way Up: The Autobiography of Suffragette and Rebel* (London: Virago).

Montague, Mary Wortley [1984] Excerpt from *Woman not inferior to Man* (1739), in Cambridge Women's Peace Collective, *My Country is the Whole World: An Anthology of Women's Work on Peace and War* (London: Pandora Press).

Nettl, J. P. (1966) *Rosa Luxemburg*, 2 vols (London: Oxford University Press).

Orwell, George [1952] (orig. 1949) *1984* (New York: New American Library).

Pankhurst, Christabel (1959) *Unshackled* (London: Hutchinson).

Pankhurst, Emmeline [1979] (orig. 1914) *My Own Story* (London: Virago).

Pethick-Lawrence, Emmeline [1984] *My Part in a Changing World* (1939) excerpted in Cambridge Women's Peace Collective, *My Country is the Whole World: An Anthology of Women's Work on Peace and War* (London: Pandora Press).

Quester, George H. (1982) 'The Problem', in Nancy Loring Goldman (ed.), *Female Soldiers – Combatants or Noncombatants? Historical and Contemporary Perspectives* (Westport, Conn.: Greenwood Press).

Randall, Margaret (1981) *Sandino's Daughters* (Vancouver: New Star Books).

Reid, Catherine (1982) 'Reweaving the Web of Life' in Pam McAllister (ed.), *Reweaving the Web of Life: Feminism and NonViolence* (Philadelphia: New Society Publishers).

Rowbotham, Sheila (1972) *Women, Resistance and Revolution* (London: Penguin Press).

Ruddick, Sara (1984) 'Preservative Love and Military Destruction: Some Reflections on Mothering and Peace', In Joyce Trebilcot (ed.), *Mothering: Essays in Feminist Theory* (Totowa, New Jersey: Rowman & Allanheld).

Schreiner, Olive [1978] (orig. 1911) *Woman and Labour* (London: Virago).

Segal, Mady Wechsler (1982) 'The Argument for Female Combatants', in Nancy Loring Goldman (ed.), *Female Soldiers – Combatants or Noncombatants? Historical and Contemporary Perspectives* (Westport, Conn.: Greenwood Press).

Strong-Boag, Veronica (1987) 'Peace-Making Women: Canada 1919–1939', in Ruth Roach Pierson (ed.), *Women and Peace: Theoretical, Historical and Practical Perspectives* (London: Croom Helm).

Taylor, Barbara (1983) *Eve and the New Jerusalem: Socialism and Feminism in the Nineteenth Century* (New York: Pantheon Books).

Vellacott, Jo (1987) 'Feminist Consciousness and the First World War' in Ruth Roach Pierson (ed.), *Women and Peace: Theoretical, Historical and Practical Perspectives* (London: Croom Helm).

Wollstonecroft, Mary [1967] *A Vindication of the Rights of Women* (1792) (New York: W. W. Norton).

Woolf, Virginia [1966] (orig. 1938) *Three Guineas* (New York: Harcourt, Brace and World; the Hogarth Press).

Woolf, Virginia [1978] (orig. 1929) *A Room of One's Own* (London: Granada; the Hogarth Press).

Name Index

ISOBEL BOWLER

Subject Index

ISOBEL BOWLER